*Flora Delaney has always been .. .....ₒ... successful retailers. This book is a must-read for all of us who works in any capacity in the retail marketplace."*

Stuart Straus, CEO, Compass Health Brands

*I've seen tremendous change in retailing with consolidation, technology advances, and a retailer's success defined by how they can better meet their customers' needs and shopping preferences in an increasingly dynamic environment. Flora is an original thinker and identifying insights is part of her DNA. Her book provides practical advice that will improve the operations and business results of any online or brick-and-mortar retailer.*

Don Kauffold, SVP Sales and Marketing, Candle-lite Company

*"If you're a small retailer, you may feel like an endangered species. But following these practical principles will give you command over new skills for winning in retail now and in the future."*

Amanda Brinkman, small business marketing expert and Host of Small Business Revolution - Main Street

*"I am so happy Flora Delaney wrote this book. It is what has been needed in the retail world. It is a real world guide based on real experience! I am anxious to buy copies of the book for my entire management team."*

Rudy Simondi, President, Flips

WATERFORD
& HOWELL
PUBLISHING
MINNEAPOLIS| MINNESOTA

RETAIL THE SECOND OLDEST PROFESSION
7 TIMELESS PRINCIPLES TO WIN IN RETAIL TODAY
Copyright 2019 by Flora Delaney.

Publisher's Cataloging-in-Publication Data

Names: Delaney, Flora, author.
Title: Retail , the second oldest profession : 7 timeless principles to win retail today / by Flora Delaney.
Description: Includes bibliographical references. | Waterford and Howell Publishing, 2019.
Identifiers: ISBN 978-0-578-44258-7
Subjects: LCSH Retail trade. | Stores, Retail. | Success in business. | Small business--Management. | Small business marketing. | Marketing--Management. | Customer services--Management. | Merchandising. | Pricing. | BISAC BUSINESS & ECONOMICS / Sales & Selling / General | BUSINESS & ECONOMICS / Industries / Retailing
Classification: LCC HF5429 .D355 2019 | DDC 658.8/7--dc23

For information contact:
  Follow author on twitter @floradelaney
  https://www.floradelaney.com

  | Bulk Discounts available. For details visit: |
  | www.floradelaney.com/book/bulkorder |

Cover design by Michael Rehder
ISBN: 978-0-578-44258-7

First Edition: February 2019

10 9 8 7 6 5 4 3 2 1

# RETAIL
## The Second-Oldest Profession

# 7 Timeless Principles
# to WIN in Retail Today

BY
FLORA DELANEY

## Why Read This Book

I'm tired of experts telling me retail is dead. It isn't dead. It cannot die. As long as people are not self-sufficient and there is a bartering system that trades money or something of value for desired goods, retail will never die. So, don't believe the pundits.

If you are struggling ... If you feel as if you and your team are working hard but you are not getting the results you want, you will find hundreds of specific things you can do today to WIN in retail. Throughout the book, look for **WIN Today** to find those immediate actions you can take to improve your business and win over customers. **WIN Today** elements act like a retail coach urging you to take steps to improve your retail business.

This book is for you if you:
- Own your own retail business– and wear many hats
- Manage a team that is always busy – but is not achieving the results you want
- Aspire to a career in retail and want to understand how it all fits together
- Need help developing inexperienced managers and new hires to succeed quickly
- Feel overwhelmed with multiple priorities in your retail operation
- Are a vendor and want to be a better partner to your retail customers

# Dedication

To the people who kindly taught me so much about this industry.
I am thinking of Gary Goff, Steve Frenda, Bob Kelly, Bob Shipley,
Don Kauffold, Dale Byrne, Jerry Friedler, Kevin Freeland, Vivian Rank,
Mike Madden, Rob Willey, Connie Fuhrman and many others.

*But especially: Geoff Kleinman.*
This book is dedicated to you.

# TABLE OF CONTENTS

## Introduction

R etail is "the second-oldest profession." As you might expect in such an enduring business, getting it right comes down to a precise command of a few timeless basics. Truth is, great retail principles are the same around the world. And – if we had a time machine – they would be the same in the past and into the future. As a retailer, I am confident that I could create and conduct a successful store in any part of the world and at any point in time if I stay true to the 7 Timeless Principles.

Before you can be a retail master, you need to tackle the basics. This book shares fundamental advice on getting retail right. Read it if you are a new store employee, recently promoted from the stores into the confusion of a corporate retail position or a store owner. The 7 Timeless Principles are true if you are a brick-and-mortar store or a digital retailer without a physical storefront. This book provides guidance and immediate actions you can take to WIN Today in retail. Follow the suggestions and your retail enterprise will succeed.

This book is meant to provide you with guidance and sound advice to help you **WIN Today.** The suggestions and insights provided will give you understanding of how the diverse elements of retail fit together and how to succeed. Most retailers will see across-the-board improvements in sales, margins, customer experience and employee engagement just by refocusing on the 7 Timeless Principles covered in this book.

These principles work as effectively with single-door retailers as with Fortune 500 giants like Walmart and Amazon. An "aha" moment in my career was when I realized I kept having the same conversation whether I was talking to a boutique owner in her own shop or the chief operating officer of a chain of 9,500 stores. It all comes down to:

1. Delivering a strong strategy
2. Treating your customers well
3. Selecting and showcasing compelling products
4. Pricing them attractively
5. Engaging a competent team
6. Being relevant to your customers
7. Running your company soundly

This book will be particularly valuable to busy people who either work in retail stores or support those people who work in retail stores. Because I know you are busy, the information is in easy-to-digest sections. They can be read and reviewed as part of a formal training session or as your own self-directed education while on breaks. You do not necessarily have to read them in order to learn and try new techniques. Keep this book handy and use it with new hires or when you need easy answers that really work for new situations you face. When you feel challenged or stuck, turn to this book to find the tools you need to move forward.

The focus is always on simple, straight-forward fundamentals and core ideas. While the book is not called *Zen and the Art of Retailing* ... it could be. Like a Zen master who teaches students through stories, the simplest principles are the most powerful.. In today's technology-driven retail sector, a gift for cutting through to the eternal truths of retail is what will set highly regarded leaders apart. Concentrated focus on these 7 Timeless Principles divides enduring retail brands from the folks who will close their doors in a few years. Businesses built around the 7 Timeless Principles will serve many future generations of customers.

In providing a concise review of retail, I have purposefully omitted critical functions such as human resources, information systems, payroll and accounting, financial management, supply chain, logistics and more in order to focus on those customer-facing retail capabilities that make the industry unique. While many of the examples are most applicable to brick-and-mortar retail, online retailers will find plenty here that applies directly to their business model. Let's face it, in a profession as old as retail, these 7 Timeless Principles are valid in every channel. The interpretation or tools may change, but the principles do not.

**Chapter 1** is about choosing and delivering a strategy. Your store's strategy is a guiding light in every decision. What you will uniquely bring to your customers and how you will defend that position against your competition are what will define your retail brand.

**Chapter 2** is my favorite topic: treating your customers well. Treat them like they were your family. I imagine you want to be fair, honest and helpful to your family – but not taken advantage of. Customer service is where you build your reputation.

**Chapter 3** is the heart and soul of both online and brick-and-mortar retailing. Selecting and showcasing products that tempt your shoppers makes your store a destination. How you treat your vendors can sustain you during rough times. Make your store or website a seeker's delight to keep customers returning.

**Chapter 4** addresses the touchy issue of making money. Let's face it. That's why we are retailers. We need to make money. Competition usually pinches pricing first. Here's how to deliver the goods and be proud of the money you put in the bank.

**Chapter 5** tackles that emotionally difficult, wonderful, terrible, rewarding, disappointing resource: people. Your team will lead you to prosperity or keep you in the trenches for the rest of your career. Leadership and management are skills everyone can practice and build.

**Chapter 6** is about the most simple hospitality in retail: marketing. In all its varied forms and channels, marketing is about inviting customers and welcoming them back. Just as you would for family.

**Chapter 7** is not as dreary and mundane as operations sounds. It is about keeping a store running like a Porsche engine. Learn the techniques the best operators use to make their store or website a focused system that cranks out happy shoppers and profit.

Too many managers think their job is "running the store." They couldn't be more wrong. A manager's job is creating the team that runs the store. It's running the system of the store. One that meets the needs of a particular set of customers better than any other store or website on the planet.

Retail can get unnecessarily fragmented. Early in their careers, employees are told to focus on buying or operations or merchandising. Software vendors and service providers expand those fractures with solutions that focus on just one thing: creating planograms or optimizing prices or forecasting promotional sales. Retail executives and owners struggle with aligning so many different perspectives within their organization. The average staff member cannot see across all the different components to understand how to integrate and prioritize resources. This book is meant to help connect the dots for people who work inside a fragmented retail organization.

Great retailers last beyond the bubbles and trends. They adapt and serve generations of shoppers. They understand how to orchestrate the intersection of every element in this book: strategy, customer service, merchandising, pricing, managing, marketing and operations.

A retailer may be excellent at selecting an attractive range of products and pricing them well, but if their customer service is lacking, they will not thrive. They might run a tight ship and have an attentive staff. But if their pricing is out of line, customers will abandon them over time. Every one of these 7 Timeless Principles harmonizes to make a retailer profitable and enduring.

For each retailer, store or manager there will be areas of this book where they excel and areas where they lag competition. To be great, every retailer must work on their fundamentals each day and with each new generation of employees.

# INTRODUCTION

Falling short in one or two areas will show up in the customer's experience. You cannot hide a sloppy back room operation when you can't find products featured in the weekly advertisement. You cannot hide an unfocused marketing campaign when new customers dry up. No successful retailer succeeds in some of these areas and not others. They are all important and they all work together.

Like a gardener, store managers must attend to every component. Gardeners know they must site their plants well, water them, fertilize them, weed them, prevent pests and monitor their plants carefully. A gardener who breaks ground, scatters seeds and then waits for autumn will be disappointed in the harvest. Store managers must know when to freshen their assortment, lower (or raise) prices, reward employees, cut back hours, drop a coupon and order more inventory to create the profit "harvest" they want.

If you are truthful, there will be an area that you simply prefer less than the others. That's natural. Everyone has things they enjoy doing more than others. Maybe you love working the sales floor or operating an efficient back room. Like most of us, you probably have delegated the tasks you do not enjoy to someone else. Or you ignore that portion of the operation. Or you put the things you do not like to do on autopilot so you don't have to think about it.

Let's say the portion of the work you most dislike is marketing and advertising. It seems expensive, requires creativity or is difficult to see results. Chances are, you are just repeating what you have done in the past. It requires minimal effort and "checks the box" for getting it done. But because the effort drains you – instead of energizing you – it isn't a focus area for you. That will be evident when you look at new customer rates. Every area where we minimize focus and resources will eventually impact the overall business.

Maybe you love marketing. You are out in the community drumming up new business and never miss an opportunity to network and build relationships with potential new customers. But inside the store, your disgruntled staff's sloppy customer service is leading to lower conversion rates and transactions. Over time, no matter how many new customers you invite into the store, the mediocre service will reduce your sales.

Do you love doing some work because it is where you derive satisfaction but ignore others because it is difficult or "not worth it?" If you cannot bring yourself to manage the website or marketing, it is time to find a service or employee who can take on that responsibility. To believe you will change "because you should" may not be within you. It takes honest self-assessment to realize what you can and cannot do on your own.

Often paying for an outside service will bring all the value we need to free ourselves of the tasks we hate.

The point is, every aspect of this book needs attention from a retailer to deliver an excellent store or website. Armed with the advice and insight from this book, you will have expert guidance on specific action you can take to make your store more profitable and fun to operate than ever before. You can make improvements. No matter your position within the store or your current conditions. Each idea in this book will help you make changes that will make you more effective, a better leader within your team and a smarter retailer. Your customers will reward you and all you have to do is just focus on 7 Timeless Principles.

## WIN Today

To address your store, first track your time. Where do you honestly spend most of your time? If it is vendor management, who is supervising the staff? If it is merchandising, who is maintaining the back-room operations? Simply track your time for a week and then look at how the rest of the store is managed. Use a time tracker like this to help you aggregate your tasks.

| Focus Area | Example | Time |
| --- | --- | --- |
| Sales and customer service | Working the sales floor, helping online customers, resolving customer issues, assembling and executing web orders | |
| Website/online maintenance | Setting up promotions and sales, managing product descriptions and images, managing online inventory | |
| Vendor management | Working with suppliers, placing orders, paying and reconciling invoices | |
| Staff management | Setting schedules, coaching and training, hiring | |
| Merchandising | Cleaning and restocking shelves and displays, changing price tags, selecting and setting up new items | |
| Operations | Receiving product, conducting | |

| | | |
|---|---|---|
| | inventory, cleaning the store and back room, remanufacturing and creating product for sale | |
| Marketing | Setting up ads, social media posts, networking outside the store, cold and warm calls | |

If you track your time for 2 weeks, as a store manager or owner, your time should ideally be split like this:

| Target | Focus Area |
|---|---|
| 15-20% | Sales and customer service |
| 5-10% | Website/online management |
| 5-10% | Vendor management |
| 35-50% | Staff management |
| 10-15% | Merchandising |
| 10-15% | Operations |
| 15-20% | Marketing |

Naturally, your time will vary. Both seasonally and from these guidelines. But if your time study shows focus areas that are over- or under-focused, consider it a warning. Use your time tracker as you complete this book.

# 7 Timeless Principles

RETAIL: The Second-Oldest Profession
© 2019 Flora Delaney

# Timeless Principle 1: Strategy

## Be What Your Competitors Aren't

Strategy is such as strong focus for a retailer in the start-up phase that it may seem permanently established once operations begin. To be honest, a strategy should be unvarying when it is a pillar of success. But to be the guide it is meant to be, a retailer's strategy needs to be communicated without end to its employees and customers.

When employees and managers understand the power of a retailer's strategic position, every decision is easier to make. It is easier to allocate scarce resources. It is easier to prioritize competing initiatives. It guides during economic lean times and reins in exuberant overspending during surpluses.

This chapter will help you reconnect to the original company strategy or give you tools to align to one. It comes first among the 7 Timeless Principles because a retailer's strategy prioritizes all other principles. It is a clear guide post for setting goals for all other principles.

One way to know that your company has a clear strategy is if you recognize and predict the company's approach in the marketplace as it announces annual plans. In a company that has a strategy to deliver the lowest prices in the market, initiatives will align with restricting operational expenses and leveraging an efficient supply chain. In a company with a first-to-market strategy, streamlined initiatives that work with innovative vendors are prioritized. In a company where customer experience is the strategic advantage, website investments, social media content and store events will be prioritized over logistics or promotional investments. As an investor, I would be concerned if a retailer I had invested in that had a stated strategy for low prices and convenient locations were to suddenly discuss investing in exclusive product design development, for example.

All retailers have to stay at par in all areas. But like a multi-leveled video game, retailing requires building stable bases and skills before advancing in market-leading strategic niches to succeed. No organization can lead the market in every area. Just as no retailer can succeed by saying that "everyone" is their target market. Each successful retailer has withstood tests by staying true to its strategy, its target market and building advantages that are difficult for competitors to replicate.

A case in point is Walmart's unvarying focus on delivering low prices every day to its shoppers. It influences everything from its real estate site selection (usually low-priced exurban sites) to its vendor relations (with a strict delivery and replenishment protocol.) Walmart does not chase new format trends or designer apparel lines to deliver profit. Its profits come from a single-minded search to plug every profit leak in the supply chain from manufacturers' production lines to bagging purchases in store. It is why it creates very accurate purchasing forecasts for its vendors who can then source components with a high degree of confidence that eliminates waste in overages "just in case." Its why cashiers have a rotating bagging carousel to quickly bag purchases without moving from their station. It eliminates relying on customers to be as efficient in loading their bags into their carts as the cashiers are in putting items purchased in the bags. (And Walmart's bags are notoriously inexpensive because there is no value created in their strategy by providing customers with a durable or beautiful bag for their purchases.)

Because Walmart's strategy is unvarying, every employee understands that their job is delivering the lowest prices possible to the end customer. That creates less controversy within the organization when making decisions. Everyone knows that projects and initiatives must be measured by the way they will reduce costs.

Walmart is an example of staying true to one vision ... one timeless principle to deliver success.

As you read this first chapter, think about your retail business. Can you clearly state its exact strategy? If you can, you will find it easier to have your ideas advanced when you link your ideas to the company strategy. You can predict the right places to invest resources that will repay in long-term stability and growth. You can identify the strengths that will confound your competitors and invigorate your staff. You can chart your own path to success.

## Strategy Is the Foundation

Strategy is your store's foundation. To begin, execute against a focused idea. To sustain, adapt that idea to new conditions. Your customers may change because of economic shifts. Your competition may change because of new distribution channels. Your product line may change because of new technology. But a strong strategy is a unique and defensible position that your competition finds difficult to reproduce.

Strategy just means: Why am I in business? What do I have to offer that is so different and so compelling that my customers should drive across town or type in my URL before anyone else's?

You do not have a strategy if you try to please everyone.

You have to make choices that zero in on your target customer and meet their needs better than anyone else. If you are a store owner or manager, it is the reason you created the business. If you are an employee, it is quite possibly the reason you decided to work for your company and not a quick-serve restaurant or delivery service. Indeed, many retail executives who began their career in the stores will tell you the reason they started out was to qualify for the employee discount on products they already loved.

Many retailers easily lose sight of their strategy. Management gets distracted and soon back-room operations overtake management time in the store. But what happens at the "front of the house" is what your customers see, remember and why they return. No customer ever valued a store because it processed deliveries at the back door quickly or had a slick time card system.

*Every successful retailer needs to create a strategy that is compelling, executable and defensible.* That means it has to be meaningful to its target customers. It has to be something you can actually do and deliver every single day with every single customer. And if you want to stay in business for long, it has to be something very difficult for your competitors to replicate.

To begin, there are five core strategies to prioritize. No retailer can maximize all of them because the cost to outdistance your competition of every one of these fronts would be prohibitive. Select one of them as your single brand differentiator and then execute against all of the others to a level that is comparable to your major competition to remain a viable operation.

### Strategy 1: Assortment

You will not be beaten on your assortment. (For Europeans, replace "assortment" with the word "range" wherever I use the American term "assortment.") This does *not* mean you will carry every SKU. You can create a differentiated assortment by carrying only ultra-premium brand items, eco-conscious items or locally sourced items, for example. If your strategic differentiator is assortment, then the *key* to being relevant to your shoppers is to focus on adhering to a unique assortment strategy under all conditions. An assortment strategy could mean focusing on the needs of the home-based business, the creative design community or the opening price point shopper. Every SKU (stock keeping unit) in the store has to be evaluated against your strategy and justify its inventory by meeting the need of your targeted shopper.

Examples of retailers who use an assortment strategy are:

- **Target** – A one-stop store for everything from groceries to auto parts PLUS exclusive designer fashion goods that are unavailable anywhere else
- **Home Depot** – Everything for the DIY handyperson: plumbing, landscaping, flooring, lumber. Not for the fine craftsman nor the large construction team. Just perfect for the suburban homeowner who wants to tackle projects on their own
- **Amazon** – Pretty much anything that can be purchased, can be purchased at Amazon

Common assortment strategies are seen at the big-box retailers who tend to ring a traditional shopping mall and are termed "category killers" for their depth of product in their particular niche. Think of PetSmart, Best Buy, Barnes & Noble, DSW or Staples.

**Strategy 2: Convenience**
You will have the most convenient store or online site for your customers to purchase what they want. This could mean extended hours, same-day delivery service, kiosk locations, online shopping, accepting corporate purchase orders (POs) or otherwise making your store or your website the easiest and fastest first choice.

Examples of retailers who use a convenience strategy include:

- **Walgreens** – In over 8,500 locations and most open 24/7, these pharmacy-based stores are practically mini-medical service stations.

- **Zappos** – This online retailer is focused on making it as easy to try on shoes (and send them back!) at home as it is in a store.

A convenience strategy is part of the overall play for all e-commerce sites since by its nature you can order any time of day from anywhere. However, the retailer has to also provide outstanding communication to its shoppers regarding the shipping status, make returns easy (and free) and be completely reliable –even during the busy days leading up to Christmas – to truly dominate the convenience strategy.

**Strategy 3: Service**

You have the friendliest, most knowledgeable people in the industry. You create relationships with your customers that no one else can replicate. You develop and reward your team members with training and an enviable pay rate to retain the best talent available. You encourage your team to provide exceptional service and monetize that outstanding service. Your customers know you authentically care for them and have their best interests at heart.

Examples of retailers who use a service strategy include:

- **Nordstrom** – Their focus on customer service is legendary. From accepting tires as a returned item (when they do not sell tires) to overnight delivery of a forgotten groom's trousers, this company strives for excellent service as its key for commanding premium prices.
- **FTD** – With same-day delivery, online and phone orders and a customizable online calendar to make sure shoppers never forget a birthday or anniversary, FTD has diversified beyond flowers to provide gift-giving services to its customers.

I know of no examples of a retailer who is both a low-price leader operating with a high service strategy. By its nature, high service requires investment in employee training, systems and support. To offset those expenses, high-service retailers are rarely discount retailers.

**Strategy 4: Price**

You have unbeatable prices. You have a reliable price strategy and your customers know that you price products fairly and offer true value. Your customers save money when they shop at your store.

Examples of retailers who use a price strategy include:

- **Walmart** – Price rollbacks are the backbone of the Walmart strategy. Aggressive EDLP (everyday low price) contracts from vendors, low-cost real estate and power buying to the extreme makes Walmart the foremost price strategy retailer.
- **Dollar Tree** – Everything is $1.00 at Dollar Tree, including food and health and beauty aids (HBA). How do they do it? Small-sized products and off-brand vendors combined with a significant amount of closeout goods direct from off-shore manufacturers. The "dollar" segment is the fastest growing retail segment in the United States during 2017.[1]

With audacious cost-cutting, price retailers do not focus on tremendous service from a knowledgeable employee base or a wonderful experience for shoppers. They rarely carry first-to-market products and will often carry name-brand items custom made for them which have fewer options or accessories than can be found elsewhere. With a focus on volume, low-priced retailers will rarely carry a full line of products and focus only on basic SKUs in terms of colors, flavors and sizes.

### Strategy 5: Experience

Your store is a wonderland and a community – not just a store. Perhaps you offer free classes, let clubs use your location for meetings, bring in guest speakers or have an onsite coffee house. In any case, your store is much more than a place to shop for your customers: it is a destination to learn and be with like-minded people.

Examples of retailers who use an experience strategy include:

- **Apple** – Its stores are a mecca for tech lovers who want to see and use the latest gadgets. Customers attend free classes. Apple was the first retailer to provide free internet access to its shoppers from its hands-on retail displays and a mobile cash register using iPads and iPhones. Apple purposefully scours urban centers for unique store locations, such as the Louvre in Paris, the Fifth Avenue glass cube in New York and Regent Street in London, which become architectural destinations in their own right.
- **REI** – A climbing wall, kayak water demos and outdoor adventure expeditions leaving from the parking lot, REI stores offer experiences for the outdoor enthusiast. REI stores are meant to inspire its customers to get outside and use their products.

The price of providing a shopping experience is seen in the details. The goal of a retailer who has invested in an experience strategy is to invite customers to visit often and linger long with every visit. It can be as expensive as marble floors in the store design to a chalkboard sign for the "staff picks" board at a local bookstore,

Dig under every puffed-up corporate mission statement and you will find the same five strategies that every retailer leverages. Most select one main and one secondary strategy.    Again, you must be reasonably comparable on the four other strategies. A customer will not put up with filthy stores or rude service for very long just because the prices are low. Savvy retailers select a strategy and then uphold it as the foremost guide in all other retailing decisions. Your choice to invest in a simple user interface on the website or a broader product selection is easier to make when you know whether your main strategy is convenience or assortment.

Once you have selected a viable strategy that you believe you can execute with consistency, you need to evaluate it from a competitive framework. Look at how you can make your strategy as difficult to replicate for your competitors as possible. That could mean exclusivity agreements with your niche product vendors, a real estate lease that is so far below market that your prices can be lower than your competition while still remaining profitable. For most retailers, the secret to strategic superiority is building a model that envious competitors cannot afford to replicate.

With your main strategy in mind, you can prioritize decisions about your store's location, promotional depth and frequency, inventory levels, delivery schedules and operating hours. Differentiating your store from your competitors can be consistently communicated with your team and all your customer-facing messages. Even your store name can support your strategy. (Which is why Dollar Tree, Dollar General and Family Dollar all use the power of "Dollar" in their name to connote their ultra-low prices.)

Communicate your focus to every employee and every customer you encounter. "Delivery on time or it's free." Or "The city's widest assortment of lawn care." Or "The lowest prices on painting products."

Whatever it is, repeat it until you can hardly stand to hear it anymore. Your customers (who may only encounter you two to three times per year) need the repetition to have your message top of mind when they are ready to make their next purchase.

The biggest temptation for small retailers is to try to be everything to everyone. They want to be the lowest price and the most convenient and have the best service and sell every SKU their customers ever inquire about. That fragmentation will lead to unplanned markdowns on inventory, unprofitable investment in employee programs and deeply discounted prices that do not drive loyalty. Remember, strategy is about making choices.

The first step is the most important: select your store's strategy wisely. Step two? Stick with it.

## WIN Today

Create a grid:

|  | Assortment | Convenience | Service | Price | Experience |
|---|---|---|---|---|---|
| Assortment |  |  |  |  |  |
| Convenience |  |  |  |  |  |
| Service |  |  |  |  |  |
| Price |  |  |  |  |  |
| Experience |  |  |  |  |  |

Place a star in the grid location that represents the two top strategies your store (or chain) is attempting to occupy. Then write the names of your top six competitors (don't forget internet pure-play operators) in the grid where they are perceived to occupy. If you are uncertain, review their advertising tag lines or public statements about what they are investing in for the future.

Share your findings with others in the organization and align on the correct grid space for yourself and your competitors. If your square in the grid is crowded, evaluate how you can occupy one where there is no competition.

## The Middle Always Loses

If the past is the best predictor of the future, we know that the world will continue to be polarized. Ends of the spectrum in politics and consumer trends will continue to grab headlines and customer attention. As a retailer, it is clear that the middle ground is less attractive than ever.

Retail reflects the same trend of the vanishing middle market. According to Pew Research, the "middle class," which represented 61% of all adults in the United States in 1971, is only 50% of the population today. At the same time, the share of income that these households control has decreased from 62% to only 43%.[2]

The middle market is crushed with competition on one side with low-price commodities and on the other side with upmarket luxury goods. For shoppers that means a growing pattern of shopping dollar channel or convenience stores (which are not the most price competitive but are convenient locations for a transportation-challenged population) or club stores and luxury stores. For the retailer who previously succeeded in navigating the middle of the road for assortment and pricing, long-term success is nearly impossible.

To start, look at the business objectively and recognize changing trends. Review sales, customer feedback and observe employee conversations to determine if there is a shift toward the upscale premium trend or the no-frills trend in your stores.

Do you think your brand could extend to the high end of the market? If so, how can you make your shop top of mind for those customers? Can you give a webinar or host an event to introduce new services to customers and differentiate yourself from the competition? Appealing to early adopters can be a prime profit driver for high-end product lines. Can you offer pre-sales for new technology or fashions? Diversifying away from the middle could make your brand noticeable with the right market. This is especially true if your shop is located where opinion makers live or work. Engage with customers who blog or have high followers on their social media accounts and give them newsworthy insight into trends to make them look smart. Together you can build credibility and loyalty with the kind of shoppers you want to attract.

The premium end of the spectrum can be served even with a conventional range of product through impeccable white-glove customer service. Same-day delivery, a customized restocking service, and first-name interactions can build loyalty among the customers who want individualized service. Many retailers aspire to this through faceless loyalty programs, but very few have the employee focus to deliver an *exceptional* transaction every time. The simple step of remembering your best customer's first names can build real loyalty.

A coffee shop I know holds a contest every quarter for one week. Baristas get a bonus at the end of the week if they were able to address 20 customers by name each shift. It is a week that employees look forward to and the tallying is a fun competition that keeps them engaged all week long.

If you aspire to deliver exceptional customer service in your shop, carefully monitor and coach employee interactions. To begin, every customer should be cheerfully greeted and asked what brings them into the shop. Careful exploration and reliable product knowledge help an employee ask the right questions and recommend the right products. Asking customers about more than replacement products uncovers sales opportunities. A simple liquor store purchase can triple in size once an employee finds out it is in support of a dinner party and offers to take a return on any unopened bottle, for example.

Finally, an extraordinary store experience attracts high-end customers. While your store may seem like an unremarkable setting, adding wi-fi and seating, coffee or hot cider, community events, attractive window displays and ancillary product lines to attract the right customer can build loyalty. In Melbourne, Australia there is a combined print/copy store and art supply house. Expensive handmade papers, sable paint brushes and easels share space with ink and toner cartridges for large-format printers. Its entryway is practically an art gallery produced by its customers. By catering to a specific art-centric market, the store dominates sales to the local artist market for printing artwork as well as their more mundane business card and invoice needs.

There is a risk that prevents most retailers from pursuing the high-end market: the fear of alienating current customers. The book *Angel Customers & Demon Customers*[3] points out that not all customers are profitable and some may need to be alienated. Consider any change in assortment, pricing or format as a gradual pivot rather than an abrupt shift to move current customers along and retain their loyalty.

In basketball, the pivot is a great move to gain relief from defensive pressure or to change the offensive dynamic. The player keeps one foot planted on the floor while moving the other to either shoot, dribble or pass in a new direction. As long as one foot remains planted, the player can spin to take in the competitive landscape and then move the ball to the next best position on the floor.

Businesses looking to change their value proposition, customer base, marketing voice or other key element would do well to learn how to pivot.

Your customers, vendors and employees will move with you if your change is a pivot. Show them that you are starting from your legacy heritage but making a change that moves into the next chapter. A wholesale conversion is very unlikely to succeed.

Examples:

**Subway's** message of "Eat Fresh" allows them to pivot to the place of any number of healthy options. Could they succeed if tomorrow they became the home of a decadent three-layer burger? Absolutely not. But, boy, would it be easy for them to pivot into frozen yogurt.

**American Eagle Outfitters** once stood for flannel, denim and Timberland boots. (When they were utilitarian – not urban hip.) Its customers were blue-collar shoppers who wanted Pendleton looks without the price. It moved to the current teen-focused apparel store by pivoting to denim, flannel and hoodies featuring everyday working man materials with teenage body cuts. Had they strayed too far (say, creating a luxe brand of high-end fabrics and styles) they would have failed.

Perhaps you believe your best move is to shift and deliver a no-frills, budget-based selection to gain market share. Cost control is the key to success. The supply chain and customer experience must survive in a very narrow cost band to deliver the lowest prices and create margin through high volume.

Retailers can keep their costs down by:
- Partnering with the lowest-priced vendors
- Locating in buildings with lower-than-market lease costs
- Carrying a small range of high-turning inventory
- Eliminating investments in slow-turning niche items
- Hiring affordable employees
- Focusing on online sales without a retail shop
- Reducing marketing costs

To succeed in the no-frills market, customers need to have at least one reliable benefit other than cost to maintain their loyalty. Cost alone is a losing framework because at some point a competitor will find a way to sell at a cheaper price. But, if your products can be reliably low priced *and* always in stock or easy to order or delivery is fast, you can use that secondary benefit to build strong loyalty when competitive price pressure comes along.

As you pivot to the no-frills market, it is important to manage your changing market position with your current customer base. Begin by making it clear that some slow-moving, higher-priced products within the standard assortment are being discontinued. Use every marketing vehicle to stay laser-focused on a new message such as "No one sells for less in the city – we beat anyone else's price on like goods by 10%" or "Always in stock on the pet food you need or its free." Select that one component that will set you apart (same-day delivery, order online for less, whatever it is) and repeat it to test if your plan will succeed in the long run.

Your brand has to stand apart from everyone else. It can be the selection of goods, the pricing, the customer service, the store experience or the convenience of shopping at your website or shop. But it has to be one thing that sets you apart and can be easily recalled by your target market to be different from everyone else.

Appealing to everyone by providing a middle ground will not succeed.

## WIN Today

Engage and energize your sales team using the coffee shop idea to inspire them to provide first-name interactions with your best customers.

## Be Something Online Can't Be

Listen to some media pundits and you could believe that online and e-commerce is the end of brick-and-mortar retail. After all, 70% of US households and 82% of US households with incomes over $112,000 now have Amazon Prime[4]. But let's take a look at a fact: 91% of all goods and services are still purchased in physical stores.[5] So why does the industry obsess about online shopping?

In short, it's because of the shift in expectations that online retail has created in shoppers. Especially young shoppers. Millennials have grown up in an age of next-day delivery and unlimited options. Online retailers have reshaped views on the importance of seeing and touching merchandise before purchasing. For young shoppers, the hassle of getting to a store for instant ownership is weighed against the ease of one-button ordering and home delivery. Young shoppers view a trip to a store differently than older generations.

Nevertheless, there are critical ways that physical stores can always beat online retailers to remain relevant and compelling to future shoppers.

**Be Social**

Young shoppers spend unprecedented amounts of time on social media interacting online. But they desire and crave more authentic interactions. Shopping with friends is considerably more appealing to young shoppers than their older counterparts. This generational trend has been true for decades. Presumably older shoppers eventually tire of shopping as a pastime. For youthful shoppers, bonding over shopping and influencing and being influenced while shopping is still a new and engaging diversion.

Smart retailers will consider how to make their store more engaging and social. Even small stores with small budgets can offer warm cider and teas in the winter to induce longer – more social – store visits and create compelling and inviting windows that call to passersby to stop. Other social ideas include offering free wi-fi, creating a fun trivia chalkboard in the store and, of course, participating in social media.

Moving beyond simple Facebook or Twitter posts, make sure your business is visible on Yelp, Snapchat and Instagram. Take advantage of social media promotions and create offers specifically for social media users. Create a "check in and get X" as a starter.

When you consider social media as one more channel to interact with your customers and not as another new task to complete, you can remain relevant to the next generation of shoppers. Be yourself in social media exchanges. Show loyalty to the home sports teams, congratulate your employees on their milestones, brag about your newest products and your personal best running time. Build a consistent personality that is cohesive with the great customer service they receive in your stores and in contrast to the "price only" cold experience of online purchasing to beat online retailers.

**Listen In**

While online stores may talk in a friendly and knowledgeable way to a shopper, they cannot listen. Only a human being can listen compassionately to a customer describe their situation and nod in understanding. Teach your store associates to ask good questions and demonstrate to shoppers that they understand their issue before offering solutions or starting to "sell." When your customers feel heard they will be more open to making purchases.

One appealing aspect of online shopping is peer reviews prior to making a purchase. Shoppers get to see product ratings and read what other shoppers think of a product before they purchase. For customers, it's like listening in on a conversation about a product they are considering for purchase. Brick-and-mortar stores can replicate that experience by including reviews in their product signs or creating their own review system. Wine stores include *Wine Spectator* ratings, for example. Even handwritten "our favorites" can help bridge the gap for customers used to looking at reviews prior to making a purchase.

**Be Friendly**

In survey after survey, customers say that they prefer being helped by a smart, friendly person rather than figuring things out on their own. Trouble is, over the years customers have become so disappointed with lifeless exchanges (Banish "Can I help you?" and "Have a nice day" from your store!!) that they no longer even expect such interaction.

Train and coach your team to give focus to every customer that walks through the door. Ensure that your team is up-to-date on the latest information for the products you sell and that they are comfortable approaching customers and beginning conversations. Genuine caring and advice from a real human being builds an authentic relationship – and loyalty.

Another way to create a friendly environment is to allow demonstrations and hands-on use of products prior to purchasing. Sell office supplies? Have working models of printers where customers are invited to print color photos and compare different quality ink, paper or printers. Sell furniture? Set up floor models and have plenty of swatches available to take home so shoppers can see their choices in their own homes. Add a well-trained store associate to the mix and you have created an experience that online retailers will find difficult to duplicate.

The key is to provide the human connection that only face-to-face interactions with other people can provide. After all, enormous companies are spending millions of dollars to try to develop artificial intelligence (AI) that will approximate that actual human connection. Those retail tech companies covet what a friendly, caring store associate can provide in the most natural way possible: a human connection.

Show off your connections by highlighting your customers and how they use/rely on your store to have a happier/healthier/more successful life. Show off testimonials and actual customers on your website or social media. Embrace what you can do that e-commerce sites cannot do. As Benjamin Golley of Today's Beauty Supply says: "Amazon can't give you a hug."

**Be the Friendly Expert**

Embrace your expertise. You either went into the business or decided to join the company you are with because you are passionate about the products you carry. As the local expert, you can ask your customers questions and then listen to their exact situation before making a recommendation. That kind of customized solution is nearly impossible for an online retailer to duplicate.

Highlight the experts in your store for different departments. Does your wine department buyer make regular trips to Napa to seek out new vintages? Make sure your customers know. Merchandise endcaps with a Staff Picks section and let each of your staff experts explain why they love the product. Make sure your customers know that you are the local expert and that you understand the local market better than anyone online ever can. Then carry that local expertise over to your website or social media accounts. When you use your website to compete on expertise and not price, you can win in the online game.

**Be Local**

Ensure your store is present at local events. Support parades, festivals, clean-ups and other local events to deepen your store's relationships with the community. Select local events that tie into your store's mission. Read-a-thons for a bookstore, walk-a-thons for a shoe store, homeless shelter support for a food store are meant to both benefit the community and also reinforce your store's image. Be sure to snap photos of these outside-the-store events to share on your social media pages. Promote your relationships with a community board in your store and don't hesitate to ask your local community to support you in turn by shopping your store.

Cooperate with other businesses within the community to create events that drive shoppers to your store. Midnight sales and sidewalk sales are common. But think outside the box by developing a cross-marketing program with a non-competing business like a pet store or restaurant. Share customer lists or promote their business on your receipts while they promote yours on theirs. Sound scary? If you don't ask: you don't get. Something everyone on your team should learn. (See "Building Your Network to Build Your Sales" in *Timeless Principle 5: Marketing*.)

**Be Smart**

As a store owner or manager, you will not beat online retailers by meeting their price or by carrying as wide a range in your store as their virtual shelves will hold. Focus on the true differentiating factors you can control that online retailers cannot match: a friendly and helpful team, a welcoming environment, relationships with customers and the local community.

While you may not use your website for transactions, you do need a website. Use it to communicate the basics: your hours, location (with a clickthrough to a map), parking pointers, phone number, etc. Then use it to show off your store's personality and brand. Tell your story. Let it show just enough to inspire customers to want to visit your store. Think of it like a dating app. You don't want to show everything: just enough to get them intrigued.

When a grumbling customer asks you to meet online pricing, remind them that you employ local people in a store that deeply cares about its customers and community. Point out your delivery program, local events you sponsor and other important programs your store supports. Remind your customer that the national or international website does not provide such services to the community and that their profits are out of state or out of the country. Chances are, they will think about you in a new way. You might lose the sale ... but you might also gain some respect, change a mind and create a new loyal customer.

# STRATEGY

## WIN Today

List six local events that you could either participate in over the coming year or could create.

1._____

2._____

3._____

4._____

5._____

6._____

Make a phone call today to begin to make progress against one of these events. Make two phone calls tomorrow. Add the events to your store calendar.

## Be Something Brick and Mortar Can't Be

Competition is cut-throat for online retailers. Competitors change their offers by the minute. Technology is expensive and changes every day. Customers have high demands. Logistic costs gobble up profits. Customers abandon shopping carts with the click of a button. And let's not get started about the turnover rate in information technology (IT) resources. To win online – against people with deep pockets: Amazon, Walmart and Target – it takes doing what brick and mortar can't.

### Be First to Market

Online retailers can unveil new items in minutes. Brick-and-mortar retailers require weeks or months to bring new items into their stores. With beauty shots and a new landing page, online retailers can introduce a new product or line everywhere at once. Assuming you have the right vendor agreements in place, you can beat brick-and-mortar retailers (and their mitigation pre-sales) every time.

Unlike a brick-and-mortar store that has to invest in expensive remodeling to roll out a new line, your online store can learn about customer demand for new products inexpensively. Work with vendors to create pop-up shops on your site to test their marketability. Develop a trend-setting reputation by always having the first of a sought-after product niche that appeals to your target market. Work with vendors to market new items in that niche better than your competition through your extended marketing or sponsorships. Make your site newsworthy for extra publicity and eyeballs.

You can be the first to serve the remote regions of the country or the planet. Brick-and-mortar retailers cannot invest in the infrastructure to put a store in Escanaba, Michigan or Emory, Texas. The population and the disposable income are not there. But in every Escanaba or Emory there are a few households – retirees, professionals, enthusiasts – who are willing to pay a premium to get the latest thing. Online retailers who discover their base and cultivate them with attention can uncover a hidden revenue stream among the most far-flung positions on the globe.

### Be the Accessible Expert

One single expert can change an online retailer's personality and credibility. Brick-and-mortar retailers have to heavily invest in training to ensure that every encounter with a store associate is helpful and friendly. Most shoppers would give them failing marks. Online retailers can create a persona that is always friendly and helpful – for every single customer.

If you do not have a viable spokesperson, you can create an encyclopedic video library to demonstrate the products you sell. Consider short recipes, repairs or fashion guides to build your brand voice and show customers new ideas for using the products they find on your site. Well-designed short videos can build bigger market baskets.

Create a mobile app exclusively for your video content with embedded "buy it now" functions. Use a "deal of the day" promotion within the app to make it important for customers to use it every day.

Customers value easily accessible online user's manuals (for ALL past products sold.) Online manuals bring lapsed customers back to your site. Host a user's forum or other community site so that customers can weave their own interconnection through your site. Ask permission to highlight a customer "project of the week" or other contests to develop your own social media content.

For fans and enthusiasts, "being in the know" is currency. They thrive on being among the first of their community to know about new models, new products, new trends. As an online expert, you can feed them exclusive behind-the-scenes videos and reports that keep them on the leading edge. That kind of insight reinforces frequent website visits and loyalty. Be sure to ask for Google ratings and reviews from your biggest fans to keep your site organically high in online searches. About 75% of all people read reviews before making a purchase decision and almost 90% of all people say they trust online reviews as much as a personal recommendation.[6]

**Be a Completist**

As an online retailer, you have the never ending aisle. Meaning you can carry every size, flavor, color and model in a line without the overhead charges of a brick-and-mortar retailer. Leaning into the long-tail strategy[7], online retailers can go deep into niches and specialty areas that brick-and-mortar retailers cannot afford. While local stores are scrambling to keep just a fraction of their SKUs updated online, digital retailers can be encyclopedic about placing every single SKU into their online catalog.

Select the niche market that is most aligned to your target market. Begin by measuring the market potential to gain market share with a particular group: the gluten free requirements of celiac patients, petite maternity wear, disabled athletes, Italian film junkies. No niche is too small if you can create a loyal following and meet their needs better than any other retailer. Once you have a stable base, delve into their unmet needs through research to find the other common points of interest that could become a subcategory within the online shop. Using this very targeted (narrow but deep) strategy, you can out-assort any brick-and-mortar store and become an online expert with a loyal community following.

### Be Fairly Priced

Online retailing has a reputation as the most inexpensive channel. "I can find it cheaper online" is a constant complaint  brick-and-mortar retailers hear from their customers. So it is critical that you know the prices across your online and physical store competitors. While you do not need to be the cheapest to gain sales, you do need to be priced fairly. That means that you leverage your operational savings (no store rent, very low labor) to set prices and margins that attract price-conscious shoppers.

Test shipping and handling fees and promotions with your shoppers to strike the right balance between honest pricing and attention-grabbing prices. Create specific value-priced promotional items that can be the centerpiece of your cyber Monday landing page. Use bounce-back promotional codes liberally with lapsed customers to keep them using your site for future purchases.

### Be Convenient

Is there anything more convenient than shopping from your couch on a cold rainy day? From "Buy It Now" buttons to mobile apps to Instagram stores, making it easy to buy is the true advantage of the digital retailer.

But being convenient means taking it further for your customers by making it easy to control where and when their purchase will be delivered. Especially for customers who live in multi-unit dwellings or risky neighborhoods. Returns must be easy to execute and, optimally, free for the customer to be truly convenient. Digital retailers who embrace convenience have to think through the entire purchase experience, including the packaging. Delighting customers is at the core of the popular "unboxing" video trend.

## WIN Today

Dive deeply into your target market to find three more niches they are naturally interested in. Find specific niches: cabinet making, children's crafts, playing video games. Look for connections by talking with customers and giving them incentives to complete surveys on your site. Share your findings with your buyers and vendors to explore a new landing page to test in the next 30 days.

## How Do You Really Stack Up?

### Using a Mystery Shopper Program to Point Out Blind Spots

A small retailer needed to create a strategy for the next 5 to 7 years. They routinely talked to their customers and team members. They conducted a detailed customer survey 2 years ago.

They concluded:
- They were the best in the market.. As evidence, a local business group had selected them to lead a conference round table on retail practices.
- The two main obstacles to increasing store traffic were poor locations that were selected over 25 years ago and lack of convenient parking.
- Their customers were high-end shoppers who did not mind paying more for the great customer service they provided.

Still,, they felt pinched by new competitors opening nearby. Profit margins were down. Sales skewed to deeply discounted product-of-the-month promotions.

After listening to the team, we set up a mystery shopper program to see what customers actually experienced in their stores.

The findings uncovered that:
- Customers were commonly ignored for up to 15 minutes upon entering the store.
- When customers asked about specific products, usually all they heard was an aisle number. Any additional conversation quickly revealed a lack of product experience or knowledge.
- Store associates were more surly and unkempt than management realized.
- Prices were competitive but not enticing. Locations were convenient and product selection was appealing – but high-end customers were happy to drive farther to engage with e a cheerful, knowledgeable team .

Think that couldn't happen to you? Think you can't be fooled? Think again.

The management team was on site every day. Their interaction with their team was so close that they no longer saw gaps in service. Management rewarded completing tasks like putting away deliveries, making bank drops and finishing the work schedule more than helping customers. At least, the team believed there was more retribution if you didn't complete tasks than for not assisting shoppers. And customers could figure that out in a single store visit.

If you are ready to uncover the truth, here is how to set up a low-cost mystery shopper program that any focused manager can create. First, do not alert your team members to the mystery shopper program. Putting them on notice will have them ratchet up to "best behavior" levels. Second, use a professional service or select people who your team will not recognize. Frankly, you can source a professional shopper service or just employ unbiased acquaintances that are reliable. Consider teaming with a local non-profit that can send in reliable shoppers in return for a donation. Then:

1. Identify your main competitors. Be honest and include the tough ones as well as the easy ones.
2. Find a professional shopper service or hire "shoppers" to complete a mystery shopping survey in return for something of value. Perhaps reimburse them for up to $50 of whatever they purchase at their assigned store.
3. Provide your mystery shoppers with specific questions to answer. And a mandatory deadline for completing their store shops: 2 weeks at most.
4. Assign a specific store (including your own) to each shopper. Do not tell them which other people nor which other stores are included in the study. Each store should be visited by a minimum of five shoppers at different times of the week/day.
5. Give each shopper the same task so that each store is tested in the same manner (for example, ask for assistance in finding a gluten-free product, the best bicycle under $175 for a child, an organic dog food, etc.)
6. Compile the answers and evaluate them analytically (in a spreadsheet or with a numeric measure that can be constant across all questions, such as 1=never, 2=sometimes, 3=usually, 4=always.)[8] Look for patterns.
7. Share your findings with your team and discuss specific ways to address each issue. Expect denial and excuses – but do not accept them. Take time to let the results soak in with your team. Reinforce the negative and the positive experiences your customers have without overemphasizing either extreme.
8. Set targets and measure against the new targets every day. For example, you can institute a new policy that all customers must be greeted within 20 feet of the door. Then measure that goal. Change how you evaluate your people and reward them to ensure compliance with new targets.

Recognize people who are meeting the new targets and make them heroes.

If your business does pass the customer mystery shopper experience with flying colors, it is time to do a similar survey evaluating assortment (count number of choices by SKU, brand and price points.) Evaluate promotions by comparing at least 6 months of advertised promotions to promotions in your stores during the same time. Evaluate prices by comparing prices on several dozen key SKUs across competitive stores each week. Each one of the store strategies listed in "Strategy Is the Foundation" in *Timeless Principle 1: Strategy* can be measured with a similar mystery shopper initiative.

Online shopping experiences are regularly monitored in the same way by counting the number of clicks it takes to find a particular item on competing sites, evaluating the order process, the shipping notifications, the delivery timing and packaging, condition of the items and the returns process. Every step can be quantitatively measured and evaluated. If you make an effort to remove your blinders and see your stores in the same framework as your customers, you can find out how you truly stack up – and determine what to change to stay ahead of the competition.

# STRATEGY

## WIN Today

Use this sample mystery shopping survey to understand and see your store from a customer's point of view:

Store name_____
Address _____
Day and date_____
Time _____
Name or description of store employee

_____

### Store Appearance
Was the outside clean – clear sidewalks, clean windows and doors, etc.? Yes/No:_____
What was the first thing you noticed upon entering the store?

_____
Was inside the store clean and attractive?
Yes/No:_____

### Initial Greeting
How long did it take to be greeted upon entering the store?

_____ Immediately

_____ Minutes

_____ I was not greeted

Was the greeting friendly and professional?
Yes/No:_____
If not immediately greeted, was the store employee

_____ On the phone

_____ Talking with staff

_____ On the computer

_____ Helping another customer

_____ No one present

_____
Other_____

If the store employee was occupied, did he/she let you know that they would be right with you? _____Yes _____No
Was the employee's appearance appropriate to the nature of the store? Yes / No
(why):_____

- 32 -

**Customer Service**
Ask the employee for <*insert your scenario here*>
Did the store employee ask good questions to find out what you were looking for? (Your situation, your budget, your experience?)
Yes / No:_____
Was the store employee knowledgeable about the merchandise? (quickly found a selection, could explain why it was a good choice, gave you several options or suggestions)
Yes / No:_____

**Checkout**
Was the checkout experience positive?
Yes/No:_____
Did the store employee thank you upon completion of your purchase?
Yes/No:_____
Did the store employee offer to carry your purchase to the car or have your purchase delivered?
Yes/No:_____
What was your overall experience with the staff in the store?
Comments:

_____

**Merchandise**
What was your first impression of the store?

_____
What is your overall opinion of the merchandise selection?

_____
Was the overall shopping experience enjoyable, leaving you with a desire to return?

_____

# 7 Timeless Principles

RETAIL: The Second-Oldest Profession
© 2019 Flora Delaney

# Timeless Principle 2: Customer Service

## Treat Your Customers Well

Whether your retail organization is entirely digital or a gas station convenience store that relies on walk-ins, it requires customers. And while every one of the 7 Timeless Principles are needed to have a well-run retail business, this is the one that will sink the business ... even if you are getting the other six right.

Every customer wants to be seen as a unique person who is valued by your company. It doesn't matter whether you use automated chatbots to solve customer issues or rely on a commission sales force to attend to customers. It really is as simple as treating customers with care and concern. Trouble is, most of the people hired in the retail sector to provide mission-critical attention for customers are being hired at minimum wage – many in their first job. Their experience as both consumers and helpful assistants may be extremely limited. Put them in a store where they see the seasoned employees gossiping at the cash register or back room and how will they learn their true role in the company?

Customer service is one of the most immediately transformative Timeless Principles. One customer at a time. One transaction at a time. Each one a chance to improve the encounter for a customer who may return because of their good experience. If your last customer was a nightmare, or if you have been rebuffed with a "just looking" from the last dozen customers, the next one can be the one that you connect with and really enjoy helping. The reason this is the first chapter after *Timeless Principle 1: Strategy* is because it is the one that can start to deliver results the same day you begin to emphasize it. This isn't a slow burn. Start to improve customer service today and you can improve your sales results today.

Retail employees who excel at engaging with their customers also enjoy their job more. They get to talk to folks, solve problems for them and make helpful suggestions. They get to learn more about the products they sell and how customers use them. Frankly, their shifts go by faster because they focus on helping the people in front of them and not on watching the clock. When customer-facing employees are in the zone, they bounce from one customer to the next, knocking them out with attention and possibly changing the course of the day for their customers.

The saying "hire for attitude, train for skill" is keenly true for selecting customer-facing staff. The best are self-motivated and positive, able to bounce back throughout the day to provide continuously excellent service. People who are strongly empathetic and able to put themselves in the customer's shoes make fast connections and advocate for their customers. Stores that are winning with customer service have more fun. Contests, inside jokes and daily (even hourly) goals make each day interesting. Managers watch to find the best combination of employees that makes the sales floor a productive buzz. Call centers track every interaction to uncover those people who seem to naturally deliver results for their customers and the company.

The timeless quality of great customer service is that it builds relationships with your customers. Real emotions that get stirred up with powerful customer service: gratitude, respect, trust. Those emotions are meaningful to all generations and all income brackets.

This chapter is meant to fire you up if you work directly with customers or to get your attention and focus if you work in a part of the company that services the folks who do. At the end of the day, it isn't the CEO, stockholders or the manager who determine the outcome of your retail operation. It is your customers. You want them to come back to you because they can rely on customer service that always treats them well.

## Excellent Customer Service for Your G-U-E-S

In the heady first days of a new employee's training, it is typical spend time covering cash register transactions, delivery protocol and how to stock shelves. Too often, the most basic driver of retail success is overlooked: customer service. Truth is, in the most successful retailers, a new employee cannot even be on the sales floor until they have been trained in how to interact with customers.

During the natural course of a year, even seasoned employees and managers become lazy about greeting and extending service to *every* customer. Top-flight store managers know that being vigilant about offering exceptional customer service every day with every customer makes the cash register ring. A simple, flexible and mandatory customer service plan that is reinforced with every employee is critical.

Begin by communicating to your team and your new employees that delivering a great customer experience is the **number one focus**. In other words, all other retail tasks (merchandising, pricing, back room operations – *any* other job) should be seen as a distraction that always should be postponed to give excellent customer service. Demonstrate that to your employees by always excusing yourself and taking care of customers so they see that customer service is a natural part of your store's culture. Challenge the team to create a new regular customer for the store with every single shift they work. Help them understand the value of having each customer re-visit the store just one more time per year than normal.

Set basic expectations for what great customer service means by remembering the G-U-E-S-T mnemonic.

### G – Greet

Use the 10/10 rule. Welcome your customers within 10 seconds of entering your store and within 10 seconds of coming within 10 feet of you. Your goal is to make your customer feel welcomed and acknowledged. Besides being polite and friendly, shoplifters will generally shy away from stores where they are greeted and engaged in conversation with store employees. So in addition to doing the right thing for your legitimate customers, you will be defending your store's bottom line. Greetings should be authentic. Include your name as a fundamental element of building a relationship with a customer. In addition to "I'm William, welcome to ABC Shop," include a true comment, such as "You look like you're in a hurry" or "It's a hot day today, right?" Just as important: smile.

And when you are busy with another customer, still greet a customer and acknowledge a customer. That sounds like "Hello there. I am with this customer now, but as soon as I get freed up, I'll be happy to help you." Customers who know you see them feel welcomed, even if you are the only one ringing up customers.

## U – Understand

Find out why your customer has come into your store today. Let them know that they can work with you – a knowledgeable, caring person – or that they can shop on their own. It's as simple as "What brings you in today?" or "How can I help you this morning?" Make and maintain eye contact. If your customer wishes to shop on their own, let them know they need only ask and you would be happy to assist. If they are lingering, return to them and see how they are doing. If they merely ask for the location of a product *walk* them to the items, instead of telling them the aisle number. Otherwise, consider yourself ready to advance to the Explore phase.

## E – Explore

Ask questions to find out what product will best meet their needs. Here is where your expertise can shine. Ask about how they intend to use something. Be genuinely interested in a recipe, party or gardening question to zero in on their needs. Focus on listening skills and product knowledge to set you apart from your competition in this stage. More importantly, it is where you can outdistance yourself from low-priced internet retailers. Once your customer knows that you understand their exact needs, they will be more likely to listen to your suggestions.

If you cannot answer their questions, make a smooth handoff to someone who can. Use names to keep the conversation friendly. "Robert is our plumbing expert. I'll put you in his capable hands and I am sure he can help you today."

Be conversational, relaxed and friendly. Remember to delay suggesting solutions until you have asked questions and your customer is sure you understand their needs. Asking questions indicates that you care about their situation and you are willing to listen.

Have an open mind. Remember that what you think is affordable may not be what they think is affordable. Conversely, do not judge what a customer can purchase based on what they are wearing or how they look. A way to think about that is to treat every customer who walks through the door as if they are a millionaire who just happens to be walking into your store on their casual day.

**S – Suggest**

Confidently recommend two or three products that will meet your customer's needs. It is good to give your customer choices. For example, a good/better/best offering could sound like "This is our highest quality paint solution because it has the most pigment and gives a truly deep color. But if you simply need this for a quick coat before you move, this is a great choice for its price and value." Or you can make a suggestion based on their earlier answers, which could sound like "Since you said you seem to often find yourself battling insect damage in your garden, you may want to take advantage of our jumbo pack which offers enough for the entire summer at less than double the price."

If you cannot narrow your recommendations down to less than three choices, you should remain in the explore phase. Continue asking questions about their budget, situation, experience with past products, etc. until you are confident that you can suggest two to three items that will exactly match their needs. Too often, store associates rush into the suggest phase and end up pointing out eight to twelve items on the shelf. If that is all they can offer, a customer is no better off than reading all the packages on the shelves themselves!

If the product the customer wants is not in stock, offer an alternative. Then, offer to order the product – and deliver it! – for optimal customer service. It is a store's best defense to keep customers from completing their sale at another store or online. Plus, home or business delivery can knit a bond to a customer like no other transaction.

The Suggest phase is also where you should offer add-on sales that make sense for the customer's situation. Having a party? Offer mixers, ice and paper goods. Going to a wedding? Do they need shoes or undergarments? Working in the yard? Suggest gloves, sunscreen or insect repellent. Before the customer goes to the cash register be sure to complete this phase by asking if there is anything else they are looking for or need. Do not assume the first reason they gave is the only one for being in the store. To increase sales, offer to carry items to the cash register to allow them to continue to shop unburdened.

**T – Thank**

Show your appreciation and thank each customer for selecting your store. Make sure each customer feels valued to build loyalty. First, ensure that they were well taken care of: "Is there anything else you hoped to find today?"

When finishing the transaction, thank the customer, bag or box their purchase and, if possible, offer to carry it to their car. If someone else will do that, make a smooth handoff: "William will be able to help you out from here. Thank you for your business today."

As you think about your competition and how to keep or build a thriving business, your G-U-E-S-T should be your focus. Make customer service the core of your store's culture to be your best every day. It takes time, but with the right reinforcement, it simply becomes "how we work here" at your store. As the process gains momentum, new employees will find themselves learning and modeling from the more experienced employees. As it becomes more natural, it becomes easier for everyone to be more genuine and have fun. And people who are having fun and gaining a sense of accomplishment are much more likely to stay in their job.

## WIN Today

Use the G-U-E-S-T model with every customer for one entire shift. Challenge yourself to recognize the phases as you and your customer pass through each one. Most people confirm that the G-U-E-S-T model makes their time on the sales floor pass more quickly and makes their job more interesting. Team members enjoy their job more and sell more product when they truly engage with customers and increase their product knowledge, creating a virtuous cycle.

Note: Just because a significant portion of the customers you engage with brush you off or do not engage with your G-U-E-S-T approach, that does not mean it isn't successful. Greeting and thanking each customer, even if they were self-directed and introverted while in the store, is still a meaningful goal when implementing the G-U-E-S-T model.

## Three Customers and What They *Really* Need

For retailers, there are three main customer types: individual consumers, small businesses (including home offices) and institutional customers like schools, hospitals and nonprofit organizations. Delivering an integrated solution for each customer type is key to a stable revenue base in all economic conditions.

Here are five ways to meet the needs of each customer type:

**Individual Consumers**

**Have what I need in stock.** As a consumer, I really don't have a schedule for replenishing stuff. When I run out, I need it. So always have what I rely on you for in stock to make your store top of mind when I need to replenish my supplies.

**Treat me well.** I have two main choices when I need supplies: the internet or a store like yours. The internet is reliable and easy – but I certainly do not get personalized service. You can make me feel special by remembering me, talking to me (and listening) and making thoughtful recommendations. Throw in home delivery or help me get it to the car and why would I choose an internet reseller?

**Set your prices fairly.** I *love* a deal and a sale. What I do not love is paying full price one week only to discover that if I had waited a few more days I could have paid 20% less! You know what I buy (based on my past sales history) so tell me when my favorites will be on sale at your store. Remind me and invite me (without shouting!) and I will reward you with my loyalty.

**Be more than a store.** Connect with me on Facebook, Twitter or the community bulletin board. I actually like knowing my shopkeepers. So advertise in my church bulletin or school newspaper. Seeing you at community events makes me trust you more than a faceless big-box store or internet reseller.

**Make me feel good about giving you my business.** Remind me that when I shop with you my money stays in my neighborhood or my planet is greener or that my kid's school benefits from your sales. If I have a problem, please don't hassle me. Stand by your products and make amends when there are issues. Really mean it when you say *thank you.*

**Small Businesses**

**Remember my timelines are short.** I don't really have a 3- or 5-year plan. I'm ashamed to say a lot of my decisions are made in the moment. So when you talk to me about return on investment (ROI) or long-term savings, I am more likely to just want to hear how you can solve the problem I have right now. Be practical. Once we establish a rhythm, we can talk about the future.

**Help me buy a solution instead of a price.** Sure, I want the lowest price I can get, doesn't everyone? But if you can help me understand how you deliver a better value, I will listen and even pay more money if it is the right thing to do. Talk to me in a language I can understand and please don't use words like "synergy" or "value proposition."

**Make me look good.** I use your products to help me in my own business. I can't afford a failure because I use cheap materials. Give me a high-quality product and help me look better than my competitors. Give me pointers to be even better.

**Reward my loyalty.** Because I am a small business person myself, I like doing business with other companies that value simple, affordable solutions. Once I make the decision to shop with you, don't give me a reason to reconsider that choice. Please don't treat me differently after I become a customer by throwing me over to a newbie sales person. When I send a new customer your way, recognize that and reward me in return.

**Recognize that I wear many hats.** Being a purchasing agent is only one of dozens of roles I play each day. Make it easy for me to get on to other tasks I have by making shopping and paying for your products simple. Remember what I purchased before and my supply requirements, my preferred payment type and deliver products to me on an as-need basis. Streamline my interactions with your shop. I will be loyal even as I quickly transition away from you each time we meet.

## Institutions

**Be patient.** I cannot move quickly. Rules and processes are in place to govern nearly every business decision. Even if you are the best supplier, I may not be able to move fast. Understand that my hands are tied and you may have to wait for approvals. But realize that once you are an approved vendor, you will be rewarded with my business.

**Help me think things through.** I need to stretch every dollar I spend so unexpected charges are a nightmare. If we can be thorough and creative by developing an everyday low price program that guarantees each purchase is as cost-effective as possible, you can win my business.

**Know that decision-makers change.** Even once you have my business, it is a good idea to keep educating our leadership team on why you are still our best resource. Our directors and managers change often and the airtight pitch you gave last year may be completely new to our leadership this year. Keep educating us.

**Align to our mission.** Nearly as important as keeping our cost down is partnership with like-minded organizations. Help us fundraise, market or donate to our causes. We need support beyond a reliable supply chain.

**Be a trusted expert.** We have so many other things to do beyond purchasing the things we buy from you. Tell us what we need to know (the good and the bad) in a straightforward fashion to help us weed through the details and get to the essential. Help us use common sense to make good decisions so we can focus on our mission.

Every customer wants to be treated as a unique individual. But if you can recognize the patterns of different shopping groups, you can be better prepared with providing the kind of service they need and build the loyalty you want.

## WIN Today

Review your top customers and see how they can be grouped into similar types. Think about the solutions you offer each type of shopper. Is there something you can do or offer them that would better meet their needs?

If your solutions and offerings are the same to all customers in all groups, devise a way to be more focused on their needs. Create a defendable offering before a competitor exploits your lack of distinction in the future.

## It Isn't Retail Without Sales

Maximizing your sales from each customer is an important part of succeeding in retail – but you need to make sure you maximize their experience along with it. A happy customer will be back for more – even if you sell a durable good that is repurchased on a very long sales cycle. The best way to improve your sales is to focus on your current customers. It takes a lot more effort to secure a new customer than to keep a current customer coming back for more.

Using the G-U-E-S-T model, always give the best service you can. Unscrupulous sales people – especially with durable goods sales like cars and furniture - can take advantage of a poorly informed customer. But as soon as they learn better, customers take their business elsewhere. And in the age of instant social media, their experience will get magnified to their network quickly. Besides, do you really want to be the store that sells to stupid customers? The store that will stay in business is the one that sells to the smartest and most influential customers. Keep your customers well informed and educated.

If you operate in an industry where shoppers' visits are infrequent, think about how you spend your marketing and adjust your marketing goals. It is unrealistic to try to build visits like a grocer could. Most specialty retail customers shop in a store two or three times a year. So with that in mind, rather than trying to increase shopper visits, maximize the sale per customer. Ensure that your sales people have a complete solution so that a television purchase is also a speaker, wiring and digital download bundle or a sewing machine purchase also includes lessons, a variety pack of thread and fabrics.

Changing outcomes can be as simple as changing your sales mindset. While you may be thinking of *closing sales,* a more effective strategy is to think of *opening customers.* Opening a customer to buying one product from you will transfer to other products. That means larger transactions and more repeat purchases. When you think about opening customers and not just closing sales, you make choices that will keep your customers for the long term.

Great retail salespeople are communicators in both directions: listening and explaining. To succeed, sell yourself, then your company, then the price. If you do not sell the first two, then all you can do is sell on price. Always remember: people want what you are selling. Your customers have choices about where to do business. But customers come to you because they need what you are selling and they think you will have their solution. Someone, somewhere will make the sale – it may as well be you!

If you make the decision to tell your customers *only* about prices, you leave yourself open to being undercut and lose customers. Any competitor can take your customers by slashing prices. When you make the choice about trust, expertise and a relationship, it will be very hard for competitors to take your customers away. Sales, then, is about selling yourself and building a relationship – not about selling products.

Salespeople are valued when they have knowledge, experience and honesty. Honesty is the most important of the three. Customers want to interact with someone who will make them feel good about their purchase. Some customers want to make an environmentally sound choice, others want a smart value-quality equation, some want to support a local business. Your goal as a salesperson is to help each customer understand how their choice fits into their goal and then find out more about other needs that could also be fulfilled.

Eco-conscious shoppers might want to know more about the ethics and values of the products you also sell. Value-quality shoppers might want to hear more about upcoming promotions where their money will go further. Community-oriented shoppers might want to hear more about local charities you support. You gain their trust by treating them individually. Then they will be more receptive to listening to your ideas about other products that will help make their lives easier.

How do you build a relationship? How do you sell? It is just like dating. It's a four-word sales course.

Ready?

Ask questions.     Then listen.

Would you expect a second date if you spent the first date talking only about yourself? Of course not. Too many retail conversations are like that.

They sound like this:

| | |
|---|---|
| Salesperson: | "Thanks for coming in today. Can I help you?" |
| Customer: | "I need to replace this cyan cartridge." |
| Salesperson: | "That's on the wall to the right. We are having a buy 2 get 1 free sale on those cartridges this week. Also, we are now carrying a new line of printers that are 10% off when you sign up for our mailing list. And Tuesday is senior discount day for customers over 65." |
| Customer: | "OK." |
| Customer: | (Grabs cartridge, completes the transaction and wonders if she looks over 65.) |

What a missed opportunity for opening a new customer! It could have gone like this:

| | |
|---|---|
| Salesperson: | "Thanks for coming in today. Can I help you?" |
| Customer: | "I need to replace this cyan cartridge." |
| Salesperson: | "Sure, they are on the wall to the right. How recently did you also replace the yellow and magenta one?" |
| Customer: | "I don't know." |
| Salesperson: | "Because we are having a buy 2 get 1 free sale on those cartridges this week and getting all the colors at once will save you another purchase in a week or so. Typically, colors run out at roughly the same time unless you have been doing an unusual print job. Do you think you have been using a lot of cyan on recent prints?" |
| Customer: | "I don't know." |
| Salesperson: | "Well the sale ends Saturday, so, of course it is up to you. You will have to replace the other colors eventually so if you want to get them at this special price, I'd recommend that." |

Customer considers her choice then grabs all three cartridges and completes the transaction.

| | |
|---|---|
| Salesperson: | "Smart move to get them at this price. We usually put them on sale twice a year, so remember that in June – or I could put your name on the mailing list and you'd get notified the next time they go on sale, if you'd like." |

(I see the start of a relationship – don't you? The salesperson is becoming a trusted advisor to this customer.)

When you ask the right questions, (*then listen!*) your customers will tell you how to sell to them. Think of how these questions lead to insight into what each customer needs:

Do you want delivery overnight or would you prefer to wait a few days to get the reduced price?

Do you have to replace this regularly or is it in spurts?

How critical is it if you run out of product? Do you have time to repurchase or do you always need to have a back-up supply?

Selling effectively comes down to four words: *Ask questions, then listen.*

## WIN Today

Write down six questions that could be natural conversation openers for customers. Create open-ended questions so they tell you more about the products they are looking for and how they will use them. Practice asking questions and then patiently waiting for customers to answer them.

Today, do two things: Ask questions. Then listen.

## Shh. I'm Listening for Sales

Think about the reputation of a great employee or coworker. Often the highest retail compliment is "they really engage with their customers." But what is the secret ingredient that elevates an ordinary customer conversation to an exceptional one? It is as simple as listening.

Communication is 90% nonverbal. That means if you are not watching while someone is speaking, you are only getting 10% of what is being communicated. And yet, how many of us try to listen while we text, while we read emails or stock shelves? As a manager, one of the most important things you can do is to coach your team members to be better at engaging and helping customers. To begin, your employees must know how to listen with intention.

### Mindful Listening

Listening is simple to practice and can be done anytime people are talking to each other in the same room.

1. Face the customer so you can see him or her speak.
2. Notice how their voice and nonverbal expressions communicate emotion and passion. You can tell which elements of what someone is saying is most important to them by their:
   - Voice rising or lowering in pitch
   - Voice rising or lowering in volume
   - Gestures
   - Expressions in the eyes and mouth
   - How they sit and lean
   - By how they hold their hands, fingers, feet and legs
3. Notice what's not being said. Can you tell when they are leaving things out?

If you notice that something has distracted you, that you drifted off, or that you realized you were spending time thinking about what you wanted to say, just come back to listening. If you need to ask for something to be repeated, do so.

This practice is especially strong with customers. The power of stopping and giving complete attention to a customer immediately gives the interaction meaning. It tells the customer that they are more important than anything else in the store.

When the customer has finished speaking, they want to know that you heard them. As the listener, you can strengthen your relationship with your customer by accurately reflecting what was said. It builds trust and encourages customers to say more, sometimes even without follow-up questions.

**How to Reflect**

When you are reflecting, you are repeating back what you think meant the most to the customer.

You can tell what was most important to the speaker by what they said *and* how they said it.

1. Only reflect back two or three things.
2. Use their words not yours.
3. Don't evaluate or translate what they said. Just reflect back what they said showing that you heard them ... that you cared enough to listen and remember what they said.
4. One way to do this is to use the person's name and then say, "What I heard you say was ... "

Employees who use this technique, open the door to creating relationships with customers. In truth, relationships with customers is the unicorn that all great retailers seek. National and multi-national retailers invest millions of dollars into customer relationship management (CRM) solutions. These analytic predictive computer models attempt to "listen" to customers by processing their sales history and predicting their upcoming needs and preferred shopping patterns. To employees that practice mindful listening, getting close to their customers and knowing them well enough to predict their patterns comes naturally.

Coaching excellent listening skills to improve customer service requires managers that employ those same skills when interacting with their own employees. Certainly, most of us would be appalled to see our employees "listening" and nodding while a customer talked without looking at the customer. Yet that simple focus is often missing in most of our conversations with our employees when they "interrupt" our tasks to communicate. Your employees will model the behavior and culture you set. So, learning how to mindfully listen when they talk will reinforce the expectation to do the same with customers.

Coaching the team to use mindful listening requires you to see yourself as a coach – not a player. A coach does not go onto the field to play alongside the team. A coach carefully watches the players, noting their strengths and the patterns that they need to adjust to become better and more valuable to the team. As a manager, shatter the illusion that you have to be focused on tasks to be productive. Set aside time to watch your team interact with customers. Are your employees listening and fully present with their customers? Watch body language and listen for your employees to reflect back what they hear before attempting to resolve issues for customers. After such sessions, give immediate feedback on what you saw.

As you coach, avoid using words like "shouldn't" and "stop." Instead, coach employees by prefacing your conversation by telling them you want them to be more effective at selling, solving problems, thinking on their feet, etc. Then explain what you saw and provide pointers on different ways to react to similar situations in the future that would be more effective. After all, that is your goal. To make them better at what they are doing so that they can succeed in their role and you can be confident in their ability to manage customers.

Finally, once you are certain that your employees are adept at listening and engaging with their customers in full focus, you must also arm them with the knowledge to answer issues and questions that their customers have.

Here are two examples when an employee does not know enough to help.

In the first, a customer spends 10 minutes describing a detailed description of a problem or request to an employee who responds with "I'm afraid I don't know the answer. Let me get James to help." The customer will only be frustrated that they need to explain it a second time to James. So, the first action is to ensure that there is continual learning on the team and that all employees have access to materials and training that builds their product knowledge. In other words, work toward educating all your employees so the situation doesn't happen.

Should there have to be a customer transition on the sales floor from one employee to the other, the way to do that is to have employee 1 explain the situation to employee 2 with as much detail as is necessary to help employee 2 "catch up" on the facts. Employee 1 should introduce the customer by name and be able to represent the customer if they have been listening well. Employee 1 should check in with the customer to make sure they agree with their summary of the situation. Employee 1 should not excuse himself from the dialog until employee 2 says "I understand. I can take it from here. Thank you, [name of employee 1]" and then give their full attention to the customer. In this situation, the customer feels entirely cared for, does not have to re-explain their situation, the employees are seen as treating each other with respect and the customer is seamlessly moved along toward their solution without being given a reason to leave the store or look elsewhere for help. If the store isn't too busy, employee 1 could stay with the transaction to listen and learn from employee 2 for the future.

In the second scenario when an employee does not know enough to help, the employee may offer too many solutions. In those situations, employees may be deluded into thinking that reading packages to the customer or shelf labels is helpful. ("Well, this one is $49.99 for a standard cleaner and this one is $89.99 for a professional cleaner.") Obvious eye-rolling answers rarely meet the needs of your customers. Instead, an employee needs to learn that professional cleaners are more attractive to customers who have high-volume situations while standard cleaners are more attractive for customers looking to minimize their out-of-pocket expense. Teaching employees more about the features and benefits of the products they sell will make them more effective in building those elusive customer relationships that build loyalty.

Finally, make it a standard of operation in your store that living, breathing customers in front of you are always more important than whomever is on the phone. When a phone rings while assisting a customer, let the phone roll to voicemail. Better yet, have a procedure in place to have the call forward to the next person on staff who can answer it without interrupting a customer transaction. Never give the impression to a customer that they are less important than someone calling the store.

A series of engaged conversations with customers build relationships which in turn create loyalty that is resistant to any competitor who has a low-price promotion once in a while. To build that kind of loyalty, all you have to do is listen.

## WIN Today

Challenge yourself to be 100% present for every conversation on the sales floor. Whenever you engage with team members or customers, stop what you are doing, make eye contact and listen well. Reflect back what the person says and use that to recommend solutions.

Watch when team members hand off customers to one another. Coach your team to make smooth customer handoffs on the sales floor. Compliment good handoffs and demonstrate how to do them with every shift change.

## The Angry Customer and You

Everyone in retail has those stories: the angry customer encounter. Sometimes funny – usually ugly. Your staff can learn strategies to prepare for the inevitable and bounce back quickly.

Working in the retail sector means handling customer complaints. It is as inevitable as opening the store and taking out the rubbish. So, it makes sense to teach your staff how to handle those conversations early in their career. If you do not spend time training and then practicing how to handle angry customers, your staff will have to learn on the sales floor. And that is never a good idea.

Here are the keys to helping your staff manage the rough waters of difficult customers.

### Recognize the Signs

Some customers can return to the store or make a phone call and have a perfectly rational conversation about their situation. Others are in a much more emotional place. If they are screaming, swearing, panicked, accusing or abusive, it is easy to diagnose the situation. Crying or chin-wobbling is another common emotional response. As soon as you or your staff recognize the signs, it is time to begin the resolution process outlined here.

If a staff member is in over their head, they need to engage a manager. Speed is important. Try to quickly suspend the dialog with the customer and find a manager. Customers will only become more belligerent if they have to repeat their story.

### Manage Yourself

First, store staff or phone reps need to separate themselves personally from the caller and their emotions. The customer is emotional, but you do not have to be. Stay calm and listen to their story. If there is abusive language or swearing, tell the customer that while you wish to help them, you cannot assist if they continue with their language. Be logical and neutral but by all means, hold firm to creating a conversation of mutual respect.

Staying cool and collected while being *screamed* at is difficult. But staying focused on the facts – not the emotions – is the only way to resolve the issue at hand. If you want to bring this ugly scene to its conclusion quickly, you need to understand what the problem is and what the customer wants.

If possible, remember that emotions like anger and crying usually are covering other deeper feelings of embarrassment or fear. In our industry, there could be anxiety over their job or reputation if they have purchased an (expensive) incorrect item for their company. Or they could be facing serious deadlines for a client and are afraid that their work will be inadequate if the final presentation isn't printed. In any case, it is important to remember that no matter what they are saying it isn't about *you* personally. The more you match your customer in pitch and tone, the longer the resolution will take and the longer you postpone the de-escalation.

Finally, be hyper-aware of your body language. Crossing your arms is a natural – almost instinctive – posture to protect yourself from a verbal attack. Force your arms to your sides. Similarly, restrain yourself from holding up your palm in a "halt!" fashion or placing your hands on your hips, both of which connote not listening. The best thing to do is look directly at the person and nod while listening to nonverbally de-escalate their hostility.

## Patience

To bring your customer around and let them run their course, it is important to give them the time to tell their entire story. When it is confusing, ask open-ended questions and continually check in with them by re-stating what you have heard and asking, "is that right?" Remember you are not prosecuting or trying to arrive at a solution at this point. Use questions to uncover their remembrance of the situation. Don't back them into a corner with leading questions. The longer you listen and ask questions, the more they will come to see that you are trying to understand their problem. Plus, you will get more details, which can help resolve the issue.

## Energy

It may be natural for some staff members to passively listen when a customer is angry or upset while other meet that same emotion with similar intensity. Instead channel your own energy to show the customer that their issue is important and urgent. Tell customers that you will find a solution for them and that it has your full attention. Be empathetic and understanding of their situation. In other words, be an advocate for the customer. Help them see that they are not alone. You are also going to shoulder their issue and together you will both try to get it solved. It doesn't mean you must apologize or take full responsibility if, indeed, the customer was also at fault (such as when they purchase the wrong item).

That sounds like:

"Well, that doesn't sound good at all. Let's work together to get to the bottom of this right away."

"This is troubling. Let me ask you some questions so I can understand what happened and then we can work together to find a solution."

"I understand. This is not a good situation. I am here to help you – so let me see what I can do."

## Compassion

When there is a solution, smile and move swiftly to complete the transaction. Let the customer know you are glad that it has been corrected. Should the issue be escalated above you, know that you have done all that you can and prepare to engage with your next customer.

Have compassion for them and yourself.

If it has been a heated exchange, give yourself time to cool off before handling the next customer by getting a drink of water. Stretch your neck and shoulders where you have been holding tension. Touch your toes. Physically release the tension in your body to prepare for the rest of your shift.

One of the best things about working in retail is being able to solve customer problems. It happens when you help them select the right item to purchase in the first place. Or help them when a transaction goes astray. It takes a special person to succeed in retail. If you and your staff stay positive in the face of difficult customers, you will have a flourishing career in retail.

## WIN Today

Make sure that staff members understand their empowerment around resolving customer issues. Many retailers will allow associates to do anything except issue refunds without involving a manager. Discuss how to handle angry customers at the next staff meeting in a positive way to keep employees from dissolving into gossip and dejection. Talk about specific behaviors that will not be tolerated, such as swearing, physical contact or destroying property. Have a plan for how to communicate and escalate such issues.

Finally, take the time to talk about how to "come down" from those emotional engagements so that employees understand how to help one another and themselves. When you see an employee in a difficult engagement with a customer, watch to see if they need assistance. Sometimes jumping in as a manager only serves to disempower your employees. Consider a code word or sign that employees can use when they do or do not need help with a difficult customer.

## Ringing it Up!

It is rare to find a delightful cashier who is personable and efficient *and* makes a customer connection! But if you think that great cashiers are born, not made, think again. Rid your sales counter of the sullen cashier who dutifully executes a sales transaction without a glimmer of personality.

To begin: hire a cashier who is energetic. A shift at the sales counter is long indeed for a person who isn't accustomed to standing and smiling. As you interview candidates, take note of their posture, their disposition and their eye contact. Ask questions about their past experience with difficult customers and long shifts. Great cashiers know that a long shift is easier and goes by faster when they see each customer encounter as a chance to talk to someone and to have a small conversation. Experienced cashiers may have games they like to do such as guessing if the person will like or hate the weather or will pay with a credit card or cash. Even that small indicator shows that the candidate knows to talk with each customer by concentrating on each person as an individual.

As a manager, you set the tone for customer interactions. If the staff sees that you are friendly, approachable and engaged with customers, they will be as well. If you think interacting with customers is someone else's job, then they will as well. Start with yourself as you think about quality customer interactions.

### The Non-Negotiables

Cashiers are the "face" of your business. As the last (and sometimes, only) person they will see at your store, you need to remind them that they should be friendly, helpful and appreciative of every customer. Remind your cashiers that while every customer is different, every single customer deserves the same thing: *a smile.* It is small. It is free. And it is the one thing you can deliver without fail for every customer.

### Be First to Greet

Just as a guest is always welcomed into the home by the host, the customer is always greeted *first* by the associate. This is easy to recognize and monitor as a manager. If a customer is the first to greet, you have an issue. Address it quickly with your staff and set the expectation that they should always be the first to greet the customer.

### Honesty, Accuracy, Efficiency

These must be present – and in this order! Cashiers must be

scrupulously honest. *Always check references.* Honesty is a matter of character. A cashier that is accurate and efficient, but dishonest is a business liability. Accurate transactions come from a combination of strong training, standard processes and detailed attention. A cashier who is distracted by phones, questions and other duties cannot focus on the primary task of accurate transaction and record keeping. Finally, with honesty and accuracy, efficiency should proceed. A cashier must ensure that they complete transactions quickly so that customers can be on their way. Too often cashiers see a transaction goal as the goal of the greedy shopkeeper. Help them see that for customers who have already made their purchase decisions, a long transaction wait steals time from them.

**Sincere Gratitude**

Customize gratitude to each shopper. Listen to the final exchange between your cashiers and your shoppers. The tone should be as bright as when the customer comes through the door. Not a downward "Thank you for shopping. Come again." as if they just finished a transaction with Eeyore. Not "Have a good one." Bright, happy, optimistic: "Thank you. I hope I will see you here again soon!" A cashier's voice should sound happy to have served and eager to see the customer return.

As simplistic and old-fashioned as these four items are, they are exactly what customers want and deserve:

1. A smile
2. First to greet
3. Honesty, accuracy, efficiency
4. Gratitude that is customized to each shopper

Execute these basics every single time with every single customer and many of your customer complaints will be eliminated.

We will not delve into the right cash levels to have on hand, identity and currency fraud, theft, bagging or sales techniques. All of those items are critical. But they can be taught and monitored. What you have to work at is creating the right environment and incentives to make each customer interaction special.

To succeed, cashiers should also have more than a basic understanding of the business.

Cashiers need to become familiar with the week's promotion and with the product sold in the store so that the customer can be made aware of any purchase that may qualify for a discount or another offer. Have a weekly meeting or a bulletin board where offers and new items are introduced to the cashier staff. Help them understand that they are not "selling" to a customer (which can be difficult for some people) but that they are making sure the customer is aware, so they do not go home and become annoyed once they realize they could have made a better purchase.

Cashier:   I see you purchased an air filter. Did you know that if you buy a second one as well, we are giving 15% off this week? That is a good deal if you think you'll be back soon for another one.

Customer: No, I didn't see that sign. Thanks.

Cashier:   Let me call someone to bring you up a second one.

Notice how the cashier makes this announcement in a friendly, conversational tone that was customized for the specific customer.

Cashier:   I saw you looking at our new mailing supplies line. We just brought that in and thought it would be convenient for customers to pick up postal supplies here as well. What do you think?

Ending a statement with "What do you think?" will surprise customers. Rarely does anyone ask them what they think. It doesn't come across as trying to sell, but to inform. By saying it, this customer will remember that your store carries postal supplies in the future.

**Name Game**

Create a contest once a quarter for your cashiers. Give away a gasoline or pizza gift card to the cashier who addresses the most customers by name. Keep a running tally where all the employees can see it. It may have to be an honor system tally – – but the important thing is that your employees will see that you are serious about recognizing and addressing customers by name.

If ever a job fit well into the Zen philosophy of being present in the moment, it is being a retail cashier. Each transaction is a fresh start. Each customer requires individual focus. Each exchange of goods for money is an opportunity to achieve flawless and smooth perfection. You may think that is over the top – but when you find a great cashier and talk with them about how they get through the day you will find it is because of this challenge of creating a perfect interaction repeatedly throughout their shift. Great cashiers want to make their customers' day better because of the encounter. They match the style and the pace of the customer but add their own imprint. And their customers return to the store again and again.

## WIN Today

Monitor cashier transactions for one simple element. Greet first. Explain that they are expected to greet a customer before the customer greets them. Every customer. Every time. Make it a part of your store's culture and a non-negotiable.

If you are the cashier, see how many customers you can serve in a row before some super-fast customer greets you first. Leaning into this competitive mindset of providing fast and customized service will make your shift go faster and give you a way to find enjoyment in the role. Once you begin, share it with others in your store and watch your enthusiasm light up the rest of the staff.

CUSTOMER
SERVICE

OPERATIONS

MERCHANDISING

STRATEGY

MANAGING

PRICING

MARKETING

7 Timeless Principles

RETAIL: The Second-Oldest Profession
© 2019 Flora Delaney

# Timeless Principle 3: Merchandising

## Sell and Show What Matters

A solid strategy and great customer service are universal requirements for every retailer. This chapter on merchandising and product selection is where a retailer separates from the competition to stake a claim for the hearts and dollars of its selected target market.

At their core, retailers are purchasing agents for their customers. They search markets to find the products their customers will most require or covet and purchase them on their behalf. Like an ancient trading caravan, today's retailer buyers bring in the latest designs and exotic flavors from the Orient so that Europe and the Americas can showcase their worldly taste. Or, like a frontier general store, retail buyers may behave like a clearinghouse of bartered locally made handicrafts and commodities. Whether your model looks more like a princely Renaissance merchant or a hipster artist swap meet, successful merchandising requires that you understand your customers completely and see the world through their eyes.

Acquiring goods that will meet your customers' needs at a profitable price point is the heart of merchandising. Selecting items is risky for retailers who start to see the world through their own eyes more than their customers. Great buyers either spend time regularly engaging with customers or work closely with their marketing team to ensure that they understand the latest trends and needs that customers desire. Buyers who allow their vendors to do all the leg work to understand their customers are the ones who overbuy unattractive new items or miss key trends.

Besides deep customer insight, another attribute of the best merchandisers and buyers is organization. To keep track of items, deals, delivery and take full advantage of co-operative marketing funds, retailers need to have a near flawless system. Merchandising takes a hit when buyers and operators are under time pressure. The urgent always outweighs the important. Merchandising is important, but in the daily grind of retail category plans, fully realized assortments can take a back seat. Half-baked ranges hit the sales floor or website and sales goals are missed.

Finally, you must be capable of making decisions when you are in the role of merchandising. Whether you are buying new items for the store, placing them on the shelves or selecting them for your advertising, you have to be able to make multiple decisions and stick with them. Many vendors say that there are two types of buyers they love: those that can decide and defend it (so they know what to bring them the next time) or buyers who cannot make decisions and take everything (for obvious reasons.) Dithering and making decisions using different frameworks (one season you stake your claim with innovative new products in new colors and the next you carry only opening price point classics in black and white) will confuse your customers and show up in missed sales.

If you are on a buying trip – to either a big market event or a trade show – make sure that you set aside time specifically to visit the new vendor entries that can barely afford to buy into the show. Those perimeter vendors are the ones who are more likely to have truly new and innovative products that will disrupt the marketplace in the seasons to come. The large anchor vendors with huge showrooms or exhibits will always have line extensions and model changes. But the true innovators and disruptors tend to come from smaller vendors who are doing something unusual. Look for the vendors who have something different to bring to the market to keep your product line fresh and interesting for your target customer. Accept calls from new vendors regularly to make sure you truly have the widest view possible of the breadth of product you could bring into your store(s) to meet your customer's needs.

While the act of physically merchandising a store is important for brick-and-mortar retailers, digitally merchandising products online is an art unto itself. It is table stakes to have customer reviews of every product, detailed product attribution and high-resolution photos from every angle. "Customers also bought" affinity algorithms and suggestions are required when there are multiple products to buy to create an entire solution. Without the face-to-face interaction of a store associate, online retailers have to make it as intuitive as possible for shoppers to find and select products that will meet their exact situation. That means there has to be multiple product hierarchies and branches to navigate to products on the site. Maybe your hardware store has cookware and power tools and camping gear. By all means, use those headers to help customers navigate, but also consider adding other solution paths like "Gifts for Her", "Gifts for Kids" or even rooms like "In the Kitchen" or "Garage" to help customers find what they are looking for.

If you are a single store or a small chain, seriously consider the benefit of putting every single item online. Most retailers who are working in their own store as well as trying to compete online find that the administration simply isn't worth it. Uploading dozens of SKUs and pictures every night can make it feel like you have to work 24 hours a day. Instead, consider highlighting a few signature items on your website and suggest that customers come in the store for more. Or use Instagram to punch up a new product and sell it for a limited time through that channel. Using your social media accounts – especially Instagram and Pinterest – to showcase your store's style and selection can attract more shoppers and be less time-consuming to manage than putting your entire catalog online to be price-shopped by customers who may never become loyal shoppers.

For most store operators, merchandising is the most fun aspect of being a retailer. A fresh selection gives you something new to show customers. Learning the story behind a product and telling its story to shoppers makes selling more fun and keeps your customers returning. Online or in store, merchandising is at the heart of retailing.

## Building a Compelling Assortment

The best retailers know to maximize their sales by making the most of every customer's visit. The more effectively you resolve issues for your customer (hunger, building a home, camping, owning a cat) the more sales possibilities exist. With each successful visit your customer becomes more closely bound to your store and your brand. For more, see the marketing journey of a customer in "Marketing Doesn't End at the Door" in *Timeless Principle 5: Marketing*.

All retailers start with a core assortment, the primary solution set that meets the needs of your target shoppers. It can be as broad as entertainment or as narrow as children's books. Even retailers like Best Buy who once had a core assortment of landline phones, VHS movies and home stereo speakers actually would describe their core assortment as technology solutions – thus providing the fluidity to change their focus from CDs to mobile phones. Diversifying your product range beyond the core can be a useful way to maximize sales, as customers are enticed to pick up a couple of additional items, along with the primary product that motivated them to visit in the first place.

Retailers who have stumbled as they diversified outside their core product sales are legion. Poorly chosen items that don't sell will end up costing you in markdowns or unsold goods later. To avoid that, begin by looking at who actually comes into your store. Who are they? What are their needs as customers? What brought them to your store? Uncover their needs and you can select an ancillary product line to suit them. The best products to diversify to are "pivot" products. They should be a natural, logical choice that complement your main products and are appealing to your target customer.

For a pet store, diversifying from cats and dogs to reptiles or fish may be the right next step. Or moving from providing products for sale to boarding or grooming services might be more appealing to a different pet owner market. It would depend on the careful observation of the customer: Are they families providing first-time pet experiences for their children or busy office workers with regular business travel? Pivoting off the main product line is key. Even if our pet retailer found astonishingly beautiful jewelry that many of its shoppers would like, making a leap from pet care to jewelry is too far to make a pivot. While that may seem funny, haven't we all been struck by odd products like microwaves in truck stops or bedding in supermarkets?

**It *Always* Starts with Your Target Customers**

To tailor your selection, take a look at your customers and their timing. If you see heavy traffic from mothers with children or over lunchtime, and you have a convenience strategy, a small selection of drink or snack items may be useful. On the other hand, if you see people on the way to or from their office, you could consider something like a spinner rack of business-oriented cards – "Happy Birthday from all of us," "sorry you're leaving," and so on.

Start with your customers and pick the products from there. Pick a group and focus on them. Don't try to please everyone because it isn't possible. There's no such thing as a universal product ... aside from toilet paper.

This advice comes with two warnings:

**1.  Do not let your vendors define your customers for you.**

As buyers look for new and unique products to pique their shoppers' interest, some vendors are rewarded with increased sales. The extreme proliferation of products (think of air fresheners, sports drinks and hair-care products) truly comes from vendors extending their production facilities and formulas, rather than a deeply unmet customer need. Validate that *your* customers are actually searching for ultra-mega strength hair spray in a 32-ounce aerosol can, rather than immediately believing your vendor's research. Suggest a test or trading out a poor-performing SKU in their line for the new item. If they do not have enough confidence in their product to agree, why should you? If you have a website, the solution is much easier as you can test the item online and then use its web sales to earn its way onto your store shelves.

**2.  Do not react to every customer request.**

Some customers will ask for you to carry everything. If you feel you already offer a compelling selection of Greek olive oils and a single customer asks for a different brand, try to find out why. Retail merchants who are too far removed from customers can react to every customer request by adding more products to the assortment. When that happens nonperformers quickly dominate the inventory investment and sales productivity diminishes. Find out why customers are making a request, evaluate the request against your current line-up and only if it is a true gap should you spend time chasing the sale.

**Consumables Keep Customers Returning**

If your industry has the good fortune of being a high-repeat business (food or gasoline) and your customers are happy with their experience, you should see them again. This is another factor to bear in mind when choosing secondary products. When given the choice, choose secondary lines that are consumable and require repeat purchases rather than once-in-a-decade accessories. What that means is that you will have greater inventory turns and cash flow by stocking a variety of screws and fasteners rather than expanding to a new line of drill bits or screwdrivers.

If, on the other hand, your retail sector is a durable good like major appliances or vehicles, every time a customer returns for a core product, entice them to pick up your consumable pivot items at the same time. Use promotional bundles or other strategies to ensure that your customer makes the connection that your store has the consumable items needed to use the core product.

If you stocked a birdbath, for example, that's a once-in-20-year purchase. It is rare for anyone to buy more than one. On the other hand, bird seed will see more repeat sales. Keep your store well balanced between single-use foundational items and consumable supplies that keep customers coming back. Hammers and nails, mattresses and bedding or printers and paper, for example. Keep a variety of choices on consumable goods so customers find something new to purchase each time.

Remember the retail golden rule: "Don't sell anything just once if you can help it."

## WIN Today

Review your current assortment and sales rates against the "durable-versus-consumable" spectrum. Look for opportunities and irregularities in your offering and address imbalances. Think through the margin implications of moving across the spectrum.

For example, the "razor and blades" business model (or bait-and-hook model) would indicate that it is better to sell razors at cost or even below cost because the profit is made up in the blades purchased for that razor over time. Other examples include Keurig coffee makers and K-Cups or inkjet printers and ink cartridges. Vertical brands where proprietary supplies and consumables are required usually follow the razor-and-blades model.

An opposite business model would be Apple iPhones and iTunes, where the money is made on the phone itself rather than the songs or Kindle and eBooks from Amazon, which are low cost or even free.

Neither model is superior – just know the difference and be intentional about which model your store will follow when selecting new product lines.

## Category Management: What Will You Sell?

Selecting what to sell drives the inventory and merchandising costs of a retailer. The number of SKUs and vendors contribute to the procurement costs. The number of times that product is handled throughout the supply chain, how far and how efficiently it travels contributes to the distribution costs. How often and how many products are promoted and have price changes contributes to sales and marketing costs. Product defective rates, returns and complexity contribute to the service costs. To be efficient, a retailer must keep all these things in mind when determining which products to assort in their stores or website.

A wrong decision is costly. For retailers, it has been estimated that it costs as much to delete an item from the product line up as to add it in. Thinking about that, it seems impossible that setting up a new item in the replenishment system, adding a warehouse slot, creating price labels and merchandising a new item can be the same as eradicating a slow seller from the mix. But the negative impact of closeout pricing is that powerful. For more on this topic, see "End of the Line: Clearance and Closeouts" in *Timeless Principle 4: Pricing*. In the US consumer packaged goods industry there are nearly 30,000 SKUs introduced each year, with an 80+% failure rate.[9] No wonder the grocery industry relies on slotting fees.

To evaluate your assortment, always start with your customers' needs and combine that with your store strategy. (Review *Timeless Principle 1: Strategy* if you need a refresher.) Look at consumer trends for value, convenience, variety, health, flavors, colors and fashion trends to gain insight into what drives your customer to make a purchase. Robust merchandising systems allow you to tag SKUs with attributes to help you look at their consumer value and analyze your sales through diverse lenses. Examples of attributes that can be helpful for tracking are designations like organic, gluten-free, made in USA, gender, etc. This is where vendor research can be very helpful. Understand how your top vendors striate customers to gain insight into how their research intersects with your target shopper. If your strategy is to be the most convenient after-work stop and your vendors indicate that 65% of its consumers want a fully prepared solution, then you should pursue an assortment plan that would carry many fully prepared items and reduce products that require a lot of preparation or handcrafting.

All merchandise decisions can be made better if you dig deeply into *why* a customer buys a product: In other words, which needs are being met? A wine purchase on a Friday night on the way to a neighborhood barbecue is very different than one for an engagement party. Fishing lures could be categorized as plastic, wood or mixed metal – but isn't it more important to know if they are for ice fishing, salt water pier fishing or bass fishing? Remember the story about the customer who bought a drill: He didn't want a drill – he wanted a hole. Understand how the products you sell meet your target customer's needs and you will make better assortment decisions.

**Clustering and Assortment Variations**

Understanding seasonality and regional (neighborhood) differences in customer demand is critical to determine if there should be a diverse or a mass approach to your assortment plan. If we were selling umbrellas, for example, we may find that our national sales ranking by color looks like the left column of the table below. Should we choose to only carry five items, we would be making a very poor decision for our southern stores.

| Umbrella Sales Ranking by Color (% of Sales) | | |
|---|---|---|
| **National** | **Northeast** | **South** |
| Black (65%) | Black (70%) | Black (45%) |
| Navy (12%) | Navy (8%) | Plaid (20%) |
| Plaid (8%) | Plaid (7%) | Polka dot (12%) |
| Polka dot (8%) | Polka dot (5%) | Peach (11%) |
| Green (3%) | White (5%) | White (8%) |
| Peach (2%) | Green (4%) | Green (3%) |
| White (2%) | Peach(1%) | Navy (2%) |

The goal is to balance the most effective selection of products with the most efficient. In our example, the most efficient choice would be to only carry a black umbrella. Nationally, we would capture 65% of our current sales with one SKU. Perhaps, we could even get more than that on desperate rainy days. But in the South, we would see a serious decline in this "efficient" choice by only capturing less than half of our current sales. Even selecting five bestsellers would be impacted if we made a national decision and did not take regional preferences into account.

Common assortment demand differences occur depending on both shoppers and the locations of your stores. College towns and college students create a different demand pattern than the norm. So do urban cores that cater to the business center. Tourist destinations, rural farming communities, ethnic neighborhoods and areas with high natural disaster occurrences all create significantly different sales patterns. For an astute retailer, that means opportunities to supply those differences.

## Category Management Planning

Most forward-thinking retailers use a category management process to align to consumer trends and demand, evaluate assortments, make sales and promotion plans and execute those plans to meet sales goals. This cycle usually occurs once a year – but it can be more or less frequent depending on the category's volatility.

The category plan reviews:
1. Past sales results for the category, key vendors and brands
2. Competition
3. Consumer trends
4. Vendor research and development (R&D) and roadmap for new products
5. Sales forecasts (for the category, vendor, key brands)
6. Supply chain metrics (on-time delivery rates, complete PO delivery rates, cost to handle, etc.)
7. Future financial goals (required profit contribution, inventory turns, etc.)
8. Customer segment goals (loyalty, repeat visits, etc.)

Most retailers have a framework or template for these category plans that help the top merchandising executives make trade-offs and decisions about future business investments. Nearly every category manager can find an unexploited niche that could yield some level of sales growth. But a unified category management process helps focus the organization on the top priorities.

Taken in its entirety, the process is usually called a category or line review. In it, the category is defined, its role within the company or store is defined, its sales and potential are assessed, and a specific budgetary goal is set. With the goal in mind, discreet tactics around adding or reducing products, changing prices, changing promotions or changing merchandising are developed to meet the goal. The costs associated with the changes are approved and the organization implements the plan. From a top-down approach, it is a proven process for capturing and sharing the best information about how to succeed in the category to remain competitive. Dominant categories with major shifts usually follow the full category review process. Smaller categories may only require a modified approach to succeed.

**Some Notes on the Category Review**

For retailers who follow a structured category management review, the first step is defining the category. The idea of defining a category each year may seem obvious – even redundant year after year. But customer tastes and habits change. Reviewing trends and changing customer behavior can capture newly-emerging opportunities so that retailers can capitalize on market shifts. For example, a retailer who defines "away from home beverage consumption" as only carbonated beverages and bottled water could overlook the trend for aseptic packaged milk consumption, plant-based milk products and flavored water additives.

Think of the implications for a retail store that defines its core category as either DVD Movies or At-Home Entertainment. In one situation, they are locked into optimizing the DVD category alone. In the second, they can evaluate gaming, streaming services, satellite television, even barware! Defining a category is all about drawing boundaries in the same way your customer does. For example, a consumer will ask "Which DVD should we watch tonight?" less frequently than they will say "What shall we do tonight?" Consider the differences in these category definitions:

- Glues and Paints versus Crafting Supplies
- Batteries versus Power Supplies
- Jerky versus Protein-based Snacks

What should come to mind are the changes in product selection and merchandising in the store or website that would better anticipate customer needs by redefining the category.

Category definition needs to be grounded in customer insights that are gained from several sources: affinity purchases uncovered while combing through market basket transactions (data mining for patterns), primary customer observational research and self-reported customer behavior. Frankly, affinity analyses can be misleading if retailers do not carry a wide enough breadth of product to be a full solution. For example, if a limited assortment grocer did an affinity analysis on birthday cakes, it may discover that the customers also purchased ice cream, paper plates and candles. It could, however, overlook that customers purchased the remainder of their needs (wrapping paper, cards, balloons and invitations) elsewhere. Primary customer observational research is expensive and time consuming. Self-reported customer behavior is notoriously inaccurate.

For most retailers, the most cost-effective way to discover unbiased shopper insights is to review the customer research of their established vendors along with research from emerging niche vendors. Niche vendors are usually the first to recognize and exploit changing customer patterns.

Established vendors less routinely recognize changes in behavior. Their focus on current product lines and customer segments can create blind spots. Take, for example, the difference between established home cleaning mega-vendors and environmentally focused cleaning vendors like Mrs. Meyers and Seventh Generation in recognizing the growing demand for less chemically intensive cleaning products.

Another example is in the rapidly declining and consolidating world of office supply retailing. Redefining the category from printing supplies to small business solution center or home office headquarters for working mothers could lead to all kinds of new product "pivots." A store could pivot to carry office décor, high-end stationery, party supplies, greeting cards, framing services, resume-writing services, copier leasing, craft supplies, photo equipment, shredders (or shredding services?) breakroom supplies or cleaning equipment. A category management process with a strong category definition requirement helps buyers create a compelling selection that meets future customer demand.

A key step in the category management process is defining the role of the category and its strategy within the store. Also referred to as a *portfolio analysis*, it helps a retailer determine how important the category is to its current and future shoppers and aligns resources accordingly. For example, at one time land line phones were 95% of all phones sold in the United States. They are still viable, but the numbers are dwindling by the day. Let's imagine you own a business-to-consumer (B2C) retail website. Even if your website had the market cornered on land line phones for homes, your sales will decline year over year. Investing more store inventory or space into land line phones does not make sense. To overcome the sales deficit, you must find a pivot business (like mobile phones) to build sales. In this case, the category is secondary and declining. However, maybe you are a joke and gag gift shop in the mall. Land line phones shaped like M&Ms, Legos and Star Wars droids are flying off your shelves. In that situation, investing in more land line phone products may make sense – as long as they are grounded in your gag gift and licensed product overarching strategy.

Here are the assortment implications for a few of the most common portfolio strategies:

| Strategy | Assortment Implication |
|----------|------------------------|
| Build traffic | Increase coverage of the highest loyalty SKUs |
| Defensive | Stock SKUs that are key to a designated competitor |

| Build transactions | Stock all proven market basket builders |
|---|---|
| Generate profit | Shift to less price-sensitive SKUs |
| Generate cash | Shift to SKUs that have the fastest turns and longest payment terms |
| Create excitement | Move swiftly on new and differentiated products |
| Enhance image | Stock limited-release and exclusive products |

**The Final Assortment Decision**

The category plan must be founded in analytics, financial data and resource productivity. The gross margin return on a dollar invested in your category's inventory for a new SKU must be balanced against the gross margin return if that same dollar was invested in more payroll hours for sales associates on the floor interacting with customers or invested in new training, new supply chain systems, new advertising or buying more Google AdWords searches. At the end, the goal is to create the most compelling assortment possible *for your target shopper within your budgetary restrictions.*

## WIN Today

Conduct a simple Pareto distribution of sales[10] analysis on your current sales. Start with the top-selling SKUs and continue through to your lowest sellers. Identify the 20% of items that typically make up 80% of the sales. Be careful to normalize sales to account for items that have had less than a full season of sales, less than full distribution or other supply chain interruptions.

Review the bottom items that make up the last 5% of sales as candidates for replacement.

## Every Product Has Its Part to Play

Talk to most retail managers about their productivity and they will usually talk about profit margins. Retail mark-ups are the lifeblood of the industry. In the days of tall ships, a merchant justified the markups to bring exotic wares to market because of the cost of the journey. One ship lost at sea could bankrupt a trader. Today's logistics operations bring products from around the world at rates unimaginable just a hundred years ago. The widespread availability of imported products means local, handmade products are more likely to command a premium than products made thousands of miles away.

But the truth is, for a well-balanced and mature retail operation, not every product should provide generous margins. Depending on the product's *strategic* role, there may even be products that will never generate a profit.

Not every product in a store's range should play the role of profit generator. Like a stock investment portfolio, each class or category of goods should play a specific balancing role. Most strong category managers follow a process that identifies a category's strategic role and then build a range or assortment that supports the role.

For your store, consider the single **primary business driver** of the store – the single category that most people think of when they hear your store's name. It is probably evident in your store name. The strategy for your primary business driver category should be to maintain a dominant assortment of SKUs and market-right pricing that is competitive without extreme discounting. Primary business drivers need to showcase national statement brands, the latest technology and opening price-point goods that highlight both value and quality.

The role of the primary business driver category is different than the role of the **traffic builder**. A traffic builder is meant to do one thing: draw customers into the store. A traffic-builder range of products needs to be surrounded by other, high-profit items to build a market basket (transaction) that is profitable overall. But the specific traffic-building SKUs within the transaction are not required to be profitable. If a category plays a traffic role, it should consist of a focused range of a select number of popular brands. Rather than carry the entire selection of products from the most popular brands, target only the highest frequency items. Seasonal products are often used as traffic builders.

One critical principle is to vigilantly retain high in-stock levels on key traffic items. Customers will sour very quickly on a store that promotes traffic builders to prompt a store visit only to be disappointed by out-of-stock product. Even without intent, most customers will see that condition as a bait-and-switch ploy. In-store or online, each traffic driver SKU should be surrounded by more profitable complementary SKUs to promote transactions that will meet minimum profit goals. Done well, the complete transaction should actually drive customer loyalty as the store benefits from a price halo around the traffic driver and profit from providing a complete solution.

There is a role for categories that are truly meant to be strategic **profit generators**. Categories that are meant to drive profit should still carry a competitive range of products that meet a good, better, best range of products, but there is less emphasis on brand names with profit generators. Which means that retailers can select secondary vendors who typically offer better margin potential than the highly promoted national brands. Customers should perceive high value and pay non-discounted rates for products that are on trend and comparable to the quality of national brands. For an office supply store, an example could be office sets – stapler, tape dispenser, pen holder – in a trendy color.

The ultimate profit generator for most retailers are their own private brands. A sourcing center can help the retailer create their own product and brands to yield remarkable profit margins compared to traditional vendors. For those retailers who have teamed up with a designer to create an exclusive private brand, they can charge a premium for the designer's brand cachet while producing a product at market parity and create an on-trend image while boosting margins. Examples include Target and their limited engagement designer shops, Kohl's and Vera Wang, Macy's and Martha Stewart – even auto parts and NASCAR-branded items.

Finally, there is another source of profit that comes from **convenience** categories. A convenience category typically completes a solution for a customer or is a low-priced impulse item that delivers incremental margins that would otherwise be purchased at a competitor's location. Everything in the maze of candy, magazines and sodas while customers queue up to get to the cash register usually are convenience items. But so are socks at a shoe store and cigarettes at a gas station. Most retailers would position their "opportunity buys" as convenience items. Vendors or distributors who offer recognizable brands at a low price point should be cultivated for possible convenience items. Think of products like gift cards, seasonal items and one-time buys. These should be minimal buys with limited quantities that might never be replenished. Give your customers new and different items and promote them throughout the store. The focus should be on the low price and the ease of purchase. Executed well, convenience items should be a significant source of margin contribution.

# MERCHANDISING

Like a well-played symphony, the strategic role of each category of product within your store should support the overall experience for the customer. Enticing and appealing traffic builders should be promoted widely outside of the store to draw in new and lapsed customers. Marketing and advertising should be disproportionately spent on traffic-building items. Traffic builders are typically sold at or just above cost. Their role is not to put cash into the bank but feet inside the store. One exception is if the product is both popular and hard to find (like the hottest Christmas toy). When demand is high, traffic builders can be sold at a reasonable margin rate.

Once inside the store, place traffic builders deep inside the store so that customers cannot simply purchase them and head directly to the cash register. Surround traffic builders with primary business drivers and profit generators. Sales associates should highlight more margin-rich products that could complete the solution for the customer. One US retailer calls it "surround the need with the want." An office manager may *need* a case of paper, but she *wants* the multi-colored sticky-note pads. Surround the need with the want.

Finally, merchandise an array of convenience items that make the trip more satisfying for your customers. If a traffic-building SKU has such a low price that there are only pennies of margin in the sale, selling a single soda may double the profitability of the transaction.

It is difficult for most retail operators to let go of the requirement that every single product must maximize its profit generation. But once they start to orchestrate their product ranges around key strategic roles, customers are more satisfied and profits improve.

## WIN Today

Define your store's key traffic-driving SKUs and create a "Never-Out Report" to closely manage their inventory levels to eliminate out-of-stocks.

If required, change replenishment triggers for "never out" SKUs so customers are not disappointed by out-of-stocks for your traffic-driving SKUs.

For each traffic-driving SKU, identify two to three complementary profit-driving SKUs and require them to be merchandised together (online) or adjacent to one another (in store) so that customer transactions are more likely to be balanced.

## Product Lifecycle Management

Just as a butterfly has a lifecycle that evolves from egg to caterpillar to chrysalis to butterfly, products go through similar lifecycle stages. For savvy retailers, managing product lifecycles yields more profit.

All products have a lifecycle: they are developed and brought to market, purchased by early adopters and (if successful) they grow and expand their appeal to the mass market. In the mass market they may thrive for decades (Cheerios or Legos) or they will peak and then decline to lose one channel after another until they are gone from the market landscape. (Remember Prell shampoo or Pearl Drops toothpaste?)

As a retailer, the key to success is to identify appealing products early enough in their development to anticipate their sales trajectory and market demand. The other critical component is to be alert to market shifts and to shed declining SKUs before they lose their luster.

### Introduction Products

Truly unique and new items for sale. New technology regularly creates new demand. Remember when the iPod and other MP3 players first came on the market? Or wireless printers? Those were the result of years of research and development and met a need that most consumers did not even recognize. Consumer trends like eco-consciousness, working from home and aging demographics can drive successful new product introductions.

Selling products early in their lifecycle presents opportunities and challenges. An advantage is that new items nearly always sell at full price. There is no need to reduce the price on an innovative new item. In fact, if the product is hard to acquire, it can be sold at a premium. Another advantage is that there is a certain cachet in selling products early in their lifecycle. Customers have historically waited in lines for the chance to buy an iPhone or a new Harry Potter book on the day of release. Developing a reputation for carrying the latest new items (whether it is technology or fashion) can build loyalty for your store.

It is important for websites and stores to support introduction products with prime placement to succeed. Customers need their usual shopping trips or online experience interjected with the new items. For stores, that means prominent placement like window displays, front displays and out-of-store marketing. For websites, pop-ups and landing page content is key.

The downside of carrying new products very early in their lifecycle is that the majority of customers will not understand them or even recognize the benefits of their new features. This means that retailers will have to spend more resources training team members, so they can explain and sell the new items. Or invest in working display models, print point-of-purchase signs or brochures so consumers can learn more about the new products. Websites may need to develop video demonstrations and detailed spec sheets online. Additionally, vendors experience an unusually volatile supply chain early in the lifecycle – especially if the product is successful. Vendors may not be able to keep up with orders and escalating sales.

Finally, the success rate and customer demand are unknown. Buyers need to have insightful expertise to separate the successful new products from the failures. Poor decisions will tie up inventory dollars and lead to clearance markdowns. It takes an especially gifted and well-educated buyer with experience in their category to reliably pick the winners.

But for a retailer who wants weeks or months of competition-free margins and the draw of carrying exciting new items, the risks may be worth it.

**Growth Products**

During a successful product's growth phase, sales rocket with mass popularity. Retailers clamor to find stock and drive sales while the product is hot. Vendors quickly diversify their offerings with new colors or adult/kid or business/personal versions of the item.

As sales escalate and volumes grow, competition increases. More vendors and retailers try to cash in on the product's popularity. Competing retailers recognize the appeal and begin to promote the product heavily and reduce the price. Escalating competition puts pressure on the supply chain. Supply chains remain volatile until sales patterns settle. Retailers see margin erosion as less sales occur at full price and promotional volume increases.

Merchandising needs to promote growth products and announce each generation or season to customers. Shelf space increases for the new products while sales and shelf space decrease for the older merchandise it is replacing. Websites may reflow the hierarchy to create pages devoted to the growth product lines.

Retailers need to take full advantage of the maturing stage of a product's lifecycle. While the margins decline, the overall volume increases and customers expect to find the product in the store. Competing vendors introduce their versions of the new product and increased competition makes the new item available at a variety of price points and features.

**Mature Products**

Once a product's sales reach its zenith the product transitions into a **mature** stage. For some "evergreen" products like paper, food, and undergarments the mature stage of a product's lifecycle can remain for decades. Vendors and retailers must work together to continue to maintain sales.

Mature products have less prominence in the store display areas as those are reserved for new products. But they may expand in their home location in an aisle or department. Web pages need less exclusive content to motivate purchases. Mature products may develop a regular promotional rhythm to stay visible to shoppers.

Special promotions, exclusive versions and new model features are regularly injected into the line to keep the product fresh and popular. Brands and sub-brands multiply as each segment is more narrowly defined. While the products may not excite customers as they once did, accessories for mature products can continue to create new sales possibilities. Sales rates are more predictable. Supply chain efficiencies eliminate previous issues from earlier in the lifecycle to maintain profit margins.

**Declining Products**

But like buggy whips, VCRs and typewriter ribbons, at some point the lifecycle of a product will decline. The "long tail"[11] of **decline** can last for months in fashion or decades in car parts. Depending on the customer base, retailers can evaluate their sales opportunities with end-of-life products as a way to enhance margins.

As a product declines, its market is superseded by a new product that solves the same problem more efficiently or with added benefits. But it will take consumers a long time to make the transition. Some, like writers who refuse to use computers, willfully stick to traditional products and those laggards must seek out suppliers at full price. So, as in the emerging life stage, the very end of a declining lifecycle of a product can bear rising margins again as products are no longer marked down to drive sales and full-priced sales are the norm.

Retailers who covet the margins but struggle with the abysmal inventory turns for declining products have options. The most common is to reduce store inventories by offering end-of-life products only as special orders or website offerings. Customer orders trigger an order with the vendor who can drop-ship the item directly to the customer. That arrangement eliminates any handling by the retailer in return for a portion of the margin. Other retailers continue to hold the inventory in their warehouse and create niche websites and catalogs for the declining product market.

End-of-life products can find new life a number of different ways:

Many end-of-life products still see volume surges at the holidays. Gift giving can be a nostalgic time. Difficult-to-find items like 45 rpm record players, red wagons and fountain pens produce sales spikes at the holidays.

Trendsetters can bring back end-of-life products. Demand can resurge as new generations discover older products. Vinyl records, manual typewriters and 1980s arcade games have all had sales boosts among shoppers too young to remember them the first time around.

Licensing and the power of branding can revive end-of-life products. Attaching a hot new brand or entertainment license can build sales. Vendors who are open to creative partnerships can create exclusive items built around niche markets and perpetuate sales for much longer than standard items alone. Partnering with beverage brands, video game titles, TV and movie markets, hot designers, etc. can make an old product popular with collectors.

Buyers faced with hundreds of new product selection choices would be wise to understand the product's lifecycle stage and make decisions based on the strategic intent of each phase in order to extract the most value possible out of each product in its range.

## WIN Today

Evaluate your merchandise through the lifecycle lens to understand the proportion of products you sell that are introduction, growth, mature or declining products. Review how you apportion prominence within your store or website across product life stages.

Select specific merchandising locations or levers to use exclusively for introduction products. Deliver focused product training for introduction products with your team. Partner with vendors to create exclusive content for your website to showcase new features and benefits.

Recognize products that are in growth and mature stages and monitor their pricing and promotions to stay competitive.

Review how declining products are showcased in your store or website. Research whether your customers still find the product appealing. Review industry trends and your competition.

## The Power of Good/Better/Best

Savvy merchandisers know how to use a good/better/best assortment of products to appeal to customers who are shopping. As a customer begins the "scan and shop" process of searching through the store for either a necessary item or a browsing interlude, the good/better/best merchandising approach is highly appealing.

This proven merchandising and selection tactic begins with an opening price-point item: a "basic" item. Let's say it is a plastic mechanical pencil. It contains one lead within the chamber, one eraser at the tip and could be refilled in the future. It is $1.99. The "better" item includes a small plastic container that contains additional lead and eraser refills. Its price is $3.49. Finally, there is a much better version that is made of a better-quality material and contains the refills as well as a second pencil for $5.99. In this example, it is easy for the customer to see how with each step up in price, there is a corresponding improvement in the product and its value. The customer will have to part with more money to purchase the "best" option, but it has a perceived higher value than either of the other choices.

The power is that there is always a choice for the customer who may be pressed for cash and needs a low-investment solution or for the customer who values a higher-quality product and is willing to spend more to get more. A smart retailer has at least three options of most items to allow a customer to feel they can make a wise choice among the options depending on their needs and values.

There is nothing magic about having three offerings. In a product line that the retailer wants to dominate, there may be 6 or 9 or 14 offerings. The important thing is to arrange the merchandising (on the store shelves or online) in such a way that the customer can easily see how stepping up and down in price generates a similar change in product features. Think of times when you have compared seemingly similar products at two different prices. Customers always wonder, "What else do I get for the additional cost?" As long as you can clearly demonstrate the difference, you may be able to carry a very deep selection of products in a single category.

In commoditized products, it may be difficult to provide three tiers of selection. It is usually done through a quantity/value trade-off. Think of 5-, 10- and 15-pound bags of flour that go up in absolute price but reduce the price per ounce for the flour with each increase in bag size. Other ways to increase the value of commoditized items is to offer a bundled purchase where a single item is one price, but two items packaged together is a lower price than purchasing two separately. This is especially useful when there are many items that are necessary to work together, and they carry varying profit margins. A low-margin dry cat food can be bundled with a high-margin box of cat treats that brings the margin of the overall purchase into a more profitable range. For example, if you only make $1.50 on the cat food, but make $3.00 on the cat treats, reducing the price so that your margin on both items together yields a combined profit of $4.00 makes it a deal for the customer as well as a more profitable transaction than if the customer had purchased the cat food alone.

One of the most important decisions you will make is determining where to set your opening price point (or lowest priced) item. If you cater to a limited income market (like students) you may want to make it a very affordable product with no bells or whistles. Conversely, if your target customer is a small business owner, your opening item may be a more functional product with a higher price point that is durable enough to last in a work environment. Review your competition and decide if you want to have items that are under, match or slightly above your nearest competitor in terms of price and quality. If your position in the market is to be the rock bottom priced alternative, you are likely to stock low-priced, low-featured products throughout the store. But if you want to stand for quality and value, you can bring in better items to be your opening price point selections.

When considering the highest price point you can offer your customers, discuss a drop ship arrangement with your premium vendor to see if they would be willing to offer their high-end SKUs for your customers even if you do not carry them in your store or warehouse. If you have selected your core assortment well, the volume will be low. But you can still capture profit and value by providing your most affluent customers with a selection that can be delivered direct to their door.

## Use Caution

There is a customer decision point you should be aware of. That is the point where a customer will abandon your store due to a lack of acceptable choices. Here are examples:

A customer with $1500 to spend on an engagement ring walks into an upscale jewelry store. The lowest priced ring is $4900. The customer will abandon the store.

A customer wants a mid-range calculator with limited scientific functions. The store offers several student calculators under $10 and old-school desk calculators with paper rolls for over $75. The customer will abandon the store.

A customer is not sure which vacuum cleaner she wants. It must be lightweight, under $120 and have upholstery attachments. The only models in stock are either lightweight and under $80 without upholstery attachments or commercial-grade with easy attachment choices but priced at $199. This is the most common scenario where a retailer offers only an opening price point and a high-end choice. (good/--/best) While many retailers (and their vendors) like to speculate that the customer can be sold up to the high-end model, studies indicate that abandoning the store is common without a relevant middle selection. Many valuable customers who could afford to purchase the high-end model will opt to shop elsewhere where they perceive that they have more choices. (And in the end, may still buy the $199 model!!)

To become a retailer that offers its customers an edited, yet relevant selection of products, consider the good/better/best approach to both selecting your range and merchandising the products in the store and online. Make sure the customers can easily see (through merchandising, signs and demonstration models) the increase in features with each jump in price. Select a smart basic model that has the minimum features your target customer needs at the right price. Select products that expand with desirable features up to the maximum price you believe you can command in the market. Carefully review decisions to eliminate choices to make sure you have an offering that keeps you relevant to the target shopper and won't send them to another store (or the internet) to make their purchase decision

## WIN Today

Select a range of products where your approach has been good/better/best and do a price comparison against your key competitors.

1. Begin by comparing if your opening price point product is where you expect compared to the competition.
2. Compare the number of choices your competition provides in each band compared to your store.
3. Review the top-end item compared to your store.
4. Make adjustments accordingly.

## How to Negotiate with Vendors

Choose your vendors wisely. Having the right products in the right place is all well and good, but of course you have to make sure they get there first. Choosing the right vendors to become your partners is crucial.

Analyze your options carefully. Try to minimize the number of vendors you work with and source multiple SKUs from the same vendor wherever possible. Vendor rationalization is the process where a retailer consolidates purchasing to just those few critical vendors that can be the best partners. This cuts down on administration and paperwork because you have less invoices, purchase orders, deliveries and so on.

But more importantly, if you have a large number of SKUs from a single vendor, that makes you more important to them and gives you more leverage. Once you've built up a strong relationship, you may be able to negotiate better terms on prices, delivery times, promotional allowances and so on. For example, you can say: "Well I carry three of your four major products, and I'm interested in doing a sale with them. What help can you offer me?" and expect far more support than if you only carried a single SKU from the vendor. If you only source a couple of items from a vendor, you will be a low-priority customer with less leverage and fewer options.

Vendor rationalization also frees your time to improve your selection. If your product offering has a limited number of vendors on the basic SKUs, you will have more time to develop unique selections for targeted items. For example, selecting one vendor to deliver all of your basic tee shirts, underwear and socks will allow you more time to develop a more compelling lineup of high-performance undergarments.

Constantly work with vendors to improve your payable terms and delivery timing. As a buyer, your goal is to commit to an order and have the purchase delivered in as short a period as possible. A short window between order and delivery allows you to create the most accurate sales forecast possible and match orders to your sales forecast.

Finally, all retailers want to delay payment for the product for as long as possible. Your ultimate goal is to sell products to your customers before you have to pay the vendor for them. For example, if you turn a product every 3 weeks, and you pay net 30, you get a week of cash float for that product every month. (See "Why Cash Flow Is More Important Than Profit" in *Timeless Principle: 7: Operations*.)

### Effective Vendor Negotiations

All successful companies rely on strong relationships with their vendors. While in constant tension, both need the other to succeed to protect their future profits. All companies should have a regular rhythm to review business with each vendor and regular market reviews to adjust the vendor mix to improve profits and supply chain efficiency.

For every retailer, the regular task of reviewing current and prospective vendors keeps their range fresh. It creates a formal setting for vendors and retailers to discuss how they are going to build a future roadmap where each one is extracting value from the relationship. For small retailers, it can feel like they are not in a strong position to negotiate. It may feel like they have to take the deals offered and nothing else. But the truth is, every sale matters to both retailers and vendors. Knowing that, even small retailers can create more value with an assertive approach to negotiating.

First, realize that the purpose of a negotiation is to explore whether or not you can pursue your future interests better through a discussion of the current arrangement. Topics that can be considered include the range of items procured from any single vendor, the price, the fill rate on your orders, delivery speed, product quality, training for you and your staff, marketing materials for your customers, online order fulfillment, market events and joint promotions. When negotiations begin with the broad range of topics on the table, there is more room for both parties to find common areas of agreement instead of focusing on only one or two financial terms.

It is easy to "beat up" your vendors in an attempt to always get the lowest price. But the truth is, the best partnerships are with vendors who provide you with more than low prices. A top tier vendor delivers on time, every time. They ship complete orders with no backorders. They accurately and proactively communicate any supply interruptions and make concessions when they create a problem. Finally, they invest in R&D and their own capabilities, so they will survive future market upheavals and bring successful new products to market. In that light, an outstanding vendor partner does more than just provide you with the lowest prices.

Most companies have a formal vendor review every 1 to 2 years. While there may be little disruption in the top-tier vendors, this review will often cull the less important vendors from your supply line and identify new vendors to test and add to the mix.

A simple four-step process for vendor reviews can guarantee success:
1. Gather information
2. Prepare a negotiation plan
3. Negotiate the contract

4. Follow up and maintain relationships

**Gather Information**

To gather information for regular vendor reviews, analyze a few simple metrics. If your organization is not tracking these metrics, put processes in place to create and track:

- Number of SKUs by vendor
- Sales (units and currency) and % of sales by vendor
- SKU churn by vendor (number of SKUs *currently* carried by vendor divided by total number of SKUs carried over 1 year by the vendor)
- % of deliveries complete – and its ancillary measurement: % of each order delivered short
- % of deliveries on time (within the window established on the PO terms)
- Payable terms (and your average days to pay each invoice)
- In-stock levels (in the stores and at the warehouse, if possible)

Upon reviewing the metrics, a clear pattern should begin to emerge that will help tier the vendors into their cohort segments:

**Gold** – The very best vendors where the focus is on sales and margin growth through preferential treatment for space and promotions. Expect high quality product innovation and support new product launches.

**Silver** – Standard vendors where the focus is on improving sales growth and supply chain efficiencies through on-time/right-quantity deliveries to reduce out-of-stocks.

**Bronze** – Smaller vendors who are highly "substitutable" who must operate to your requirements or risk being replaced.

**Prepare a Plan**

Use these tiers to set up the preparation stage. Strategically think about your opening position. Do you need extended terms? More on-time deliveries? Faster order completion? A larger volume discount? What concessions are you willing to make to improve the relationship and the business? Consider your order rate. Are you often placing last-minute emergency orders? Is your pricing in line with the market? Think about the promotions and sales you could support to bring about an overall sales improvement for your vendor partners.

A "negotiation" may feel more elevated than your dialogue, but remember that a negotiation is simply a back-and-forth discussion to reach an agreement where some of your objectives are shared and some are opposed. To the degree that you can move your vendors to see that most of your objectives are shared, you can build toward agreements to concede on items that are not shared. The key is to focus on the entirety of the relationship – not just price or volume.

Amongst the items that could be discussed are margins, returns, price protection, promotional and display allowances, training for store personnel, payment terms, volume discounts, minimum order size, delivery charges, merchandising assistance, etc. Arriving at the negotiation table to discuss more than price will send the signal that you are looking to improve the entire partnership. You need to have a number of possible goals as you arrive at the negotiation table. Take time to predict their goals as well so that you can establish clear areas where you share common interests. Perhaps you both want to sell more to men or you both want to reach a more upscale customer. Be prepared to re-focus on common interests or outcomes and not positions when communication becomes strained.

Great negotiators preview the negotiation in their head prior to the meeting and anticipate requests, constraints and objections.

### Negotiate the Contract

During the negotiation, expect to see emotions as people defend their territory. If you have a number of different items to discuss, you can tack your way to your final goal just as a sailor must do when facing strong headwinds. If you only talk about one item (price) there is nowhere to build common cause when the negotiation gets difficult. Remain fact-based, find points of agreement and build on those, understand the value of trade-offs and, when you must, make some concessions in the short-term that can be addressed later.

Have a plan going into the negotiation with a BATNA (Best Alternative To a Negotiated Agreement.) To walk in with a strong BATNA (if this does not work with Vendor X, I already know the terms to switch to Vendor Y) you will have confidence and power to negotiate a new deal with Vendor X. A BATNA can prevent poor decisions in the moment. With a strong BATNA, you will know when to walk away from the table.

The more prepared you can be to inform your vendors of their status with you (sell-through, return rates, promotional sales lift, on-time delivery rates, order-completion rates) the better prepared you will be to attain your goals from the start of the process. It is not considered good business to share any competitive information with your vendors where they would be given insight into their competitor's prices or sales terms. However, it is common practice to compare each vendor to the average for their category.

For example, it would not be ethical (or in some countries, legal) to provide vendor-specific information:

| | Cost of Goods Sold (COGS) | Average Ship Time | Supply on Hand |
|---|---|---|---|
| **Vendor A** 1 liter water pallet | $42.36 | 18 days | 31 days |
| **Vendor B** 1 liter water pallet | $39.95 | 12 days | 22 days |

It would be ethical to provide an average for the category:

| | Cost of Goods Sold (COGS) | Average Ship Time | Supply on Hand |
|---|---|---|---|
| **Vendor A** 1 liter water pallet | $42.36 | 18 days | 31 days |
| **Average** 1 liter water pallet | $40.15 | 10 days | 18 days |

When provided with this information, it would be completely appropriate to discuss how to improve delivery times and reduce inventory with Vendor A while explaining that should the price not come into alignment, it will be difficult to continue keeping their SKU in the range. Of course, this assumes that the product quality and marketing for Vendor A is similar to all other vendors in the category. Armed with knowledge, a retailer can enter into a negotiation with confidence, no matter the size of their operation.

A good negotiator must balance hard and soft tactics. Negotiate too softly and it can be easy to lose a winning position. Negotiate too hard and you risk harming the relationship or losing it all together. Mature negotiators are soft on people but hard on problems. Keep the focus on solving problems and not assessing blame. The goal is to help each side gain insight into the other side's position and constraints. The more you can understand who you are negotiating with and what is important to them, the better position you will be in when you arrive at the negotiating table.

If you know their bonus depends on new item placement, while you need faster order shipments, can you secure a commitment to reducing days off your orders in return for bringing in a new line? If they need to improve their overall volume, can you replace a competitor's line with their product in return for a volume discount? It's cliché to say look for the win/win in a negotiation. But good negotiators put themselves in their opponent's seat and see the what could be placed on the table to entice them into a compromise.

**Winning Negotiation Tactics**

Successful negotiating requires thoughtful preparation and a planned goal as well as a BATNA. Because this is a human interaction, remember that emotions will be at the table as well. Everyone prefers to work with people they like and respect. Keep the conversation amicable and honest. It is completely reasonable to tell a partner that while you truly like them and their company, you cannot persist with the current arrangement and consider yourself a good buyer. Explain what needs to change. Then listen to their response. Listening. Nodding. Restating their issue but remaining firm in your "ask" will help them see that you comprehend their situation.

An overlooked key to effective negotiations is to give yourself time. Arriving at an optimal contract in one session is rare. It can take weeks and often months to complete. Be persistent. Set a follow-up date at the end of every discussion if there are still open issues. Work at making progress during every round.

Another good practice is to have at least one more person at your side during negotiations. Here are two critical roles that one or more people can play during vendor discussions:

The first is the subject-matter expert (SME.) The SME may be the person who manages receiving who can discuss the problems in shipping that are causing product defects. Or the accounts payable expert who can elaborate on invoice reconciliation problems that should be addressed. Inviting another voice at the table to discuss their area of expertise and provide factual evidence for a point of negotiation will help you demonstrate credibility with your vendors. A note: Prepare your coworkers with the role they are to play in the meeting and make sure you are aligned on the message to deliver.

A second important role of someone at your side of the table is to take detailed notes on points of agreement. Each meeting should end with a summary of what was agreed upon, its timing and the follow-up required. If a second person can be tasked with concentrating on that, you can focus on creative problem solving with the vendor.

Finally, one of the best tools to have in entering a negotiation is honesty. Bluffing may work in cards, but making false statements in a negotiation will eventually catch up with you. Your vendors (while competitive) are a tight community. Reputations are shared. Keep yours fair, honest and respected and vendors will know to come to the table prepared to bring you their best offers.

**Follow Up**

Finally, take detailed notes and document the negotiation. After each round or discussion, send out a note that documents what you heard and where you believe there were agreements and discord. Typically, there are two (or more) final documents that would come out of a vendor negotiation:

1. New terms and agreements that are signed for a specified period of time. Both parties agree to continue business under the new terms.

2. Notes and documentation on items *not* included in the agreement. For example, a plan to jointly review forecasts once per quarter, on-site training for new technology, promotional events, joint agreements to address any issues in the future, metrics to be shared and tracked by month, etc.

Well-documented negotiations can become the building block for future meetings and new agreements. After all, vendor negotiations are not a battle ground. When managed in a professional manner, they become the roadmap to improved relations and profit for everyone involved.

## WIN Today

Review the metrics you have available to evaluate, review and compare your vendors prior to beginning a negotiation. Use the metrics to create a scorecard for your vendors to divide them amongst the gold/silver/bronze levels discussed above.

If a vendor is shared across multiple buyers, make sure that the designation is true across all areas of the business. It can be common to have a vendor partner at a gold level in one category but a silver or bronze level in a different one. Team up across the company to provide one unified viewpoint for the vendor and leverage gold privileges to entice them to improve areas where they are performing like a silver or bronze vendor.

## Four Rules to Master Visual Merchandising

In the world of retail there are so many places that management can focus that sometimes the most basic items get overlooked. Merchandising is broad. It includes product selection, assortment planning, vendor management, sales forecasting and visual presentation. Visual merchandising is focused on how product is presented to the customer in a store or online. In many ways, visual merchandising is the goal line of a football field. Getting your product (the ball) within the last two yards does not score a touchdown. You have to get the ball all the way across the goal line.

You may select a profitable assortment that is appealing and priced competitively. But unless it is organized from a shopper's perspective, easy to understand and clearly signed, it may not achieve the sales you expect.

### Rule 1 – Make Products Easy to Find

Your store or website is a destination where customers arrive with an intended purpose. In today's busy world, a customer passing by who decides to stop in just to browse is rare. Even online shopping is intentional.

For customers entering your store, they step through into the threshold and pause and scan the store from wall to wall to get their bearings and create a map inside their head. They are looking for cues about where products are located and how the store is organized. How to navigate from their current location to where they believe they will find their desired product. This can happen quite rapidly, and some customers may not even break their stride as they create their mental map.

One of the first components of good visual merchandising are "way-finding signs." Aisle markers and category headers frequently serve the purpose. Smart retailers who flex their product range create sign holders that can accommodate interchangeable signs to hold down costs. A change in location can be as simple as sliding out a sign and replacing it with a new one.

Another strategy for helping customers orient themselves to the store environment is to use peripheral walls. Walls can accommodate over-sized brand logos if brands are a primary shopping driver. Or peripheral walls can have very large graphics of products or customers using the products. These lifestyle photos help shoppers find their way.

Online, the product hierarchy should be easy to navigate and obvious from the landing page. Filters should make it fast for users to narrow their choices to the items in stock, the correct size or color or on sale. Filters need to remember previous choices and not revert to an unfiltered selection as shoppers review items to keep them engaged with the site.

**Rule 2 – Organize Products for Buying**

In stores, once a customer finds the correct aisle, they need to quickly understand how products are organized. The goal is to find a specific item (or narrowed consideration set) to purchase. Here is where brick-and-mortar retailers stumble.

Each customer will approach the purchase from their individual framework. So, if the customer was interested in looking for a pencil, there are a number of ways that pencils could be mentally organized by the customer: mechanical versus wood, by lead softness, by color or licensed character set, by price point, by quantity. Each customer may identify a different way that they think about pencils that makes sense to them. As a retailer, your job is to present those pencils in a way that closely aligns to how most customers shop for pencils *and* makes it easy to impulsively purchase more pencils (or more expensive pencils) than planned.

Smart brick-and-mortar and online retailers consult the consumer decision tree (CDT) to understand how their target customer thinks about making a pencil purchase. Consumer decision trees are corroborated mental frameworks for how customers organize and compare groups of products.

For example, the cat food CDT may be:
    **Life stage**: Kitten, Adult, Senior or Special Needs cat
      **Canned**, Dry or Moist
        **Brand**: Iams, Science Diet, Blue Buffalo
          **Protein**: Tuna, Salmon, Chicken

Let's say the CDT indicates that the first decision a pencil customer makes is whether they want a mechanical or wooden pencil. A smart retailer would separate mechanical from wood pencils. That would make finding all of the wood or mechanical pencils easier. To make the sale complete, lead and eraser refills would be merchandised beside the mechanical pencils. To organize wood pencils, a retailer could pile packs of pencils on the shelf. A retailer with strong visual merchandising skills might place multi-colored pencils in a clear acrylic vase at eye level. Besides being an eye-catching display, it might induce more impulse purchases. Propping matching pads of paper, thumbtacks, paperclips and markers helps create a total market basket for customers.

Online, pencils should follow the CDT as well. The "customers also purchased" feature online can help round out the complete sale.

Retailers must think about and approach merchandising as a customer would. Too often retailers think about the *process* of merchandising and want to make re-stocking the shelves the paramount decision in merchandising. When a retailer organizes the product to induce buying (instead of reducing re-stocking costs), sales improve.

### Rule 3 – Showcase Products

As in the pencil example above, great visual merchandisers know how to present products to create eye appeal and interest. Basic art and design principles translate directly to visual merchandising in stores.

**Levels create interest.** Get products up off of shelves with props and holders to give shoppers something appealing to look at. Use blocks, create pyramids, and use easels of every size to create levels.

**Curves create flow.** Even the unvarying rectangle of books can be merchandised in curves when stacked in a spiral pattern. Our eyes and minds prefer to see things bend away from us rather than stop abruptly.

**Colors unify and harmonize.** The most mismatched items look harmonious if they are the same color. Showcase colors that are complementary (across from each other on the color wheel, like blue/orange or pink/green) or analogous (color wheel neighbors like blues with greens or lilacs with pinks).

**Stores are three-dimensional.** Shelves of products (and especially pegboards with flat products dangling from pegs) can create unbroken planes of merchandise. Break up planes with alcoves, fin signs that run perpendicular to the plane or shelf extenders to use space more fully.

**Surprises are remembered.** Customers will remember products that are displayed in an unexpected fashion. That is why window displays often juxtapose products in a unique way. A dress made of newspapers with an umbrella made of paper plates are not for sale – but they are intriguing and draw customers into the shop.

Showcasing products online is in the hands of the design team and photographers.

**Design themes.** Design campaigns around themes and new arrivals to make a statement. Themes like "summer barbecue" can showcase everything from clothing to food to insecticide and dining accessories. Use cohesive, eye-catching graphics, palettes and fonts to capture the mood of the themes. Change themes regularly to keep the site fresh.

**Use an expert to build a house brand.** Designers, TV personalities and celebrities can give credibility to a selection of products that share a common appeal. Even the senior merchandising executive can become the sites expert. Provide tips and tricks or inside news bites to create a voice within the site. Invest in the expert to build a following.

**Invest in high-resolution product photos.** Be sure to have many orientations. Consider a 3-D motion camera so site visitors can control the camera angle and zoom. Allow customers to see each static shot in every color. Include action shots or videos. Showcase products in a solution set.

**Be entertaining or educational.** Since you do not have the advantage of customers touching the product or seeing it in real life, compensate by making your site entertaining or educational. Be a perfectionist in providing measurements and specifications. Use iconography to help customers see when a product is made from recycled content, GMO-free, weekend or business appropriate, etc.

### Rule 4 – Never Look Empty

Brick-and-mortar merchants know that a shelf or display that looks full will always be more appealing than one that has many holes and looks "picked over." True, some customers avoid purchasing the first item, as it would disrupt a perfect presentation. But nearly *every* customer will avoid purchasing the last item since it infers that others rejected it.

On shelves or pegs, merchandise should be pulled forward to give a full and well-cared-for look. On endcaps or displays, product should be redistributed to always look well-tended. Use blocks or false backs, if necessary, to keep product prominent and near the shelf edge. As products sell down to a point where they no longer look appealing, farm them back to their home location and replace them with heavily in-stock products. If you expect a replenishment shipment soon, consider creating a sign that alerts shoppers to how fast your great deals sell and that you will be back in stock. Nothing instills confidence like knowing that other shoppers find your store and products desirable.

Online, review how many products can say "out of stock" or "on backorder" to understand their chilling effect on purchases. If a vendor is not able to deliver product quickly, determine if it should come off the site until it is back in stock. Test to understand when informing a customer that a product is on backorder will move the customer to a substitute product or to abandon the site completely.

The extra care that visual merchandising requires is paid back by making your store or website a pleasant environment to shop. Great visual merchandising makes shopping fun and pleasurable, sells more full-priced items and brings customers back to the store or website for the joy of spending time evaluating products presented with imagination and care.

## WIN Today

Brick-and-mortar stores:
1. Make sure way-finding signs are visible from the main entrance and accurate. Aisle markers should include the most iconic products in the aisle. (A hand tool aisle should say hammers, handsaws, screwdrivers instead of vise grips or pliers, even though those products may be in the aisle.)
2. Organize how products are merchandised. Size, flavor or color choices should be in the same order from brand to brand. Beware of vendor-supplied merchandising that always places brand at the top of the organizational pattern. Truth is, brand is not a driver as much as vendors claim. Salad dressing shoppers probably want to shop by flavor and price (Italian vs Ranch vs French, then price) more than brand and flavor.
3. Find one to two areas in the store where you can boost visual appeal. Ask a creative team member to provide ideas. Keep the focus on the products. This is not a time to *decorate*. Visual merchandising is not decorating the store. It is about showing a product in action in an unexpected way. Light fixtures as mannequins, a tree made of kitchen utensils or an oversized tea pot pouring acrylic tea into a normal-sized tea cup are arresting images that get a customer to stop and shop.

Online stores:
1. Review your product hierarchy and image libraries. Make improvements to bring high-engagement products to life.
2. Consider creating an expert store-within-a-store from products curated by someone of merit. Internal or local experts who want to extend their reach are affordable options.
3. Make sure that store themes are well planned and differentiated with a unique design motif that complements the brand.

# MERCHANDISING

## The Productivity Zones of Your Store

In your home there are rooms that are used several times every single day by every resident: the kitchen, the bathroom, the entryway. Some areas are seldom used: the attic, the spare bedroom or the laundry. The same is true in stores. Savvy retailers make sure their high-traffic areas are as productive as possible and find ways to make sure customers visit the less frequented areas to keep the entire store as productive as possible. After all, the rent is charged for every square foot of the store – so every square foot must pay its way.

The most productive area of a store is typically the most visible area of the store.

Everyone enters the store, so naturally, one would expect the front of the store to be the most productive. In fact, customers typically need about 6-10 paces to acclimate themselves to the environment of a store. They step inside and psychologically they need a few steps to adjust to the lighting, temperature and acoustics of their new environment. While their body continues to take steps, their brain is making many adjustments that prevent them from considering a purchase. The entryway is the area to welcome customers and make them feel comfortable.

Once adjusted, customers begin to navigate the store. Their eyes sweep from side to side above the shelves to understand and orient themselves to the store. They try to understand how the store is organized and create a path in their mind to achieve their goal for entering the store. It is at this point that they actually begin "shopping" or considering merchandise and purchases.

Spend time watching your customers and try to identify where the "shopping" journey begins in your store. Decide if your store is too bright, too loud, too dark and make adjustments so that your customers orient themselves as quickly as possible once they step inside the threshold of your store. Watch how shoppers orient themselves. Make hand baskets convenient for them. Baskets or carts placed too close to the door will be overlooked.

In the United States, where large supermarkets are the norm, grocers have developed the "milk, eggs and bread" merchandising strategy. Between routine buying trips, most households run out of milk, eggs and bread and need to have a return visit to the store once or twice a week to do a "quick run" for just the essentials. Grocers have strategically placed those necessities at the back of the store in order to make sure that customers must traverse the entire store to get to their destination. What happens along the way? They see cookies, snacks, fruit and ice cream -

which can all be added to their cart as an impulse purchase. The simple $5 purchase escalates to $20 or more.

You can adapt this strategy for your store by making sure that your shoppers see as much of your merchandise as possible on their way to purchasing the most popular items. A large graphic on your back wall that clearly indicates that the popular items are located in the back will help customers understand their pathway once they are oriented to your store. A clear sign will also help minimize questions from customers every day that start with "Where is ...?" Pay close attention to the route customers take to the back and note the "hot zones" along the way where you could highlight new products, niche or seasonal products and great values or closeout product to increase purchases.

The area immediately facing the landing area in your store is where new items and promotional items with a high-profit margin should be placed. This is where nearly every customer will begin their shopping journey. Do not let this critical location stagnate. Selections should be fresh and change regularly. If your strategy is to have a deep selection of products, reinforce your brand by highlighting a changing variety of products in this highly productive hot zone. If your strategy is everyday low prices or low-priced promotional values, routinely showcase your best values. If you carry the latest new items – and your customers are early adopters of new technology – make sure your newest products are showcased here.

One of the most productive areas of a store is at the cash register. If you have a store where customers routinely queue to wait to their turn for the register, flank the queue with impulse items that do not require much consideration to purchase. Trial size products, small and colorful products and "want" versus "need" products are good candidates.

At the register, there should be items within easy reach of your employees that could be suggestively sold to customers to help them complete a satisfying transaction. Employees should pay attention to each customer's purchase and engage with customers so that they can ensure that each customer leaves with what they need. For example, re-usable bags are a good choice for a suggested sale. A customer purchasing shoes may also need a shoe care kit. And every salon suggests shampoo and sprays at the register. Savvy merchandisers regularly showcase a variety of items at the cash register. A stagnant selection at the till will erode impulse sales over time and weaken productivity.

It is important to help your employees at the register understand that their role is to help customers make a completely satisfying sale. Consider a customer purchasing a smoke detector for their home. They purchase the smoke detector only to get home and realize it will not work without a battery. How frustrating! If the store associate had only informed them of that, they would be pleased with their shopping experience instead of exasperated. Your employees should understand their primary role is to help their customers make a satisfying purchase – not run credit cards, count change or bag up products. Those steps are the means to the end.

As you watch your customers shop, note where they change direction and make corners. Where a customer changes direction, they readjust to their surroundings as they did as they entered the store. Corners are natural productivity zones for merchandise displays. Endcaps and perimeter walls are strong candidates for changing merchandise to highlight promotional products and sales. In some stores 50% of all sales in an aisle can come from the products on the end of the shelving run.

As you evaluate the sales of new, seasonal or promotional products, if sales are below expectations review where they are merchandised. If they are not in one of your productivity zones, move them to a highly visible area of the store to give them the best possible merchandising. After a month, if sales have not improved, there is a different problem to solve: perhaps the price is too high, the customers do not understand the value or functionality of the new product or they simply are not interested in purchasing it at your store. Consider other ways to stimulate sales such as a price decrease, selling it online or bundling the item with a proven seller.

While a majority of your store can be static and merchandise should have regular home locations, the productivity zones of your store – the store front, cash register, endcaps and natural corners – need to be organized and fresh to stay as productive as possible.

## WIN Today

Spend an hour watching customers enter your store and note where their "shopping journey" begins. Align your displays to showcase the key items at every hot zone as well as at other natural corners in your store.

If required promotional locations are directed from headquarters, make sure that the most important ones are truly aligning to your shoppers' traffic patterns. Take steps to inform your headquarters of the highest value locations for your store so that they can plan accordingly.

## Showcasing in Physical Stores

Excellent merchandising increases your bottom line. It's as simple as that. Two stores could have the same product at the same prices with the same customer traffic and the one who does a brilliant job of showcasing and merchandising the product will have higher sales than the one who does not. How merchandise is presented to your customers is critical. Like a silent sales associate, great merchandising helps customers find what they need and entices them to happily make unplanned purchases.

Merchandising that practically compels customers to make a purchase happens when team members care about maintaining powerful merchandising and are held accountable for excellent execution. To succeed, you need communication, planning, direction, follow up, measurements and rewards.

Store teams are tuned into your customers and what they learn every day can provide valuable input. For example, talk with your team about your store's hot and cold zones. We've already talked about hot zones like the opening rack, the area for queuing to the sales counter or a wall of new arrivals. Review those areas with your team and communicate that it is a priority to tend to them and merchandise them correctly every single shift. Then look at the "cold zones" – those infrequently shopped areas in the store – and try to increase their shopability. Consider creating outposts to highlight accessory items to improve awareness with your shoppers.

### Adjacencies

One of the most effective ways to increase unplanned purchases is to make complicated sales easier through smart merchandising adjacencies or suggestions online. Review your category assortments as if you were a customer solving a problem – not a buyer selecting products from a set of vendors.

If you are a working mother, a problem you may have to solve is making fast, healthy breakfasts. A grocer who looks at products by category will scatter that mom's purchases across the store: making her shop the bread aisle for bagels, the dairy aisle for cream cheese, yogurt and milk, the produce section for bananas, the cereal aisle for cereal or granola bars and the refrigerated case for eggs, juice and bacon. Enlightened grocers are installing refrigerated outposts into their traditional cereal aisle to make a breakfast aisle that contains everything for the busy parent to pick up breakfast solutions in one place. What it means is that grocers who are willing to invest in the extra fixtures and complexity reap additional sales in accessory items. For example, when a busy parent who initially planned to only pick up cereal and milk sees other selections in the same aisle, he may add on a loaf of raisin bread, a bunch of bananas and a few cups of yogurt. In effect, the unplanned purchase doubles the intentional shopping list *and* makes the shopper more satisfied by providing a complete solution in one easy-to-shop location.

Smart adjacencies are critical for building additional sales without the need for team member assistance. They are most effective when approached as a customer solving a problem.

### Stocking

If a customer cannot find an item or see it, it will not sell. In 2002, a study on retail out-of-stock (OOS) levels of fast-moving consumer goods (FMCG) products found that the overall level of OOS in developed countries world-wide to be 8% and that 75% of the cause was due to retail store practices (as opposed to up-stream supply issues.) On average 30% of the items that were OOS were purchased at another retail store. The implications suggested that retailers on average lose 4% of their annual sales due to OOS items.[12]

Your store team needs to be vigilant about eliminating "holes." Any product from the back room needs to be moved onto the sales floor. Stores with small back rooms store product as upstock, stock that may be stored on the top-most – unshoppable – shelf of a set. It is best to move that product into place after hours since ladders are required to access it. Be aware of visual out-of-stocks as well that occur when products on the top and bottom shelves are so far back as to be out of your customer's line of sight.

Among the daily tasks you should expect from your store team is front facing the merchandise. All products, either on a shelf or peg hook, should be pulled forward to the front edge of the shelf or peg hook to increase their visibility and abundance.

The presentation side of the package should always be facing outward and right side up. Older stock should be brought to the front of the shelf or peg hook with newer product placed behind it, thereby rotating your stock. This assures older stock, that may have older packaging, is sold first. Not only is stock rotation a good practice, it is a legal requirement for perishable products and can be prosecuted in some states.

When front facing, review product packages that may be in need of repair or are damaged. Use hangs tabs (which are plastic adhesive tag tabs – see www.do-it.com) to fix packages that will not hang from peg hooks when their peg holes have been torn out. Tape any boxes that are broken or torn. Consider a price reduction on any damaged boxes to ensure the item will sell. As you front face, return all orphan items that are not in their correct home to their proper location in the store.

Before leaving the aisle or store location, note empty locations for re-order. Then review all shelf labels for accuracy. Shelf labels give customers price information and should be clean, easy to read and accurate. Store associates receive valuable information about product description, the item number and the current price. Even if there is no stock, the shelf label should remain visible so customers know you carry the item. Consider creating a standard tag that says "Sorry, this item is temporarily out of stock" with a place for an associate to write the date the product went out of stock (and was re-ordered) for easy record keeping. Those tags inform your customers that you are aware of the situation and have ordered the product – making your store look more professional. Remove old promotional price stickers immediately.

**Special Locations**

While merchandising, you may uncover clearance items that no longer have a home. Move them to a designated area in your store for clearance. Successful locations are a back endcap, a flex area, a table, a rolling wire "baker's" rack or a dump bin. Show your customers the value of the clearance item with a "was/now" price sticker to show the value of the discontinued price. Clearance product offers incredible values to customers. Make sure they see it. (See "End of the Line: Clearance and Closeouts" in *Timeless Principle 4: Pricing*.)

Flex areas and endcaps are those temporary locations that highlight new items, seasonal items or great values for your customers. Because of the visibility, studies have shown that endcaps can increase the sale of items without special pricing up to 25% just by placing them in front of more customers.

Typical endcap merchandising strategies include:

**Bulk endcaps** where the entire end is one item or one brand. This is a good tactic for a consumable item (like paper towels, laundry detergent or soda) where an attractive display of a large volume equates to a good deal to a customer. The retail phrase is "Stack 'em high and watch 'em fly."

**Theme endcaps** combine related items to create a theme – back-to-school, Mother's Day, family game night, lunchbox favorites. Again, these do not have to be sold at a promotional price to generate additional sales.

**Solution endcaps** collect separate pieces of a solution together for a customer to make a one-stop shop. Examples include blank formal invitation stationery, matching envelopes, sealing stickers and metallic pens together for a bridal invitation solution. Or bug spray, sunscreen, towels, beach toys and small coolers for a beach outing. Or pasta, sauce, bread, cheese and wine for an Italian dinner.

Increase impulse sales – without increasing overall inventory – with merchandising strips and wing racks to highlight natural sale partners. Merchandising "clip strips" hold 6 to 12 items on clips or hooks at regular intervals that can be affixed to shelves. Used as secondary locations for impulse items, natural cross-merchandising increases sales. Batteries near flashlights and tape near wrapping paper are candidates for clip strip merchandising. Wing racks are usually 10 to16 inches wide and use the sides of endcap shelves. Wing racks can be corrugated display shippers or a more permanent fixture that uses the sides of shelf ends. Use cross-merchandising to place items in several locations in the store where they can be purchased on impulse by a customer.

The counter at the cash register is usually the store's premier location for impulse purchases. As customers wait they have time to consider products they may have passed by in the store. High-margin items with a low price are most attractive, which is why candy, soda, travel-sized goods and magazines are merchandised there. Of course, space is limited. Have a plan. Do not let the register become a cluttered dumping ground for everything in your store that is under $5.00.

Some stores outsource their cash register merchandising program to a single vendor who acts as a direct store distributor and merchandiser (called a service merchandiser.) Typically, they buy the right to sell items at the cash registers and manage the inventory on a consignment basis. This is particularly useful for retailers who do not want to manage the fast-turning inventory and mandatory merchandising required to keep cash wraps looking fresh. Most supermarket magazine programs are managed in that manner.

## Display Fixtures

Drive impulse sales with attractive outpost fixtures throughout the store. To create outpost impulse fixtures, purchase a display fixture that is utilitarian and straight-forward. Fixtures are a costly investment. For retailers to control their presentation, it is important to plan a fixture that can be used to merchandise many different kinds of products and fits within the look and feel of the store.

For example, avoid large displays that can only be used in one area, in one way. (Like an umbrella fixture or a poster fixture.) You will want to move it around so look for locking casters. Fixtures should be versatile and durable. Durable fixtures allow you to put product on a display that supports your store brand rather than buying a prebuilt display for a single purpose. Retailers are tempted to accept a "free" fixture from Nike, Under Armour or Pepsi but quickly realize they want to use the fixture for other products. Too often they end up throwing the specialist display away, especially if that particular brand doesn't sell well.

A generic fixture with a holder for a large-format sign that can accept a color graphic can be made to appear like a branded display by simply changing the graphic element. Savvy retailers charge their vendors for the right to be displayed in such a location and create the correct branding to support both the vendor and the store's image. Thus, the same fixture can be used as a Marvel display, a Martha Stewart display and a Jell-O display for the cost of a printed sign.

Aesthetics are also important. An attractive, well-ordered store will give a much better impression to customers. Bear this in mind when choosing your displays and shelving and try to maintain a palette that fits with the theme of the rest of the shop. If your store has weathered wood fixtures with hunter green trim and a vendor offers a free red wire display rack, consider the effect on your customers. Sure, it will attract their eye, but your customers will probably stay clear of it because it will connote a "cheap" aesthetic.

## WIN Today

Make sure the process of proper front facing, stock rotation and package repair is learned the first week on the job for every new hire.

Review your back room for old display units that you or past management have been holding. With permission from your management, discard displays to free up back room space. Eliminate old signs and graphics from past promotions as well.

## Planograms = Consistently Appealing Stores

Perfectly stocked shelves that are easy to fill, easy for customers to shop and correctly balance inventory with sales demand. That is the dream. Inevitably, managers realize they need "planograms." Implementing the principles of a good planogram can make your store more attractive and more profitable.

Think of planograms – or schematics – as maps that guide a store associate to place merchandise on shelves or peg hooks. When done well planograms make it easy for customers to find what they need, induce impulse purchases and make sales more profitable. Sometimes vendors offer a preferred merchandising planogram to showcase their brand when they introduce new items. But only well-resourced vendors are able to customize their planograms for each store. Most retailers do it themselves.

Planograms should make the store easier to operate and more functional. They should be easy to execute with very limited changes required by the store team to complete the task. Most desirable are easy "swap out" planogram changes where a single SKU is changed over; such as when an ice cream flavor is replaced with a different flavor of the same size. That is easy to execute because the rest of the shelf is undisrupted by changing shelf heights or re-flowing merchandise within the freezer case. All a store associate needs to do is remove the old product and either send it back to the vendor or place it on a clearance location at a reduced price then change the shelf tag and place the new flavor in the empty space.

More troublesome is when there is an abundance of old product on the shelf and no location to liquidate it or when the old product is sold (leaving an empty "hole" in the shelf) and the replacement product has yet to arrive. In that a situation, the store manager must either leave the location empty or fill it with product that is available in the store but will not necessarily create incremental sales. For a store manager who is evaluated on store sales, getting new products into the store is critical.

Of course, not all planogram changes are a simple "swap out." From time to time, there are major disruptions to support customer expectations or new company initiatives.

An example of a complicated planogram a retailer recently implemented created a birthday party section within the store. Looking at the opportunity to increase sales beyond invitations and favors, the retailer pulled together gift bags, cake decorating supplies, disposable paper goods, thank you notes, decorations, candles and gift wrap into a complicated aisle that was vertically merchandised by theme: princess, dinosaur, cowboy. The planogram took several evenings to complete because of all the adjustments that had to be made to sections that were left empty by the new birthday center in the baking aisle, paper goods aisle and card section. But once it was completed, the store saw an increase in sales in its new "birthday center" category. It became a customer solution that had previously been hidden within the sales reports. With new focus and an integrated merchandising plan, it continues to grow in sales because of the careful management of the revolving themes to keep pace with kids' fickle interests.

To get to that point, the retailer had to look at the breadth of its product selection across categories through its sales reports and recognize that busy parents were purchasing items from multiple places in the store in the same transaction in a regularly recurring pattern. This is called an affinity analysis or market basket analysis. Typically, retailers who have access to "big data" and data mining tools can run reports against transactions looking for what else is most commonly purchased when a certain item is included in the transaction. Thus, a retailer might uncover that when a cake mix is in the transaction the next most common item in the transaction is a can of prepared frosting, then the next is eggs, then the next is milk, then the next is pre-sweetened cereal, then the next is fresh bananas. All of which helps a grocer identify the customer as a likely parent with children and could help a grocer determine the kind of promotions to send to the customer. Or how to merchandise store shelves more efficiently to meet that customer's needs.

A simplified analysis would look at customer transactions in the following way: Assume you are an office supply store and your most popular ink SKU is a black ink refill cartridge. Run a report that ranks the other most common purchases with that SKU and physically identify where in the store your customers have to walk to find those SKUs. Naturally, you will see other ink colors and paper. Those are the easy and natural connections. Look for the other less obvious connections. For example, what else do your shoppers purchase? Mailing labels? Packing tape? Staples? Stamps? Do you need to pull together a mailing center for all the products customers need to send parcels? A wedding section for all the items needed for brides? An office center to set up a home office? Look at affinity reports to help you find the natural connections that customers are making when they are solving a specific shopping occasion's needs and you may find new ways to merchandise or cross-merchandise products in your store. Merchandising by solution sets can increase sales without increasing your inventory.

If your new merchandising plan is complex and takes products from several places in your store, it will take planning to reflow the store without disrupting business. Think through the adjustments and break them down to discreet tasks to keep customer service levels high throughout the change-over. Major planogram changes usually occur after store hours so that associates can empty shelves, wash and clean them, rearrange the fixtures and then complete the new planogram. Store managers are typically given a limited number of hours to complete the tasks or a budget to hire a temporary third-party labor force to help complete the work. A planogram change that is not well-planned can waste time and money and be a disappointment for customers who may not return.

Retailers may select among many computerized solutions for creating planograms. All require basic data about fixture dimensions, product dimensions and sales history or sales forecasts to create optimized merchandising. The financial investment in this kind of system is usually beyond what a small chain can afford. However, most vendors have access to a system at their home office and will offer some level of support for creating planograms even to small customers if they believe they can benefit from increased shelf space, inventory levels and sales. Ask your best vendors for planograms and you are likely to get a recommendation for merchandising their product.

Retailers who create Category Captain programs expect vendors to create planograms that include competitive product. This is a standard operating process for grocery, drug and mass merchandise chains in the United States and less common in specialized retail organizations. Category Captains are vendor-funded resources who typically work onsite at the retailer offices. Category Captains truly are servants to two masters: the vendor that employs them as well as the retailer. Their role is to act in the retailer's best interest while planogramming and doing other category analyses for the category they participate in. They should approach their work with insights and customer research for their category. The program works when the Category Captain is ethical and held to strict standards to remove bias from their merchandise plans.

Even without a formal planogram development application or a vendor Category Captain, ask your best vendors about the recommended ratios for facings of one category to another and evaluate whether you have a sales opportunity. For example, if your vendor recommends all-purpose flour facings at a 4::1 ratio to whole-wheat flour, but your sales show a 6::1 ratio, you may have an opportunity to improve your whole-wheat flour sales by increasing its visibility. When evaluating a planogram, look beyond the individual SKU placement and try to understand its merchandising principles. Is it merchandised by price segment, color, occasion, brand? Then apply that merchandising strategy to create your own planogram.

To keep merchandising consistent across stores, it is a good practice to designate one store to be the "prototype" store. At the most basic level you can merchandise your prototype store then capture the "planogram" with a photo and a line listing that can be shared with the other stores. Tweak facings and placement to test new merchandising and analyze its impact on sales. Many retailers who have begun setting their high-profit private label items on eye-level shelves and have dropped branded items to lower shelves have seen an increase in their category profits as customers naturally tend to consider items at eye level before all other items in an aisle.

Finally, good planograms need to be easy to maintain and self-serviceable for customers. (There are exceptions such as loss- prevention cases for valuable items like expensive over-the-counter medications.) It needs to hold enough inventory between stocking sessions to meet customer demand. It should be easy to merchandise. Sometimes efficiency is built into the product development such as when a case can be cut open and slid onto the shelf for customers to help themselves. But remember to balance speed with customer's expectations. For example, it is far easier to open a case of books and stack them on a table than to create a spiral stack on the floor. But for many bookstores this attractive – and time-consuming – stack adds visual excitement for merchandising new titles.

Organized merchandising will usually be acceptable if it makes sense to customers and makes their shopping trip an easy one to accomplish.

# MERCHANDISING

## WIN Today

If your store uses planograms, compare the most recent planograms to the actual merchandising in your stores. Evaluate if you are in compliance. If your merchandising does not reflect the planogram, understand if it was due to poor execution and understanding from the team or if there are true obstacles to executing the planogram as it was designed.

If the issue is training and understanding the importance of setting the planogram accurately, that is your role as the store leader to correct and reinforce. If there are true roadblocks to executing the planogram, be sure that the people who made the planogram understand why it is impossible to set as directed.

If your store does not have planograms, think about how to document what the shelf sets and fixtures should look like. Consider using photos and text to capture "best practices" for your store. Focus on the high-visibility areas first like front-facing fixtures and endcaps, how to integrate mannequins into apparel displays, etc. To be long-lived, do not be specific to the exact product in the photos, but talk about the principles of good merchandising and display requirements you expect.

For example:
- Products should be merchandised from smallest to largest left to right.
- Place white clothing on the left, colors in the center and black on the right.
- Every product should have a minimum of two facings.
- Products with multiple facings on peg hooks should be merchandised in vertical blocks, not horizontal blocks.
- Lowest-priced items should be on the bottom shelf.

None of these are necessarily right for your store, but the idea is that there should be documented merchandising rules that replace formal planograms for your store.

## Make Sense of Your Store Signs

Being a good merchant is like being a good communicator: select a single message and hit it hard. *What* your message says, *where* you place it and *when* a customer encounters the message are key to keeping your stores easy to navigate and free from "visual pollution."

Focus on singular messages. What is the *one* thing every shopper passing the outside of your store needs to know? What do they need to know as they enter your store? Shop your aisles? And, finally, check out and leave the store? Match the message to the vehicle: put your hours and seasonal promotion on the door, a hot offer in the window or an exterior banner and your return policy next to the cash register, for example. It is unnecessary to complicate our very simple industry. Customers come into stores to (1) find what they are looking for, (2) be pleasantly surprised to see something unexpected and (3) execute a purchase. Pretty simple. And universally true across merchandise lines.

As a general rule, stores contain too many messages, signs and information "attacking" their customers. Sign creep happens to retailers as they allow every program and every offering to customers to have equal weight. Successful retailers (think of Apple) focus on one message – or at least one at a time. Prioritize signs and place them in a hierarchy, based on their roles:

**1. Inspirational/brand signage** – Remind them where they are and all they could be by purchasing from you. These are iconic brand messages that are considered permanent signs. In addition to your company name and logo, they could include a mural of happy customers using your products, an organized desk/home/garden, a delivery van or an environmental message about recycling resources if those are core to your brand. On websites, this is usually the major image on the home page.

**2. Department/wayfinding** – Herb Sorenson in his book *Notes From Inside the Mind of the Shopper* says 80% of the time a shopper is in a store is spent navigating the store instead of actually considering an item for purchase.[13] They are simply trying to find what they need. Make it simple. Online navigation should be intuitive.

**3. Category or brand** – The next step in navigating and way finding. Now that I have found the plumbing department, where are the faucets? Then kitchen faucets not the bathroom faucets.

**4. Pricing/promotional** – Pretty simple. Make it easy. *One* color and style for everyday pricing. *One* style and color for promotional prices. Not a different color and style for every promotion your marketing team and vendors have set up for the quarter.

**5. Informational** – Again, make it standard and restrain yourself from justifying an informational sign for every new SKU added to the assortment. It has to truly be something that needs to be explained. Oh ... and it actually has to matter to your shoppers.

Turn a critical eye to your stores. Look for locations where customers are bombarded with information and messages that make sales clumsy or confusing. Even simple messages ("Buy two pairs of sandals and get a pair of sunglasses free") can be confusing when they are on an endcap with a mix of beach towels, sunscreen and SKUs that do not qualify for the promotion.

Messages should be presented to customers on a "need to know" basis. For example, shoppers do not need to know your store hours at the cash register. They need to know it at the front door. They do not need to know that you have a return policy of 30 days while they are shopping in the aisles. They need to know that at the cash register. It is unhelpful to place notices about a vendor being out of stock on a key item at the cash register – when customers really needed to know that at the shelf so they could make an alternative selection.

Your role should be to approach your store as a shopper advocate. The goal is to always provide shoppers with the relevant information they need to simplify their purchase.

**Visual Pollution**

One source of visual pollution is vendor-provided point-of-purchase (POP) materials and "free promotional fixtures" that seem to reproduce like rabbits in stores. Think of the variety of messages, styles and vehicles that aggregate when vendors are allowed to affix window clings, door banners, fixture toppers, endcap signs, floor adhesives, in-line offers, floor stands, display-ready cases and other items in stores. To find the most common example of that, look at a convenience store. Soda bottlers, beer distributors, snack vendors and gum/candy merchandisers clutter aisles, cooler doors and counters with so many messages and products it is often difficult to conduct the transaction at the cash register. This is also where you will find red, black, blue and white wire racks left over from old promotions being re-purposed on the sales floor, making the entire store look like a yard sale.

Visual pollution is as common in small stores as large ones. In the United States, Suncoast Video – a chain of DVD stores that were often under 1,000 square feet – regularly had more than 40 different promotional messages at any one time. Shoppers were expected to wade through movie studio signs promoting 20 or more titles on sale for one price, *plus* new release signs, *plus* loyalty point marketing signs, *plus* discounted price signs, *plus* free-with-purchase offers, *plus* magazine subscriptions, *plus* Netflix offers, *plus* club member offers, *plus plus plus.* It was distracting. And what is the natural reaction to so many different messages? To ignore them all.

Skilled retailers have to learn to say "no" to secondary messages and focus on the primary messages that are most important. To make that distinction, remember that secondary and tertiary messages are often relevant to just a small segment of the shopping public. They may be fabulous offers, but their appeal is very limited. A good retailer will find a better way to reach that valuable niche market through email campaigns or targeted loyalty programs.

For example, a pet supplies retailer will nearly always make dog and cat food the primary message. Dog and cat consumables are the categories that bring most people to a pet store. That means fish, birds and other pet messages are always going to be given secondary status. The solution: create a bird- or fish-owner sub-community and address offers for bird and fish food directly to that target group. Use social media, opt-in email campaigns and microsites to direct messages and offers to niche groups and leave large scale, in-store messages to the high volume/broad appeal offers. Translate that into your store. What are your broad-appeal offers? Realize that despite a great offer to your niche markets, you can never really increase overall store sales by cluttering your store with an offer with a very narrow target market.

Messages may seem redundant to you. You see the offer every day throughout the year. But your customers may only be in your stores every few months. Your messages must be simple, located on a "need to know basis" and concise to inform shoppers without overwhelming them.

MERCHANDISING

## WIN Today

For most stores, there are too many signs and messages for customers. Focus on the most important messages that will communicate your store's strategy and boost sales.

Make a list of the key messages, then:
1. Walk your store and look for every sign or message displayed to your customers. Are they in "need to know" locations?
2. Take down all out of date and redundant messages.
3. Move messages and signs to where they will be most helpful to your customers.
4. Look for your broad appeal messages and your targeted niche messages. Work on a plan to communicate the targeted messages directly to the audience that will act on the message.

# 7 Timeless Principles

RETAIL: The Second-Oldest Profession
© 2019 Flora Delaney

# Timeless Principle 4: Pricing

## Make Money – But Stay Competitive

For all the pride that most retailers take in sharing their exciting merchandise and great customer service, retailers can become suddenly shy and ashamed to discuss pricing. Too many retailers believe they have to have the lowest price to attract customers and ring up sales. Knowing they are not the lowest on every item (even Walmart isn't the lowest price on *every* item) they can become subdued about their pricing.

Pricing is just one of the 7 Timeless Principles and it does not have to be the lowest to be an asset. The value equation for customers is price + quality (or utility.) Thus, premium-priced products (like Dawn dishwashing liquid) have a commanding market share despite competitors at less than half its price. For consumers, the search is always for the best value for *what I intend to spend*. If customers always wanted and expected the lowest-priced products, we would all be driving a Kia and Mercedes-Benz would have gone out of business years ago.

As a retailer, it is most important for you to stay in business. That seems like a ridiculously obvious point. But many local store operators create their own demise by pricing their products below what they need to survive. If you set your prices so low that you cannot keep your doors open, you need to be honest about your value delivery to your customers.

Make sure that you are leaning as heavily as possible into the other six Timeless Principles and then take credit for that. If you are offering personalized service, there is a value to that. If you have products that customers can take home today, there is value in not waiting for a delivery truck. If you allow customers to try on selections before purchasing, there is a value to not getting something home and then having to send it back. If products can be serviced or repaired in your store, there is a value to that. Finally, if you carry exclusive, hand-crafted items, realize that there is no other competition. There may be similar items (as in an Etsy shop where multiple sellers carry similar items), but there is only one place they can get the exact item you carry. There is a value to that and it isn't the lowest price possible.

Rarely does a retailer need to make pricing the center of its strategy. Setting your prices to be the most competitive in the market is like building an acting career out of being the most beautiful actress in the world. There will always be someone who comes along who is prettier and younger and will take your place. Instead, make pricing a reinforcing attribute of your store. Prices should reflect the value customers can rely on with your store.

Smart retailers make sure that their prices "ladder" so that customers can see a good/better/best selection to capture the most sales. Customers must always be able to see the reasonability for price increases across an assortment.

While pricing isn't unalterable, it requires consideration to change it. Following competition for every price move up or down a few cents may not make sense when each price change requires a thousand stores to print, find and re-ticket every item in every store. The sales generated by a price move of a few cents may not ever overcome the cost of employees having to make the change in every store. Online, price changes are much more malleable yet, there is still the possibility of upsetting customers today who spent more yesterday on an item they can get for less on your site today. Price protection and a strong pricing policy need to be in place to cover those situations.

Retailers need to be competitively aware but may not need to match competition on price. With one caveat: be as vigilant about when your competition raises prices as you are about when they lower prices. If you are regularly reducing prices to stay competitive in the marketplace, be aware of when prices return to previous levels or begin to rise so that you can recover margins. As a retailer, your margins are the only thing that keep the lights on. Your pricing must always provide you with the stability to stay open.

# PRICING

## What's the Right Price?

One of the most important decisions a retailer makes is pricing. Prices talk directly to customers. They communicate the value of the product and the customer's acceptance that her needs are being met. A pricing strategy is necessary whether you are a dollar store or Cartier. To begin, select your pricing strategy. Your pricing strategy reinforces your brand promise and strength. See "Strategy Is the Foundation" in *Timeless Principle 1: Strategy* to see how pricing can reinforce the convenience, assortment, service and experience. If your retail strategy is to set up price as your greatest strength, then you make a promise that your prices will be the best in the market.

### EDLP or Every Day Low Price

Retailers who follow the EDLP strategy derive their profits by reducing their operating costs to such a degree that they are able to thrive on thin margins.

Ways of doing this include:

- Deliberately selecting a location with a below-market lease (purposefully selecting a C or D real estate location)
- Minimizing marketing costs
- Employing lower wageworkers than competitors (perhaps creating a serve-yourself model)
- Capitalizing on an efficient supply chain

Another successful model to follow if you have selected a lowest-price strategy is to carry completely unique products that are difficult to price-shop. Admittedly, it is difficult in today's internet-comparison shopping environment to create an assortment that cannot be researched by a device-enabled customer. But selecting a range of handcrafted or made-to-order items that can support healthy margins can be the foundation of a profitable assortment without negatively affecting your low-price image.

To deliver on your promise of low prices, you will need to regularly comparison shop your competitors and adjust your prices.

Be vigilant to two situations:
1. Competitors have reduced prices on high-visibility items and you may need to reduce your pricing to remain in a leadership position.
2. Competitors have raised prices, leaving you the option to either adjust your price and regain margin *or* keep your price low and promote your

pricing as another example of how you surpass the competition.

With a low-price strategy, your marketing messages are easy to plan: constantly reinforce that your prices won't be beat. A guarantee to meet or beat a lower price in the market will give your customers confidence in your promise. This is actually one of the easiest marketing messages to create and repeat. It is a simple matter of saying one thing over and over. (Walmart started saying "Always Low Prices" in 1962 and has really never veered from that message. Price is the Walmart strategy.)

Risks to the EDLP strategy are that you must have the operational efficiencies to support the low prices and still remain profitable. The other risk is that your competitors will set your prices to some extent. Should they decide to create a price war (selling items below cost) you need to have the financial means to outlast them or abandon this strategy.

If you selected any other strength from our first chapter: convenience, assortment, service or experience, you have other pricing strategy options.

**High/Low Strategy**

In a high/low pricing strategy, everyday prices have healthy margin rates to offset low promotional pricing you offer from time to time to attract customers. Usually, the promoted items have universal – not niche – appeal. Smart retailers find ways to promote different items throughout the year to appeal to a wide variety of customers and maintain an image of good deals throughout the store.

Promotions are designed to attract new shoppers and remind past customers to make a return visit. In a well-run high/low operation, low-priced items are balanced with high-margin items to make the overall transaction profitable.

Timing promotions to coincide with vendor price reductions helps maintain margins throughout the entire promotion. Vendors reduce prices during their "drive periods" to increase their market share through coupon drops, advertising cycles and sampling to increase the impact of their investments. Vendors also reduce prices at the end of a model year and sometimes when component prices decrease their production costs.

Many high/low retailers are able to maintain their margins through an analytic practice called **forward buying**. Forward buying is an inventory replenishment practice of intentionally buying a larger than normal volume when vendors offer deep promotional discounts or prior to a price increase. Forward buyers analyze the discount, the sales rate, the perishability of the product, the cost of money[14], and the warehousing costs to determine the optimum amount to purchase on deal to extend low-cost products into the future.

For example, imagine a canned juice manufacturer offered a discount for a month if the juice is featured on the front page of a grocer's ad at a reduced price sometime during the month. The retailer is likely to evaluate exactly how many extra weeks of sales the ad would deliver. Let's say in the 1-month period the retailer expects to see double the demand and can sell an average of 2 months of juice. Instead of buying 2 months of juice, the retailer may buy 8 months of juice: 2 months to cover the promotion and 6 additional months to sell at regular price but retain the larger margin.

This is dramatically different from the EDLP retailer. An EDLP retailer wants to smooth out both the customer demand and the supply chain peaks and valleys in an effort to create a more efficient overall system. An EDLP retailer would attempt to negotiate with the juice vendor to reduce prices all year long to reduce price and sales volatility.

Risks to the high/low pricing strategy are "cherry pickers" – those customers who come in to only purchase sale items and only during promotions. Without profit-building ancillary items in the transaction, those are unprofitable customers.

There are two things to do with them:
1. Induce them to impulsively purchase high margin items, or
2. Give them to your competitors (known as "firing customers")

This is a controversial tactic. But analyzing cherry pickers shows that they will quickly move to other promotional sellers once you curtail your offers to them. Firing customers means sending less offers to the general public and striating offers so that your best customers qualify for your best promotional offers. "Buy More, Save More" events help reduce the number of cherry pickers.

The other risk to the high/low pricing strategy is "training" your customers to only shop at your store during promotions. This leads to peaks and valleys in your store traffic.

A way to combat this is to time your promotions to be out of synch with repurchase cycles. Universally, most retailers see predictable peaks and valleys in their transactions on key shopping weeks – typically the 1st and the 15th of the month when most paychecks for employers and the government are issued. Offering a promotion that occurs on the 7th and the 21st interrupts the usual purchase cycle and can increase off-week shopping.

There is a hybrid between EDLP and high/low pricing: the price halo strategy.

**Price Halo Strategy**

Retailers looking to price their items competitively and still manage to eke out a sustainable profit would be well served to get a key value item (KVI) analysis and follow a *price halo strategy*. The SKU-level KVI analysis helps identify which products disproportionately drive customer's price-value perception of a retailer. They are the first products that drive store switching when pricing is the determining factor in selecting a store or website.

A KVI analysis is based on:
1. Behavioral data
   - Sales
   - Household penetration
   - Purchase frequency
2. Attitudinal data
   - Customer awareness of specific products
   - Accurate recall of their prices
   - Significance in price comparisons between stores or websites

Products that index high in KVI require special attention from retailers for both everyday pricing and promotional pricing. These items are the critical "price halo" products that set the price image for the entire store. In a successful price halo model, the "halo" of the low prices on the KVIs shines across the entire store creating an image of low prices – even for "blind" items. "Blind" items are products whose prices are not generally known by the majority of shoppers and are, thus, price inelastic. See "Scoring Big Profits on Blind Items" in *Timeless Principle 4: Pricing.*

Examples of KVIs for grocers in the United States (at time of publishing) include:
Unbranded
   - 1 gallon milk
   - 1 dozen eggs
   - 1 pound bananas
   - 1 pound grapes
   - 1 loaf white bread
   - 1 pound ground chuck
Dairy

- 6-ounce Yoplait Yogurt
- 16-slice Kraft Singles American Cheese
- 1 pound Land O'Lakes Butter
- 1 pound Parkay Margarine Sticks
- 1 pound Oscar Mayer Bacon
- 1 pound Ball Park Franks

Frozen:
- 1.5-quart Breyers Vanilla Ice Cream
- 8-ounce Cool Whip
- Lean Cuisine Single-Serve Dinner
- 12-inch Tombstone Pizza

Dry
- 14-ounce Cheerios
- 40-ounce Heinz Ketchup
- 30-ounce Hellmann's Mayo
- Kraft Mac & Cheese Blue Box
- 26-ounce Ragu Sauce
- Campbells Red Label Soup
- 18-ounce Jif Peanut Butter

Drinks and Snacks
- 12- and 24-pack Coke, Diet Coke, Pepsi and Diet Pepsi
- 18-ounce Oreo Cookies
- 10-11 ounce Lay's Chips
- 12-ounce Doritos
- 20-pack Capri Sun

Health and Beauty Aids
- 500-count Q-tips
- Nice 'N Easy Hair Color
- 12.5-ounce Pantene Shampoo
- 30 count Band-Aids
- 40 count Tampax

Household
- 4-pack AA Duracell and Energizer Batteries
- 150-ounce Tide
- 96-ounce Clorox
- 100 count Ziploc Sandwich Bags
- Huggies and Pampers Diapers
- 8 count Bounty Paper Towels

KVIs will change by market – to accommodate strong regional brands – as well as by time of year. Holiday items like Halloween bagged candy, turkey, cranberries, stuffing, marshmallows, cream cheese, sugar, flour and other key items rise to the top of customers' lists as they search out traditional ingredients and compare them to the prices in their memory. Each customer segment has its own KVIs. It may be Levi's, one ream of basic copy paper, Purina Dog Chow, 2" x 4" lumber, or a dozen red roses.

Understanding how your customers identify "a good deal" is important when developing a price halo KVI list. Conduct a competitive survey and evaluate the market pricing for those items – both every day and on promotion. If you match or roughly match the margins and prices on those items, your customers are likely to evaluate your prices as being fair and competitive.

Remaining focused on KVIs is an execution risk. Be disciplined in selecting a narrow number of critical items. Do *not* let the competition distract you into reducing prices on so many other products that your profitability suffers. Your promotions may feel repetitive as you feature the same items over and over. But if you have selected the most universally appealing products, they will still succeed. The way to keep promotions fresh is to also showcase new items. Include them at full price to create a total solution for your customers.

Price your selected KVI items equal to or below your competitors. Maintain those low prices and clearly sign and promote KVI low prices every day. On the remainder of your product range, follow standard high/low pricing and keep promotions and price reductions infrequent and shallow.

In a successful price halo model, the "halo" of the low prices on the key items (which are most frequently shopped and most appealing) shines on your entire store. Customers perceive low prices – when, in fact, only a small percentage of your items have the ultra-low pricing.

**Blind Items**

Assuming you have selected KVIs or that you compete well with your high/low strategy, the remaining products likely fall into the "blind item" category. Blind items are products that customers do not know the prices of immediately or items that are difficult to evaluate across stores. Examples include boxed holiday cards or appliances with varying features. These are items where margins can be slightly higher to compensate for lean margins on the known-value items.

One of the most profitable analyses a retailer can undertake is the price elasticity analysis on blind items. This is relatively easy to test. If you have an online channel, you can raise the price on a test item over a week or month and evaluate its sales compared to previous weeks. If you have location identifiers in your login, you can even target the test to a specific market. If you are a brick-and-mortar retailer, select two groups of stores. Normalize the stores sales to one another and to their historical trend. Then increase the price in one set of stores on a potential blind item and see what happens to sales.

In our first example, the price increase in store group 2 adversely affected sales. Even though sales increased, sales did not increase as much as in group 1 where the price was held steady. This test would show that the item being tested is price elastic and as prices increase, sales will reduce. This is not a good candidate for a blind item price increase to enhance margins.

|  | Historical Sales Prior | Sales After Price Increase | Results |
|---|---|---|---|
| Store group 1 (control) | $1200 | $1500 | + 25% Pre/Post |
| Store group 2 (Test) | $2400 | $2800 | +16% Pre/Post |
| Difference | 200 Index | 186 Index | |

In our second example, the price increase in store group 2 did not affect sales. Sales remained stable despite a price increase. This test would show that the item is price inelastic. This is a good candidate for a blind item price increase to enhance margins. This example purposefully shows a test where sales are declining. Blind item pricing is more common at the end of life for a product when its sales are naturally declining and there is less promotional activity and advertising for the product.

|  | Historical Sales Prior | Sales After Price Increase | Results |
|---|---|---|---|
| Store group 1 (control) | $850 | $700 | - 18% Pre/Post |
| Store group 2 (Test) | $600 | $560 | + 7% Pre/Post |
| Difference | 70 Index | 80 Index | |

**Cost Plus Strategy**
Another common pricing strategy is called percent markup, keystone or cost plus strategy, where a retailer is very clear that their markup is, let's say, 14%. Many online retailers choose this strategy. They set a margin rate and a minimum dollar profit requirement for any item sold. Products are priced at whichever method provides the higher price to the customer. Costco in the United States is a brick-and-mortar retailer known to employ this pricing strategy. They make its costs clear to its customers by pledging to never mark up a product more than 14%. One benefit is that it is very easy to execute. To employ this strategy, retailers need excellent cost control and a customer base that understands the strategy.

**Competitive Pricing Strategy**

A dangerous strategy is competition-oriented. This strategy pegs specific competitors and sets prices according to the competition, which is easily done online where like items can be shown in a grid comparing competition prices. (Think of Progressive's insurance pricing, for example.)

Let's say a retailer decides to set all of the prices at -4% below a specific competitor. Of course, this takes a certain level of control away from the retailer using this strategy. A competitor who decides to engage in a price war can cause tremendous problems to other businesses who are employing this strategy.

**Lead Generating Strategy**

If you sell handcrafted items or deeply customizable items, perhaps prices should not even be publicized. Artist and designer websites often describe products or services available for sale but instead of a price, a button says "Request Pricing" or "Learn More." Customers who are interested in the item must engage in dialogue with the retailer or producer to define specifications before prices are set. Customizable systems like children's play sets, boat docks or handmade home decor regularly use this strategy to handle pricing. Each job is priced on its own merits.

If you sell items that require delivery and set-up, customization or are made-to-order, obscuring pricing until you know the details might be safe. Just remember, that customers can be intimidated by "ask for price" notices and you can inhibit sales without some price ranges for customers to consider.

Every store is under pressure to match and beat competitive pricing. Here are tactics for managing the strain while maintaining your profits:

**Regularly shop your competition for price changes.** Be alert for price moves and make your adjustments accordingly. You will lose credibility – if not customers – if you are out of step with marketplace prices. Be as vigilant about noting when prices rise as your customers are about noting when prices drop to maintain your margins.

**Determine which competitors you will and will not match.** If you have a delivery program or a deep community involvement and following, then matching an online retailer with no customer support may not be necessary to maintain your market. Decide which of your competitors are relevant and which are not. Monitor all of them. But only make price adjustments when your truest competitors make price moves.

Have an FAQ or train your team to explain why you do not match some competitors.

**Make your pricing policy clear to your team and your customers.** If you will meet or match competitive prices, state it with messages on your website, the check-out lane and on your receipts. If your team members are empowered to adjust prices, clearly document when and why. Make sure that you have a way to track those price adjustments since they can become an invisible form of "shrink" that can occur without a good point-of-sale process.

**Remember that pricing alone is a non-defendable strategy.** Someone will always be able to sell a product for less money if they have deep enough pockets. Focus on the ways your store adds a value beyond price to keep customers returning even without the lowest prices every day on every item.

**When you do promote a sale price, make a *big* deal about it.** Make sure your customers know when you are giving them an excellent value either through promotions or clearance pricing. As long as they know that you regularly offer them values, they will be less likely to be attracted to a competitor based solely on price.

## WIN Today

Create or commission a KVI analysis for your store. Identify the critical items that need to be monitored for competitive price changes.

Create a business rhythm and accountability for competitive price shopping the KVIs. Update competitive pricing based on the volatility of the category. (Milk may be every quarter or month while flour may be once a year.)

Create a test for blind items to find pockets of untapped profitability. Test merchandising and pricing changes to help underwrite lower prices on more visible items (KVIs.)

## Competitive Pricing Strategies

In our online, shop-from-any-device market, price is the prime focus for competitors, vendors and customers. Most retailers proudly claim that their prices are as low as the competition.

However, a pure price focus is a dangerous marketing position for any retailer.

Truth is: a retailer that focuses on price can *always* be beaten. It just takes a competitor who has deeper pockets and the fortitude to suffer losses long enough to put its competition out of business.

Savvy retailers combine a low-price proposition with another key strategic point of differentiation: a wide (or niche) range of products, expert service, same-day delivery, knowledgeable assistance, environmentally sustainable recycling, an after-hours or online community, etc.

Retailers who struggle either:
- Focus entirely on price and barrage their customers with a lowest-price message to their own detriment, or
- Attempt to claim every benefit listed above – and cannot deliver.

A good marketing tactic to differentiate and create a *clear* position in your customer's mind is to focus on two strategic value propositions: price and assortment *or* service *or* delivery *or* inventory, etc.

But we certainly cannot ignore the fact that most customers are attracted to their preferred store because they believe they receive a fair value for the price they pay. Which raises the question:
*How can we communicate our low prices effectively?*

### Everyday Low Price (EDLP)

Sell products at the lowest possible price without sale pricing or other "gimmicks." EDLP is particularly effective when selling to other businesses (B2B) who can rely on re-ordering with you at the best price every time.

An advantage is that EDLP retailers usually have a lower cost of advertising. It also prevents problems when customers pay full price one week to see their purchase advertised for a lower price the next.

The danger of the EDLP strategy is that it can be difficult to entice new customers without a glitzy promotion to try your location. Additionally, it takes a disciplined manager to not be tempted to meet loss leader pricing from the competition. It is tempting when competitors advertise an ultra-low price on a product because they can make up the profit margin on other full-priced purchases in their stores.

Finally, to be truly effective using this strategy, you must have a significantly reduced operating model to sustain your low prices. Walmart, for example, achieves its low prices with an extraordinarily efficient supply chain. If you have an owned store (no rent cost), volunteer assistance (low labor costs) or an energy-efficient building that allows you to operate with extremely low utility costs, you may be able to keep and hold the EDLP position in the market.

The point is, you have to have some operational leverage to sustain and *win* with an EDLP pricing strategy.

### Price Match Guarantee

A common online and storefront policy is to match any advertised price by a competitor as long as it is offered on the same item and within the same market. It offers customers peace of mind that your store will not gouge them and may keep customers loyal. It somewhat relies on customers to be too lazy to research other prices.

Many retailers purposefully load their assortment with uniquely featured items so that there are no other "like items" in the market. Examples include special bonus packs, on pack offers, unique colors, sizes and packaging. It is most common in consumer electronics and appliances, where button shapes and sizes can change a base unit to a different SKU for a Home Depot versus a Best Buy appliance by the same manufacturer.

But of course, there is the danger that customers will find lower prices.

In fact, this policy encourages them to look for better prices elsewhere. And with smartphones that is easier than ever.

The subsequent interaction with a customer to reduce the price at the register or refund a recent full purchase price takes time for both your store associate and your customer. These can be touchy negotiations, especially if your store associate is not gracious or the customer misinterprets the offer or the competition's price. It is common for customers to bring in a "similar" item price – but not the same item – then demand that you reduce your price to match it. So from a high level this seems like a smart offering, but in the reality of daily operations, it can be a costly policy to uphold.

### 110% Price Match Guarantee

A variation of the price match guarantee is beating your competition by 10% should your customer find a lower price offered elsewhere. Again, the same benefits and dangers apply as with the former price match guarantee. But customers will be rewarded to shop solely on price *even more*. This is not the behavior of a particularly loyal group!

Giving an extra 10% on an item is no more work on your store associate's behalf (changing the sales transaction price) and probably goes much further to communicating to your customers that you will take care of them no matter what the competition does. So in many ways, if you are planning on meeting competitive prices, going with an additional 10% probably doesn't tremendously change the outcome. You will still have customers who take advantage of this policy but your low price positioning cannot be questioned.

Another option is to promote the 110% price match policy only during a high demand period, such as back to school or holidays. Offer this policy for a limited time during a highly promotional season to restrain your regular customers from being enticed by competitors who will increase their promotional pricing during the "high season."

### Accepting Competitor's Coupons

If you have a competitor who regularly employs direct mail, email, mobile or other non-public offers to its best customers, this is a way to entice those customers to try your store. This can be especially effective if you have a more convenient location or better delivery service than the competitor.

Often, competitors stay in business for years and seem to do little to no advertising. What you may not see is a targeted direct mail or email campaign that keeps customers engaged with limited offers. Advertise that you will accept competitive coupons to lure your competition's best customers to try your stores.

The main risk is that you are opening yourself up to an unknown level of activity. Many stores limit this offer by excluding e-commerce retailers or limiting the offer ("Limit one competitive coupon per customer").

## WIN Today

Any of these methods for promoting your price value advantage, will require additional steps to succeed:

1. Diligently review competitive prices to ensure that you are not caught unaware of price reductions in the market.
2. Train all team members to conduct an efficient reduced- price transaction.
3. Fully educate your team members on your competitive pricing policy. Be sure they can effectively and politely communicate it to your customers.
4. Repeat and reinforce your messages to your customers to make it memorable. You may see the message and think it is obvious, but your customers may see it just two times a year.
5. Deliver your secondary message to your customers at every occasion. Do not rely on low prices alone to build loyalty. Always connect your low prices with friendly service, same-day delivery, in-stock assortment or great selection to help customers remember why they should return to your store or website.

## The Truth About Value

The current jargon in marketing is "putting the consumer at the center of the equation." It means making sure that every decision is made in light of how users approach your store and your products. More than saying "we sell high quality footwear" it means deeply understanding and supporting what customers truly want and delivering it in a way that makes profit.

Given your daily interactions, you may think your customers want a low price. But what they really mean is that they want **value**. The value equation (value = price x quality) has other aspects as well:

> **Save me time.** Easy parking. Fast transactions. Automatic re-orders.
> **Be dependable.** Be in stock. Have regular hours. Have smart capable employees
> **Entertain me.** Teach me something. Have an enjoyable environment. Be clever.
> **Make me beautiful.** Make me look good. Make my work look good.
> **Make me seem smart.** Remind me that I am saving money. Give me the newest technology. Tell me which products are non-GMO or organic.
> **Give me status.** Treat me better than other places. Give me access to events and discounts because I am your shopper.

...Value is in the eye of the beholder.

Value for *you* as the retailer is understanding the **lifetime value** (LTV) of the customer and the cost of customer acquisition and churn. The simple calculation of the lifetime value of your customers, average acquisition cost and churn rate is at the core of sophisticated marketing analytics for the most advanced retailers in the world. And it is within the grasp of *every* retailer in the world to master.

For example, if the average consumer purchases 16 bags of dog food per year at an average cost of $20 per bag and the average customer is in the dog food market for 25 years, that customer would have a lifetime value of $8,000 – on dog food *alone!* Let's say the cost to acquire a customer is $25 (based on marketing spend to get a customer to try your shop for the first time). Acquisition costs vary but $25 would not be out of line for many retailers.

If the average customer stops shopping at your store after 4 years, the churn rate would be 16% per year. The lifetime value of that customer is reduced only $1280. To fully extend and maximize the value of each customer, be willing to spend the same to keep that customer as you would to acquire replacement customers over their lifetime.

In our example, that would mean spending roughly $150 over the course of that shopper's lifetime to retain the full $8,000 in revenue that customer represents over their time in the dog food market. From that framework, that is less than 2% of the money the customer will spend with you over their "lifetime."

So if you extend that reference, imagine what you could do with $150 per customer to build unbreakable loyalty to your store.

Take a look at the value of "save me time." Convenience can mean more than just a nearby location. It means considering their purchase before they do. True convenience would mean automatic replenishment at a rate that matches their usage. While no retailer can presciently predict a customer's usage rate, it is possible for retailers to set up regular replenishment cycles that shoppers can control.

In the United States, many pet food, coffee and cleaning supply retailers have set up home or office delivery that customers control online. They select the item they want delivered and estimate their delivery timing (with weekly choices from once per week to once every 8 weeks). Customers are incentivized to stay in the repeat delivery program by getting price discounts every two to six deliveries. Using our example, you could offer a $5 discount off the fifth bag of dog food purchased as a perpetual customer retention offer to reduce customer churn. If a customer knew they could always count on that discount, there would be a natural inclination to maintain loyalty to your store or website.

Other ways to save a customer time is to track usage and suggest maintenance and tune-ups just as an automobile dealership would. With an understanding of the typical life cycle of a lawn mower or laser printer, you could alert your customers and provide access to what they need before they realize they need it. Help them avoid a costly repair or interruption to become their loyal supplier. Shoe stores could remind parents that children should be fitted for new shoes every 6 months. Pet owners could be alerted to monthly flea and tick applications.

**Market segmentation** is another tool for marketers who understand the value of putting customers at the center of their equation. Understand your market segments – small businesses, schools, hospitals, salt-water aquarium owners, freelance workers, busy moms, brides, etc. – then what they most value to make your store and brands relevant in ways that a clumsy marketing campaign cannot. To offer every segment the same promotion ($3 off $15 or $7 off $30, for example) does not recognize the different weights customer segments place on various elements of the value equation.

For a creative freelancer, the most valuable element may be "make me look beautiful." So a printing and services retailer who provides 24-hour access via online uploads to high-end printing with a quality guarantee may be far more valuable and build greater loyalty than a price offer.

For a purchasing agent in a hospital who must justify their role in the organization by demonstrating ongoing value, the most valuable element may be "make me seem smart." A just-in-time delivery program with contracted protection against price increases may be more important than a price promotion.

Do not be deceived into thinking that only more "glamorous" products than yours can be marketed to customers in a way that will build an emotional attachment and loyalty.

For example, very few people would find chain saws to be a product that builds a user's esteem. A chain saw manufacturer with low brand awareness and an undifferentiated product line initially focused on *the quality of their saws.* Advertising campaigns and tag lines reinforced the saw's quality and reliability in the field with little effect on sales. They were just like every other chain saw brand. When the company changed its focus to the chain saw *users who save time and money* because they invested in a high-quality saw, it had a great effect on its market share. The campaign focused on the accomplishments of the smart users who finished their work quickly and with precision because of the saws.

Exactly the same levers could take any undifferentiated product to high brand awareness. A smart retailer will produce marketing campaigns about the creative, savvy, frugal, smart customers it has and how they rely on their store or brand for all their needs to replicate the same strategy.

That is truly putting customers at the "center of the equation."

## WIN Today

Pull customer data from your POS system for a handful of core SKUs that defines your store and drives traffic to your store. Analyze the average transaction size, customer repurchase cycle and the other items that are most frequently in the transaction with those core SKUs.

If you have loyalty card data or other identifying data, look at the return shopping frequency of those customers and their churn rate. Estimate their lifetime value by multiplying their average transaction size by their shopping frequency per year by the number of years they stay loyal to your store. Even a customer who is loyal for 3–4 years can quickly be a valuable asset.

Once you understand the lifetime value of your customers, re-evaluate your marketing spend and redistribute money from programs meant to acquire new customers to programs meant to retain loyal customers.

## Scoring Big Profits on Blind Items

Smartphones make it easy to compare prices. You might think that all customers know the competitive market price of every item. Nothing could be further from the truth. Most consumers only truly know the price of a few fundamental items they regularly purchase. All others are considered blind items – products that customers only have a very rough idea of their price or value.

As a retailer, you are tasked to be sharp on those key value items (KVIs) and keep your price within striking distance of your competition. Customers demand value and retailers stay awake at night thinking of how to meet their demands. Perhaps you can only eke out single digit margins on the key products. Typically, they are the promotional products that are most conspicuous in advertisements.

But there are blind items where you can make up profit. Blind items can be priced 40%–400% higher than the KVIs.

Here are 10 indicators that you have a blind price item that could be a strong source of increased margins:

1. **It is a hand-crafted item.** If the product is created by an artist, baker, florist, designer or other hands-on service, the price/value equation is nearly impossible to compare across providers.

2. **It takes extra handling for the customer.** If you shave steps – and time – off a process for a customer, your price can be difficult to compare across the market. Adding delivery is one example. Online and brick-and-mortar retailers create a tiered pricing system. Delivery is $15 with no minimum order, $5 with a $75 order or free with a $125 order. This tiered system not only helps retailers cover their costs, it incentivizes customers to increase their overall purchase. Another example is carting away old mattresses or appliances when you purchase a new one.

3. **It is a natural add-on item.** Examples include sharp prices on paper but larger margins on envelopes or competitive pricing on cat litter but higher prices on litter trays.

4. **It is seldom used.** The price of a laminator or paper shredder is much less well-known than the price of an ink cartridge, for example. Same with pricing on ice scrapers versus windshield fluid. Customers who repurchase consumables often are more aware of their prices than the less frequently purchased durable good.

5. **It is a repair or replacement item.** The price of a replacement assembly item or belt is not known nor advertised. Bundled within the labor of making the repair, replacement parts can be one of the most

margin rich product lines in your shop. For many hardware stores, the service center repairing lawn mowers, grills and power tools is more profitable than selling the units on the sales floor.

6. **It has luxury or status appeal.** Ask anyone why the iPhone can command top prices, and chances are people will concede that it is a status item. The truth is iPhone resellers usually make 3–6% profit on them because Apple can demand rigid adherence to its pricing policy. Where resellers can make money is on high-end phone covers and accessories that have a cachet for the consumer. Another example is Montblanc pens, which function the same as an opening price point pen, yet command hundreds of dollars.

7. **It is seldom promoted.** Also tied into the theory of "the long tail" this is especially true for aging technology products and maintenance items. For example, if you are still selling typewriter ribbons or dot matrix ribbons, chances are you can command margins of up to 300%. Look for on-trend retro products such as re-issued toys and limited-edition licensed products to keep margins rich.

8. **It is not in season.** Shredders at tax season are much more price sensitive than shredders at other times of the year. The same is true with gardening supplies. If you have the room or are willing to stock and sell products off season, they can often be sold without a discount.

9. **It is an of-the-moment item.** If the product can be tied to collecting or a hot property, it can command a higher margin. But this is a risky strategy. A Summer Olympics t-shirt or cup can transition from prized collectible to dusty closeout in weeks or days. When selecting entertainment properties or likenesses, always err on the conservative side.

10. **It is not sold in a mass merchant.** Finding niches where your product line is different from mass merchants will preserve your margins. Retailers find niches to purposefully go deep in an assortment because a mass merchant will not. An example is art supply houses with high-end mechanical pencils and engineering tools, artist papers and other materials that are not typically carried in mass merchants. Another is the woodworking and hardware company that purposefully carries the most esoteric wood species and furniture making finishes that a mass hardware outlet cannot stock.

Obviously, you have to carry the volume-driving products that require you to price competitively. And chances are your highest volume SKUs will compete with mass merchandisers simply because they sell at a higher velocity than the more obscure items. But if you price correctly, the sale of those selected niche items can put more money in the bank (as profit) than a dozen high volume products that keep people coming to your store. That is true whether you have an online or physical store.

Somehow, however, most retailers are hesitant to raise prices – even on products that customers purchase without a notion of their price in the market.

Here is a true story: A shopkeeper in Kansas was investigating a neighborhood competitor who sold similar products. He came around the end of an aisle to see reading magnification glasses ("readers") priced $5.00 higher than in his own shop. A friendly customer watched him and said "You have much better prices on those. I would go to your shop and buy them for $5.00 less." To which the shopkeeper replied, "Well, you better hurry and get there – because as soon as I get back, the prices are going up $5.00."

While it is a funny story, the truth is, retailers are quick to reduce prices to match competition but not nearly as quick to raise prices to match the market. As a general rule, blind items can be as much as +10% above competitor's prices up to about $4.00 without an adverse effect on sales. That is why they are called "blind" items.

And to the degree that you are below market on such items, chances are your customers do not give you credit for low pricing. Customer do not recognize low prices for items that they do not purchase frequently. They are unlikely to know the market price.

Price rounding on blind items can be another rich vein of profit. A guideline to pricing is to always round *up* prices as follows:

| Price Band | Ending Price |
|---|---|
| $2.00 to $9.99 | End in .49, .79 or .99 |
| $10.00 to $19.99 | End in .99 |
| $20.00 to $49.99 | End in X1.99, X2.99, X4.99, X6.99, X7.99 or X9.99 |
| $50.00 and above | End in X2.99, X4.99, X7.99 or X9.99 |

The psychology of those ending digits is important and can mean significant improvements in profits at the end of the year.

Be thoughtful in raising prices by watching two things:
1. The *left* digit is most important. A price increase of $39.99 to $41.99 is just $2:00, as is $44.99 to $46.99. Yet the perception to the customer is much more severe when the number turns from thirties to forties. Be

judicious in raising prices but be careful in raising left-most numbers.

2.  Several frequent small price increases are more palatable than one large price change. Adjust pricing over a year instead of re-pricing everything at once. Select your niches and be prudent. Watch the effect. Test the price elasticity yourself by raising prices slowly and monitoring the marketplace and customer reaction.

Savvy retailers know their customers judge their value on just a few limited products. Keep prices sharp on those key value items to maintain a strong value impression with shoppers. Then look for blind items that can help you subsidize the lean margins on KVIs by adjusting prices on blind items. It's a strategy that works.

## WIN Today

Evaluate your pricing using the price guidelines above. Move the *last digit* of your prices to eliminate odd pricing that ends in numbers between .01–.08. Evaluate your prices by starting with slow-turning products in each category first.

Visit your competition. Contrary to urban myths, stores are public places where you and your employees can note prices without anyone "calling the police." Be swift, be polite and quickly take down prices. (Very easy to do with online competitors!) Look for a minimum of two dozen items where your prices are below market and make an adjustment.

## End of the Line: Clearance and Closeouts

It happens to every retailer. Despite your best attempts to predict customer demand, eye-catching merchandising and competitive pricing ... you are stuck with a glut of inventory that isn't selling. There are key practices that can help you move through that product quickly and possibly prevent future disasters.

First, take a look at the inventory:
- **Is it in unsellable condition?** If the packaging is torn or worn you cannot expect to sell it at full price.
- **Is it seasonal?** There is nothing more tired than a Valentine's product in March. If your seasonal goods are of a high value *and* were not for sale during the peak of the season (due to a vendor's backorder, for example) it *may* be worthwhile to store the product until next year. But if the product is of low value or was on the sales floor throughout the season, it will not sell any better next year. Time to close out.
- **Is it too unconventional for your store?** It may be the finest cheese slicer in the world, but if you are a sports equipment store, it may just be too far removed from a customer's expectations to sell well in your store.
- **Is it too early in its life cycle?** Consider the stores that attempted to sell personal computers in the late 1970s. The product was simply too early in its life cycle to attract customers. Similar issues happen in new technology all the time. Unless your customers are early adopters, wait until technology products hit the masses before bringing it into your store – no matter how revolutionizing your buyers tell you it will be.[15]
- **Is it too trendy?** Colors, patterns and licensed products all have a dangerously short shelf life. There is a reason white, black and gray are called "basics." Their appeal is universal. If you are left with neon orange or turquoise products while the basic colors have sold out, you need to adjust future purchases accordingly.

If you answer "no" to all of these questions, think about how to reduce the price to a point where your customers will find it attractive. Try as you might, it is impossible to perfectly predict the fickle desires of customers when selecting assortments. Combined with churning technology and fashion lifecycles, your job as sales fortune teller becomes more difficult.

After peak seasons, you may have excess product sitting on your sales floor and tying up inventory dollars. Here are good practices for moving out clearance goods from your store.

**Practice 1: Re-Value Your Inventory**

This is possibly the most difficult psychological transition to make as a retailer. You bought a case of goods months ago at $150, planning to sell it for $300. Customers have not been interested in the product and today you still have nearly all that product on the sales floor. Remember that inventory is not like fine wine – it does not get better with age. If your customers were not interested in the product in November, it is highly unlikely they will like it any better in February.

At this point you must try to determine what price will move the products off your shelves and into your customers' baskets. Instead of thinking "I have $300 or $150 worth of product on my shelves" you need to dramatically shift your view. If the customers are not buying the product, you actually have a product worth $000.00 and your goal has to be how far from $000.00 you have to price the product to recoup some portion of your initial investment. Actually, one could argue that non-selling merchandise has a negative value since every day your inventory is locked in product that is not selling, you give up future sales potential you could get if you could invest your money (and your shelf space) into more appealing stock.

To do that, consider the following:

- **Elasticities** – Highly inelastic products will require a dramatic cut in prices to sell. Examples would include sweaters at the end of winter or discontinued scents of deodorant. You will need to mark prices down to perhaps 75% off just to entice customers to consider a purchase. Contrast that with elastic products (like mobile phones) which don't require much of a discount at all to activate demand.
- **Seasonality** – If the merchandise is highly seasonal, determine when the next seasonal demand is likely to occur. If the storage costs outweigh the clearance discount, mark it down. Expect damage to a percentage of the inventory to occur in the transition to storage. And remember that labor and handling costs are not free. Store associates who pack up and store product are not available for customer service and sales. If you received product too late to meet the current season's demand, storing the product may be worthwhile.[16] But if a school pencil pack was in your store for the entire back-to-school season and did not sell, chances are it will not sell next year either.
- **Basic needs** – If the merchandise is a basic need item – copy paper, garden gloves, dog leashes – there is an ongoing need for the item.

Excess inventory on a product like this is an excellent candidate for a promotional price – instead of a clearance or closeout price. Slow but eventual sales may outweigh speedy liquidation costs.

- **Technology changes** – If the product supports a technology in retrograde (DVDs or Polaroid film, anyone?) you may have an opportunity to keep the product on your shelves at regular cost if you have the patience for recouping your investment. According to "long tail" theorists, selling products at the very end of their market lifecycle is not a matter of reducing price to incite demand. To succeed, target your offering to the interested few who are willing to pay *any* price to stay supplied. Long tail items are the best candidates for a warehouse program where they can be featured online and shipped directly to customers at full price.

**Practice 2: Merchandising**

Clearance and closeout merchandise is an ongoing retail dilemma. A best practice is to create a permanent clearance or closeout location. Gathering all of your clearance product together creates a "treasure hunt" destination for bargain shoppers and accelerates depleting the inventory.

Online, create a "Clearance" tab for value-seekers. In the store, use signs shouting out the value. Examples include using a back-facing endcap or standalone display rack and placing a permanent "Up to 75% off" sign over it. Some retailers keep the bottom right or left corner of the category "home location" or planogram available for clearance or closeout product.

Even if the product is marked for final sale, remember that it is still your job to make the product as appealing as possible. Half- opened cartons, dusty or dirty products and broken goods create a negative halo image for all products marked for final sale. Even an item in pristine condition will look tawdry surrounded by other damaged goods.

**Practice 3: Returns Policy**

If your store will not accept clearance or closeout products for future returns it is good practice (and possibly a legal requirement in your jurisdiction) to publicize this statement to the customer.

Consider at least these three locations:
1. At the cash registers
2. Checkout screen online
3. On receipts and packing slips

At the end of the day, your goal is to keep your store inventory fresh and compelling. Once you see slow sales, take proactive steps to address any obvious issues. Correct poor positioning, poor signage and above-market pricing. But if the product is simply not of interest to your shoppers, come to terms with your customers' decision. Move quickly to liquidate the product and move on to something more appealing.

**Merchandising Clearance and Closeouts**

To make closeouts easier to manage, here are the specific steps in an established closeout procedure:

In your merchandising or POS system, flag the item as a *closeout*. This should automatically disable any re-orders that may be in your replenishment system and prevent any new inventory additions.

Items in *closeout* status, should be flagged on your return and refund policy as being sold "as-is" and ineligible for return on all customer's transaction receipts. (See practice 3 above.)

A pre-defined closeout markdown schedule should begin once the item is flagged. Typically, there is a distinct markdown cadence that occurs once per month and can be easily color-coded with stickers on price tags. For example, the cadence can be set as:

1. Closeout status first month = 25% off original price (yellow sticker)
2. Closeout status second month = 50% off original price (blue sticker)
3. Closeout status third month = 75% off original price (red sticker)
4. Closeout status fourth month = write out of inventory as unsellable

This would be a fairly aggressive closeout cadence. Some products may take 6–8 months to reach the write-off stage.

The stickers are used to avoid re-pricing items. To make it easier on your store associates, use colored sticky dots and adhere them to the product or price tags. For example: January = red, February = blue, March = yellow, April = green, etc. Then customers can be told to look for the color-coding and follow the schedule to understand their prices. For example: All orange tags are half off, blue tags are 25% off. This avoids associates having to re-sticker products each month.

Group all like items and closeouts together in one location to make it easier for customers to find bargains. Help associates corral closeouts to one location and place any policy notices about returns, refunds and "as-is" sales nearby.

With some sales history, you should be able to predict your markdowns by month. A markdown analysis should help you uncover predictable patterns.

For example:
- At 25% off, 50% of the inventory sells
- At 50% off, 40% of the remaining inventory sells
- At 75% off, 60% of the remaining inventory sells.
- Full write-offs occur on 10% of the original inventory

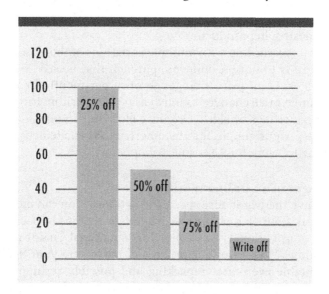

With a predictable pattern, your closeouts can be managed to reduce their negative impact on your profit margins. Monitor the remaining slow-selling inventory to forecast negative sales and profit impact each month. Top-flight retailers conduct this forecast each week and manage the closeout funnel very carefully. They ensure that there is never a glut of closeout inventory entering the funnel that will adversely affect profits in the months to come. They delay some lines and brands from moving to closeout if there is too much inventory at the end of a season, for example.

To further refine your closeout process, consider setting up a standard closeout cadence (to be used on normal model changes, planogram changes and standard vendor deletions). Then, set up an aggressive closeout cadence for highly seasonal items (Easter, Halloween, Christmas goods) and a less-aggressive cadence for basic slow sellers with a long shelf life at the end of their lifecycle (paper goods, non-trendy kitchen décor, etc.). You can vary the cadence by having multiple stepped-down price rates (15%, then 25%, then 33%, then 40%, then 50% off) *or* by changing the length of time that an item stays at a price point from 1 month to 2 months – or 2 weeks.

Resellers will often take unsellable inventory off your hands at pennies to the dollar. Be sure that your original sales covenants with your vendors will not be broken if you resell their products. Usually unsellable goods are packaged into lots that are only minimally defined (five pallets of children's school products, for example). This is usually a last chance effort by a retailer who has made serious miscalculations in inventory. But for those who are requiring some way out of an inventory mess, resellers are better than destroying product.

The key to succeeding with multiple variations of the closeout cadence and procedure is to have a uniform approach that is easy to execute for store associates. Limit price changes to once per month for closeouts, if possible. Handle price changes as much as possible within the POS system and not on paper tags or signs. Organize closeouts in one merchandising location. Keep signs simple for customers. Build excitement around the value and the treasure hunt for smart shoppers.

**What Changes in an Online World**

If you have the warehouse space and patience, you can move all items from the sales floor to a shipping consolidation point (a back room in a large store or a regional warehouse for a national chain) and sell the products online. Monitor online prices and make sure your net sales will still be profitable even after repacking and possibly reshipping product from the stores to a new shipping point. If you have the expertise and the capability, you may be able to sell component parts more profitably than selling the original unit intact. Again, you will have to review all of your vendor covenants to ensure that you can sell products online using your own website or an eBay or Amazon storefront.

Use your closeout values as clickbait for online shoppers. Highlight a brand name, a style and a price in email and banner ads to entice bargain shoppers to your "Clearance" page. Then engage your affinity engine to recommend other products on the site to boost the transaction. Consider a policy change to eliminate clearance products from free or reduced-shipping offers if customers cherry pick your clearance products at a profit deficit.

## WIN Today

Aggregate and consolidate your closeouts to one location in your store or online and make sure signage is clear for customers who are looking for bargains.

Review your returns policy and make sure that it is clear which items can and cannot be returned at the end of their life.

## The Cost of a Price Change

Before changing prices, consider the cost of making those price changes within your stores. No price change is free.

In stores, IT systems have to be synchronized, new pricing labels have to be printed, promotional messages may need to be edited and employees will not be able to do other customer service tasks.

Online, price changes have to synchronize with marketing and promotional campaigns. Price changes can disrupt customer messages that are already in flight.

Before making changes ask:
1.  **How profit-accretive is the change and how long will the change last?** A permanent price change that increases margin while maintaining sales velocity is far more digestible than a short-term change that may depress sales.
2.  **If the change is due to a vendor's price change, do you *have to* make the price change to meet competition?** When vendors announce price changes, a smart retailer waits to see what the market does with the supply cost change. Move too soon on a price increase and you may decrease your market share. But move too soon on a price reduction and you could erode your margins faster than your competition without customers rewarding your brand with sales.
3.  **Can you protect your inventory?** When a vendor increases prices, always request a protected order cycle so you can place a final order under old pricing. If a vendor decreases prices, ask for pricing protection for the inventory you already own as a credit on your next order.
4.  **Should you forward buy?** When a vendor announces a price increase, use a forward buying model to determine the size of your final order before the price increase goes into effect. Forward buying is helpful when a vendor offers extended dating or a promotional price discount for a specific period of time. There are sophisticated financial models that sit behind forward buying models. But at the heart of it, they balance the price increase with customer demand to protect a defined number of weeks of stock before inventory costs rise.
5.  **Can you predict what your competition will do?** Estimate what your customers will do and what your competition will do once the price change is in place.

**Price Decreases**

With a price decrease, it is *critical* that you are very public about the new price. Make sure shelf prices and even external marketing calls out price decreases so your customers are aware of your cost cuts.

If it is caused by a vendor reducing their prices, make sure that your messages communicate your pass-it-through transparency. This will put pressure on your competitors to do likewise.

If you are going to take a number of price decreases on products throughout the store, consider shelf edge "violator" signs. They will highlight all the products with new reduced prices for customers looking down the aisles.

Online, create a graphic that is eye-catching so that shoppers scrolling see "new low price" messaging across every page. Make a campaign out of the price reductions. Create a graphic element that can be used in banner ads, email campaigns and on landing pages.

Your goal is to have your customers appreciate that they are getting new lower prices from you and to build an emotional bond that encourages trust and confidence in your ethics and value. The worst outcome for a retailer who takes price decreases is when customers do not notice the changes: the retailer doesn't get credit for them and sales volume or loyalty doesn't increase.

**Price Increases**

Price increases are much trickier. As a rule, those are done quietly and slowly.

Retailers should have a reason behind price increases when asked. (Cost increases from vendors or increased taxes and licensing, for example.) Carefully monitor what customers do with the new price change. Are product sales the same? Is it because customers did not notice or because competitors raised prices as well? Are category sales the same because customers transferred to another product in the category? Does the category decline overall? Maybe customers are making their purchases elsewhere.

Carefully monitor customer and competitor reactions to the price change and be prepared to put mitigation tactics into place. You may need to find a new vendor with a lower price point, increase promotions temporarily or step up loyalty campaigns.

One way to transition into a price increase is to change how you communicate prices.

Let's say you have been selling yogurt at 99¢. Now your costs increase and you will have to price them at $1.29. Begin selling the yogurt at 4/$5.00

instead of 99¢ to move customers up to the new normal. Bundle pricing on items that are often bought in multiples (or could be) can help acclimate customers to new pricing.

Another way to address price increases is creating bundled pricing on complete solutions. Rather than communicating a price increase on backpacks, create a back-to-school price bundle. Offer a backpack, lunch box and school supplies for a single price. Use the margins on the other items to create a value perception with customers. With the backpack pricing embedded into the bundle, customers who are price-sensitive can still find a value in your store.

Finally, there is a certain level of disruption that price changes can have that ripple across your stores, website and customers. Price increases can erode customer loyalty and confidence if not well thought out, timed and executed. When de-emphasizing pricing (during cycles when prices are rising) lean into your other strategic strengths of assortment, convenience, service and experience.

Remember, as a retailer, you are expected to make money – but stay competitive.

## The Cost of a Price Change Is Nothing in the Online Channel

Well, nearly nothing. With real-time price changes, online is *the place* to experiment with pricing and price elasticities. If you have the luxury of selling at two different prices online and in store, the online channel can be the laboratory for determining the optimal pricing before making investments in the store.

Small-scale, targeted experiments can help you evaluate the change in demand when a price change occurs and where the customer demand shifts. Learning if you can still retain the sale but move it to a different product in the assortment is key. Remember that your online prices can impact sales in your stores. But if you operate under a different banner name online or can use a different storefront, you can learn and share those findings to improve your price image both online and in the store.

## WIN Today

The easiest way to reduce the cost of a price change (decrease or increase) in a store is to make them infrequently and efficiently:

1. Create a regular cadence for reviewing price changes and set a schedule for changing prices that can be accounted for in creating the store team schedule.

2. Document the exact steps required to conduct an accurate and timely price change.

3. Select team members who should be accountable for printing out new price labels, distributing them to the correct store locations, destroying old price labels and testing new pricing at the register.

4. Make sure that price changes can occur before or after normal store hours to avoid the embarrassment of changing prices in front of customers.

## 7 Timeless Principles

RETAIL: The Second-Oldest Profession
© 2019 Flora Delaney

# Timeless Principle 5: Marketing

## Invite Customers and Welcome Them Back

Marketing is the simple act of inviting customers to come to your site (physical location or digital) and asking them back again and again. Called *customer acquisition and retention*, marketing has always been about projecting an image that you can deliver against again and again. In our Timeless Principle model, let's imagine an orange cart in ancient Morocco. The owner of the cart places it in a highly visible location in the market. The oranges are placed carefully so that the most flawless sides face out (great merchandising). The owner pays a young musician to set up nearby and play music to attract attention to his corner of the market. There is a sign above the cart that reads "fresh picked this morning." This is the marketing promise. Fresh oranges. Clean. Inviting. As the owner, he remembers his customers by name and always offers the best ones to his best customers. Customer service? Yes. But smart marketing as well. Because marketing is the creation of a promise that is fulfilled.

Marketing is the general heading for all messages about your store or your website. In other words, it is your brand statement to the market and then the consistency of that message over time. It is the promise of your brand radiating from your strategy. In brick and mortar, it is everything from awnings to shopping bags. Every lever that you pull to tell potential customers about yourself and where you are located is a part of marketing. Even your store manager is marketing when they are out on the town and wearing their store shirt. Online, marketing is every single touchpoint that makes an impression on your potential customers about your site and its goods.

Marketing must reflect your store's specific strategy with personality: fun, quirky and nerdy or sophisticated, smart and lavish. Your store's personality comes across in the logo, tagline, colors, font, words and people that customers see. While there are only five strategic differentiators, there are limitless ways to communicate them through marketing. And, while a strategy should be timeless, marketing campaigns can (and should) change. Thus, a luxury brand can run a season-ending campaign that focuses on value or a convenience retailer can run a marketing campaign that highlights their broad assortment range.

Really, any touchpoint is marketing – which should be part of the day 1 training for people in your call center and your store staff. Every single touchpoint with a customer informs their opinion of your company and how you view them. Treat them with respect and gratitude and they will reward you with a return shopping visit. But in every aspect, your brand must also stay authentic to be believed. Recently, retailers have been caught in situations where their marketing messages are invalidated by their practices. Take the example of the big-box retailer that tried to promote their sustainable and ethical supply chain only to have their customers learn that their apparel is manufactured by underpaid children in southeast Asia. Or the retailer that highlights acceptance and inclusivity in their ads only to have their benefits policies deny coverage for LGBTQ partners. When customers see that marketing efforts (the promise) are not being held up by actual practices by retailers, the results can be disastrous.

Social media is the ultimate in the border between marketing and authenticity. Customers expect retailers to behave as if their personalities are real online. That means absolutely consistent messages. If your brand is fun, trendy and breezy, your social media account should not weigh in on politics (ever) or quarterly earnings reports. (Create a second account @mybrand_corporate to handle those messages.) And if you choose to use social media you *must* engage with your customers on those channels. Reply, "like" and repost items that reinforce your commitment to the community. If you are a small retailer and find it impossible to juggle everything, outsource your social media activity to a marketer or freelancer who can provide your brand with consistent messaging.

Marketing really means putting the customer in the center of every engagement. Sound familiar? It's a lot like Timeless Principle 2: Customer Service. The difference is that marketing messages go out to a broader audience and need to resonate with people to such a degree that they take action. Don't worry if prospective customers scan your website to compare prices or read customer reviews. Isn't it great to be in their consideration set? Don't worry if a coupon could be used on clearance product, making it sell below costs. Chances are, they will buy other things as well because of strong customer service. Those are small items in the broader scale of marketing to your customer. Give customers a reason to come to your store and then invite them to return. Stay true to your brand promise and values in every marketing campaign and your customers will respond.

## Marketing Doesn't End at the Door

Maybe for some businesses the role of marketing ends once the customer comes in the door. Dentists and lawyers have businesses like that. Their marketing campaigns are built around targeting and attracting customers to get them to come into the office. But smart retailers know that marketing is a sequence that continues into the store and includes the experience in the store, at the checkout – and even if products are returned.

The marketing journey of a customer looks like this:

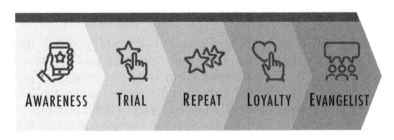

**Awareness** campaigns simply let prospects know you exist and what you stand for – *the brand promise.* For many businesses, it is a logo, a tagline and an address repeated in as many channels as possible. Awareness is the cost of entry to even become a part of a customer's consideration set when they are ready to make a purchase.

**Trial** campaigns are usually spurred by a promotion or a convenient location. A promotion is the reason to come into the store *now.* Coupons, special sales and limited-time offers create a sense of urgency and a call to action that get customers to open the door.

**Repeat** visits, over and over. For customers, a delightful first visit leads to a second, third and fourth visit only if each trip is consistently appealing. For products with long purchase cycles, the time between visits can be weeks or months. In furniture, for example, it can be years. So impressions in the store or online must be long lasting. A customer is considered to be in the "repeat" phase for as long as necessary until the customer would say that ABC Store is the *only* store I go to for ABC supplies.

Customers in this cycle are in a *retention* pattern. Retaining customers is key. Retained customers are customers who are not shopping at your competition even if you are not their only choice for the products you sell. To keep customers repeating, retailers rely on lapsed customer emails, bounce-back offers and regular check-ins at birthdays and anniversaries.

These retention loyalists can reduce your customer churn rates and become your stable customer base.

**Loyalty** stage customers only consider one store to shop for their needs. One "brand" if you will. They have had such pleasant and consistent experiences that choosing which store to visit is no longer a decision. It is automatic. When a customer builds a relationship so deep that they literally think of a bakery as "my bakery" instead of "the bakery" they have become a loyal shopper. Customers are *purchasing* loyalists in this stage and are usually open to expanding the solutions they purchase from your store. These customers are targets for add-on services and solution bundles or extended contracts. These purchasing loyalists can help you grow your average revenue per transaction.

**Evangelist** customers are your best marketers. They are the people who recommend your store, share your sales and posts on social media and enthusiastically endorse your business. Clever marketers push loyal customers to become enthusiasts by offering incentives to "like us on Facebook," "review us on Yelp" or give special friends and family coupons to loyal customers to share. These advocate loyalists help you build your customer base.

But a misstep along the journey and customers move backwards along the sequence. It is why stores that were once popular wane. Customers re-evaluate their loyalty when "the service isn't what it used to be" or "they never have what I want in stock." When fundamentals do not meet expectations, they can ruin years of customer development along the path. Successful managers realize that the marketing journey is not just the elements outside the store that bring a customer to a store (or website) but the entire journey.

The challenge is sharing marketing plans with staff so they know about offers happening and how they are supposed to support it in their role. The wrong time for store associates to find out about online coupons or special pricing is once a customer brings it to their attention. A coordinated communication plan is as important to delivering an excellent experience to your customers as any other operational plan. If your store associates know the steps to opening, closing, and stocking the store, they also need to have a communication system to learn about the active marketing campaigns in the market.

Begin with a marketing board in the backroom that is updated with all advertising in the marketplace. Include online offers and customer loyalty campaigns as well. Clearly highlight the start and end dates for each offer. Keep the board up-to-date.

Then, make sure marketing offers, prices and brand issues are included in every staff meeting. Talk about *why* it is important – not just what to do.

Talk about living your brand promise at every staff meeting.
Every.      Single.      One.

Select a store associate who is in need of new challenges and delegate marketing communication to that person. Ask them to do half of the staff meeting updates. Do not have them do it all – or it will quickly be seen that it is not really important to you. Make them the first stop for staff questions about marketing.

Finally, to be clear about the importance of the brand experience, put measurements in place. Your staff will begin to adjust and understand when you consistently share measurements that show the results of their efforts.

Begin with basics. If you are concerned about sharing actual numbers, you can share percent change versus year ago numbers to begin. Track the percent of transactions that included promotional items. Measure a rolling 12-month customer count or transaction count. If you have the ability to segregate promotions, you can even show them the impact of specific promotions such as percent of transactions with a coupon or a loyalty program. What gets measured, gets done. Show your team that marketing results are being measured and that they can impact those results.

It is your role to coordinate the customer experience so your business can succeed. Marketing creates the brand promise. But it gets delivered "on the front line" – in every interaction with your customers. A brilliant advertising campaign or an entertaining website can be sunk if the brand promise is not evident in each customer encounter.

Whether or not you choose to use this model and advice in running your business, the truth is that your customers are always on a journey. It is up to you to make sure the journey arrives at your store.

## WIN Today

Create a physical or virtual marketing board where each staff member can see current marketing campaigns you are employing and competitive campaigns. Make marketing a standing topic on staff meeting agendas.

At a staff meeting, introduce your staff to the customer journey graphic and the steps along the journey. Then ask them if there is a brand of something that they buy automatically (cigarettes, shampoo and coffee are good places to start). Or ask them to recommend a place for lunch and *why*. Draw the parallel about their journey in becoming evangelists for their favorite brands and the journey your customers go on when they shop your store or website. Explain that the evangelist customer becomes an advocate of the brand when they have gone through the journey. Explain how their job supports that journey.

## Promotions That Sell

The key to attracting new customers and retaining loyal customers is a strong promotion plan. Price promotions are a common part of every retailer's marketing plan. In the customer path from *awareness* to *trial* to *repeat* to *loyalty*, strong product promotions give customers an urgent reason to visit your store or website and make purchases. While *branding* builds awareness, *promotions* are a call to action.

### Building Promotional Events

**Create a calendar of events.** The first step in creating promotions is to create a basic calendar of events. Savvy retailers align their promotions to customer buying patterns and give them reasons to purchase. For example, January is key for organizer, storage and clearance sales; March is spring cleaning sales; June is graduation events; August is back to school and October and November are holiday ramp-ups. There are also mini-events and created events that might impact your target market. Examples of mini-events could be Breast Cancer Awareness in October, Formula One racing season beginning in March or spring break.

**Create goals for each event**. Build your promotion to deliver on those goals. For example, if your goal is to collect 250 new emails during the event, give a discount to first-time customers when they sign up. If your goal is to increase sales of a particular brand or line of product, be sure to promote the best-selling items in the line to create a widely appealing product selection. Goals should be clear – and clearly communicated to your sales staff.

Examples of good goals are:
- Increase canned soup sales by +25%
- Launch a new accessory line and generate $1000 in revenue from it in week 1
- Sell 2 pounds of candy for every Easter basket sold
- Increase the average weekly transaction count by +15%

For consumable products, a goal may be to pantry-load customers by promoting in multiples. Customers tend to purchase in the multiple of the promotion. Thus an item on sale for $1.25 will not sell as many units as the same item on sale at 4 for $5 – up to a point. (Obviously, while that is true for consumable items like pens or soda, it is not true for cameras or televisions.) Pantry loading is a good way to gain market share, but do it with a plan for recapturing those customers as they come back into the market to repurchase.

The point is that the goal should be something you can specifically state and measure.

**Select items that support the theme.** Each promotion's objective should balance appeal with profit. Most retailers categorize their products as either "traffic-drivers" (items with broad appeal that bring people into the store) or "profit generators." Selling even a few profit generators can offset the price discount on traffic generators. Low priced products with broad appeal will bring people to the store or website where new items ideally sell at full price

An example would be a price reduction on a product, like car batteries, when combined with a full-price service, like a tune-up.

Another common practice is to physically surround the sale-priced item with full-priced accessory add-on items in the store. A display with sale-priced guitars can be merchandised surrounded by full-priced sheet music, pedals and amplifiers.

**Manage promotion frequency.** Promotion managers should understand the purchase cycle of the customer. If customers re-purchase about every 8 weeks, a promotional cycle of 6–7 weeks will anticipate their needs and keep them returning to the store regularly.

**Forecast sales and inventory needs.** To succeed, retailers must accurately forecast expected promotional sales. Remember with a promotional goal to increase sales by 40% during the month of June, you must purchase more than 40% above your average quantities in June. Purchase enough to account for variability in the sale (some SKUs will sell more than +40%) and to come out of the sale in a reasonable in-stock position. Retailers who do not have enough stock to cover customer demand in the final days of the sale risk short-term lost sales and disappointed customers.

**Measure the promotions.** After the promotion, measure and maintain a record of the result for future promotional improvements. Refining promotional effectiveness in the future requires a record of the past. Good records include the items on sale, their average (baseline) sales and sales lift during the promotion, the wording of the offer, the marketing channels used to promote the sale and the location of the sale item in the store or its online page rank. Maintaining a detailed record is the only way to measure tests when store locations are changed, price ratios are changed or different marketing channels (radio, newspapers, banner ads or email campaigns) are used.

For online retailers, measurement is much easier in that A/B offers can be devised and measured in real time. Use online results to inform brick-and-mortar promotions in the future.

**Track the competition.** Finally, keep records of competitive promotions. Even the best conceived promotion can be a dud if a competitor is surprisingly aggressive.

A library of promotional prices kept on file will let you review your promotional plans against market prices to ensure you are as competitive as possible. All retailers tend to follow a similar promotional calendar year after year. If competitor X advertises all sweaters on sale the third week of January this year, chances are they will do the same next year. That knowledge puts you in a good position next year to decide whether to advertise sweaters the second week of January (to intercept the promotion) or to advertise a different item the third week of January to appeal to different shoppers.

At some level, every retailer must engage in price promotions. Following these guidelines can transform promotions from a necessary evil to a business-building strategic advantage.

## WIN Today

Review upcoming promotions and ensure that you can articulate the specific goal of each promotion. Make sure your team members understand what the goals are (introduce a new line to current shoppers, sell a pallet of seasonal toys, increase average units per shopper from three to four units, etc.) Review how you are monitoring your promotional sales as well as your competition.

Start to build a calendar of your competition's promotional cycle by category. Use that calendar to predict their sales and inform your timing in the future.

## Basic Customer Retention Programs

A customer retention program keeps your best customers loyal to your store or website. For most retailers, loyal customers represent 20% of the transactions but 80% of the profits. Loyal customers are those customers who make your store their first choice for the range of product you sell *and* are most likely to purchase at full price.

For stores who have done the work to create a customer database, use it to delve into your customers' habits. Evaluate your customers to identify their importance and then create inducements to reward them for their patronage and secure their return business.

**Analyze their annual value.** Identify those customers who represent the top 10% of your sales, then your top 25%, and top 50%. These are your platinum, gold and silver customers.

**Create an app.** Solution providers are accustomed to creating account-based apps and if you have purchased a loyalty program or CRM, they are likely to have an app offering. Depending on the size of your business and the profitability of your loyal customers, develop an app to:

- Make it easy for your customer to see their points and status
- Push your promotions to the app
- Allow customers to use digital coupons that are scannable from their device
- Redeem points online or in the store
- Create a virtual shopping list and
- Order online and track delivery status
- Access electronic receipts

**Go "old school."** If you do not have the technical resources or must justify the investment through a proof of concept, you could use a paper-based or home-grown solution.

Send customers letters or emails notifying them of their new status – along with a membership number and a printed (or printable) business-sized card. IF you have an app- push a notification when they reach new status levels.

Either create a single reward plan to retain them or offer a tiered rewards program to give them incentives. Examples would be: free delivery to silver members and above, free delivery plus 5% off every day for gold members, free delivery plus 10% off every day for platinum members.

Inform the rest of your customers about the rewards available if they were to join the loyalty program and let them know how they can achieve preferred status.

**Tried and True**

If you do not have a database, create a simple punch card system where every $10 in purchases receives a punch. After 20 punches, the user can get $15 off their next purchase (a 7.5% promotion cost.) Or you can offer a free item after 10 or 12 similar items are purchased. This works well with low-value, highly consumed items like bird seed, paper or coffee.

Offer special customer appreciation events for your best customers. This is an especially powerful practice for improving sales during historical lulls in your calendar. You can offer a special after-hours sale or a sale on selected items.

Some retailers succeed in creating events that do not involve sales. Pet stores have a Halloween costume contest. Office supply stores invite their best commercial customers to a free business seminar by a local banker, Realtor or investor. Craft stores host a photo event for customers to learn how to do digital photo books. Fabric stores bring in a sewing expert to demonstrate new sewing machines or techniques. If you have the space, offer to host relevant community groups in your space. Include wine and cheese if it is after hours or coffee, tea and sandwiches during the afternoon.

**Provide early access.** Give your best customers early access to the newest products to influence trend setters. First-to-market events knit you closer to shoppers who typically pay full price to have the latest and greatest products. Invite your vendors to host special introductory events when their new lines come in. Designer trunk shows have been a mainstay in high end boutiques for decades. Take a large step outside your comfort zone to make real connections with your best customers.

**Reward-a-friend offer.** Your best customers are also your best resource for finding new customers. Send your best customers two 20% off coupons. Ask them to pass one on to a prospective customer and use the other one on their next purchase in your store. Leave room on the prospective customer coupon for customers to identify who gave them the coupon. When one is redeemed, send the original customer *another* set of coupons as a way to say "thank you" and to encourage them to pass on the coupons to yet another prospective customer. As long as your current customers keep inviting new people into your store, there is no reason to end this cycle. Turn your loyal customers into evangelists for your store!

**Give every customer a bounce-back offer.** Treat each customer like a preferred customer by inviting them back with a limited-time discount. Use bag stuffers or register-receipt messages to invite customers back to your store within 30 days to receive 10% off their next purchase or some other enticement. Be sure to train your staff to tell every customer about the offer during the purchase transaction.

These ideas are easily translated to online stores. Use social media to host real-time events. Offers are included either on packing slips or as timed post-sale email campaigns.

All of these tactics are excellent means for retaining customers. Naturally, authentic appreciation will always be the basis for a loyal customer following. Coach your employees to treat each customer with respect and gratitude for their business. Set the standard whenever they see you interact with a customer.

For more advanced customer retention, analyze your best customers to look for patterns and common characteristics. Are your best customers most likely to be schools? Medical offices? Retirees? From a specific neighborhood? If you can find two or three groups that seem to have a common attribute, focus your marketing on finding more customers that fit the same profile. Start to see which customers are most likely to evolve from "occasional shopper" to "loyal repeater" and give them reasons to make return visits.

### Making Promotions Pay

If all of these discounts and offers make you fear for your ledger, know that all retailers who use these offers understand "breakage rate" and "market basket."

**Breakage rate** is the difference between the number of offers circulated and the number of offers redeemed. For most retailers, the breakage rate on a mailed promotion is 98%. In other words, only 2% of the offers in circulation will be redeemed. The breakage rate will be smaller if the offer is better than normal. A free ink cartridge worth $19 is much more likely to be redeemed than a 5% discount on paper, for example.

**Market basket** can help justify the cost of the promotion. The market basket is the average total transaction when the promoted item is included in the transaction.

For example, imagine you were to offer 50% off a pair of $60 jeans. What if the average market basket for transactions that included those $30 jeans was actually $85 because your customers usually also purchased $55 of other products? Then the overall offer and sale may be profitable when the promotional cost is spread across all the items in the market basket.

While new customers are always a goal, remember that your most loyal customers are key to your store's profitability and long-term stability.

Our next topic busts a few myths there as well.

## WIN Today

If you do not have a customer database, build one. It can be as simple as collecting emails or phone numbers at the register and connecting them to transactions. Work closely with your IT security team to safeguard customer data. Identifiable customer data must be encrypted.

Monitor what others are doing on your behalf. The law makes clear that even if you hire another company to handle your email marketing, you are still legally responsible to comply with the law. Both the company whose product is promoted in the message and the company that actually sends the message may be held legally responsible.

If you have a customer database, begin the analysis to understand the platinum, gold, and silver levels (top 10%–25%–50%) of sales. Devise programs to give platinum customers outstanding service. For example, a store I know does not deliver. But when one of its platinum customers held their annual summer barbecue, they delivered the food and helped set up a beer and wine bar at the guest's home, which nearly doubled the total sale – already one of the largest of the year!

## Why Low Prices Can't Create Customer Loyalty

It costs more to attract a new customer than to keep an old customer. *Harvard Business Review* pegged the cost of selling to a new customer at 5x to 25x more expensive than selling to a current customer.[17] When retailers create their marketing plans, they define and understand what each campaign is meant to achieve: appealing to new customers *or* to established customers? Promotions are typically meant to attract new customers, while *loyalty programs* keep past customers returning for more.

The most common tactic to attract new customers is to reduce prices on a hot item to entice them to make an initial visit to the store. The problem is that once the customer has an experience with the store, rarely will a low price induce the customer to return. Price is not the main reason for customers abandoning a store. It is actually due to poor customer service according to an Accenture Global Customer Satisfaction report in 2008.[18] According to Bain & Company, a customer is four times more likely to defect to a competitor if the problem is service-related rather than if it is price-related or product-related. What that means is that a price promotion to attract a new customer will not be the most effective tactic to get that customer to return again. So the marketing efforts to build customer loyalty (points, bounce-back coupons, rewards programs) may be money spent on the wrong thing if the customer experience isn't superior.

Customer experience binds a customer to their favorite retailer or website.

When planning promotions for your store, every promotional investment needs a defined goal. Determine if a promotion is meant to attract new customers or to reactivate lapsed customers to keep messages and goals focused. Remember to think of every past customer as a lapsed customer. Too often retailers are lulled into complacency by looking at re-purchase cycles and forget that during dark periods past customers are being wooed by competitors.

Price promotions and pantry-loading tactics are effective for attracting new customers and keeping them out of your competitors" store (or website) for the short-term. Examples of pantry-loading promotions are aggressive case pricing and "buy more, save more" promotions where the savings is stepped (for example: Spend $50, save 15%; spend $80, save 20%). This entices customers to buy a longer-term supply and keeps their supply cabinet filled with items purchased at your store and not the competition. Taking customers from the competition in the short term can be necessary. Getting aggressive on large quantities can be a smart strategy. Of course, it also means less return trips to your stores and can be a problem if the shelf life of your goods can reduce customer satisfaction when they use the product.

Those promotions are very different from loyalty programs where the goal is to knit your customers close to you and create such a point of differentiation from your competitors that they would not consider shopping elsewhere. The most cost-efficient loyalty program is excellent customer service. Make no mistake, any other reward program will be undermined if the customer experience is not helpful, friendly and respectful.

Loyalty programs can be technically enhanced though CRM databases, loyalty cards, smartphone apps and tech-savvy websites. But retailers with smaller budgets can still compete by being authentic and creative while engaging their customers. Rewards and recognition (think of silver, gold and platinum customers on airlines and the rewards they receive) are not the only ways to build a loyal customer base. The truth is, customers seem to be tiring of loyalty programs. Retailers saw a huge surge in membership in 2015 when US memberships topped 3 billion. Specialty store loyalty programs were second only to credit cards – even surpassing airline programs. But, active membership has dropped by 4.5% with only 42% of members actively using their accounts and redeeming offers.[19] What once seemed like a unique offer has become a hassle for customers who now have to present cards or remember passwords to qualify for the best price. Retailers who got lazy and use price as their main reward now have customers who are unimpressed and find the loyalty game stale.

Savvy retailers are creating compelling loyalty campaigns by integrating mobile, social, local and experiential elements into their loyalty marketing campaigns. For example, some give their customers points for more than just making purchases. They can earn rewards by sharing their data (or updating it) to keep communication channels open and accurate. Simply updating email addresses and mobile numbers with Delta recently gave flyers 250 additional miles. Gilt regularly offers its members a way to "invite friends" with a special email code. The customers pass the email code on to their friends and when those friends add their email to the database, the original customer is rewarded with Gilt Dollars to spend. Connecting to more customers in the right target market to the brand has a value for retailers and they appeal to their best customers with more rewards.

Social applications like Pinterest, Facebook, Yelp and Instagram are custom made for engaging content from retailers. Giving customers a fun and visual way to engage with the brand is why smart retailers are creating active accounts on many channels of social media. If you have a single account on Facebook, for example, that is a good start. But social media can be thought of like magazines. Just because you are actively advertising in one magazine title doesn't mean everyone who reads that magazine will see your message. Using a social media content management engine to take a single message and replicate it across multiple social channels does not take any more work than creating a message for a single channel – just as creating an ad does not require more work to create it if you choose to run the ad in multiple magazine titles.

Events and experiences are rewards that are the most differentiating for retailers. Sneak-peek events, new release parties and customer appreciation events create rewards that are meaningful for customers and build long term loyalty. Examples of ways to reward loyal customers include a customer appreciation after-hours party, free (or discounted) gift wrapping service or free home delivery or discounted delivery pricing. Offer small business customers special events for office managers or other key decision makers (with manicures, massages and gift bags underwritten by vendors) to create a deeper relationship with critical business influencers than price discounts. The goal is to make price less relevant and relationships more authentic. To stay top of mind for key purchasers, retailers need to bring creativity and a unique framework to the market.

## Win Today:

Either discuss expanding your social media channels with your current marketing team or look into easy-to-use replication engines like Buffer, Falcon, SocialPilot and more.

If you are personally managing your social media accounts using only one or two channels, consider engaging an intern or a media-savvy part-timer on your staff to work with you to expand your coverage. Be sure you clarify how to gain approval for the content.

At your next staff meeting, discuss the importance of customer experience combined with fair prices to keep your best customers returning. Ask for recommendations about how to improve the experience for your best customers from the people who interact with them the most: your staff.

## Are Advanced Loyalty Programs Worth It?

L oyalty marketing programs are affordable for even the smallest retailer. Chances are your inbox is being hit with a slew of offers from technology companies, POS companies and local marketing firms offering to set up a loyalty program. Is your shop ready to succeed with an advanced loyalty program?

First, *loyalty* is meant to build repeat shopping visits or customer engagements with the business at hand. In order to decide if the investment in *repeat* visits is the right one, we will revisit the customer journey:

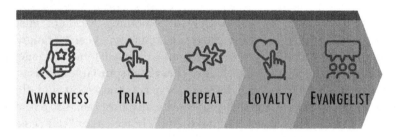

Before a customer becomes a *loyal* customer, they have to be *aware* of your business or services, conduct an initial transaction and then include it in their ongoing consideration set for ongoing purchases. So, from a marketing standpoint, the awareness and trial offers need to be effectively in place before any investment in loyalty makes sense. A very new company should prioritize investments in awareness campaigns and deeply promotional offers to encourage a trial transaction before investing in loyalty systems.

From the customer's point of view, the primary requirement to return to a business is an **outstanding customer experience** with that business. To that end, perhaps the greatest "loyalty" program a business owner can put into place is customer service training for all employees. Investing in a loyalty system without first ensuring that your employees are consistently anticipating and providing friendly, helpful, competent service is misaligned and a waste of money. This is about more than just conducting "sales" training. There have to be sustaining platforms in place to ensure that customer service is reinforced and modeled every day by all levels of management. Once the customer service experience is in place and supported by everyone from the manager to the new part-timer, a loyalty *system* may be the right answer.

Loyalty systems (and their underlying technology) are meant to build habitual behaviors based on rewards that are valued by the customer and profitable for the business. The rewards may be free goods (buy 10, get the 11th free), discounts (10% off everything  for our loyalty program members) or other rewards (convert purchases to frequent flyer miles, get exclusive access to limited-edition items or tickets to events). It is simple enough to do the break-even analysis to decide if the reward is a positive advantage for the business. The test comes in determining if it will change and reinforce behaviors for customers or just reward them for behavior they would do already. The reward, therefore, needs to be hefty and desirable and stretch customers.

Rarely is a "10% off every day" kind of program going to build a more loyal customer on its own. Over time, customers will see it as the standard offer. However, there is real power in combining excellent customer service with an everyday loyalty program. If employees can be taught how to adeptly weave the loyalty program into their customer engagement, they can have conversations with customers that spur larger transactions. For example, "I see you are deciding between these $50 and the $40 products. Since you are a member of our loyalty program, the $50 choice would be $45 for you. Does that make your choice easier?" Or "I see you are getting two of these today; if you purchased three, your next one would be free when you return. Would you like to do that?" In these kinds of engagements, the customer comes away feeling that the sales associate really "looked out for them" and they had a great experience where they were reminded of their prestige and power in being a loyalty member. Meanwhile, the transaction size increases and there is an upward spiral of positive brand interaction being built.

Unfortunately, in all too many cases, the loyalty program discount occurs at the register and the customer is rewarded with a "pleasant surprise" in spending less than they had planned. That brief benefit is not detrimental, but because it did not happen earlier – at the purchase decision point – there isn't an opportunity to use the loyalty program to increase the transaction.

The common systems available today – points earned toward future discounts or offers – are only accretive if combined with the kind of customer service described above. Customer loyalty is built on service and experiences, not points and offers.

Some loyalty programs are effective in positioning your business as a good citizen or community caretaker. Programs that are as simple as a school parent-teacher association (PTA) donor day, when a portion of all profits are donated to a school, are effective in building traffic and building an emotional connection to customers (which builds loyalty). Additionally, the charitable entity does most of the marketing for the business. Some technology-enabled services provide a similar outcome, like GoBuyLocal.com, which allow customers to earn money during their transactions and contribute that money to a local nonprofit. By highlighting the connection to the community, local businesses can build a differentiated marketing platform from national competitors. If the business understands its customers and their emotional motivators, a charitable loyalty program can be more motivating than cash discounts. From my experience, this is a great way for local guys to compete with the national players.

If your company is ready to implement a loyalty program, there are two critical system integration points to help in your decision. How does it integrate with your POS system and how does it integrate with your CRM system? Let's be clear: your "CRM system" may be as simple as Constant Contact, Mailchimp or Robly. Or it may be more robust like Salesforce.com or Zoho.com.

To begin, contact your POS provider and ask about loyalty programs they support. Selecting a loyalty program that works with your POS system without custom integration and programming will get you started quickly and without expensive development fees. Best practices include loyalty points, status and promotional messages printed on receipts. There should be a cashier message from the system terminal to ask about loyalty membership and an alternative look-up (with a phone number, for example) for customers who do not have their card or account information. Test the alternative look-up to be sure that it is not sluggish and will not slow down transactions during busy times.

Then, work with your marketing plan to determine how you want your loyalty program to interact with email messages or other promotional messages to your customers. There should be data feeds to automate welcome emails, birthday offers, lapsed customer ("we miss you") offers after a specified period, loyalty reward notices and other events so that the POS system, the loyalty program and marketing campaigns are synchronized.

Finally, the system has to be affordable, produce a positive return on investment in under a year, stable and scalable for future growth plans. Due diligence requires interviews with current clients as well as past clients who cancelled their service. More advanced considerations include mobile platform support for smartphones and tablets, standardized and customized report generation and integration to loyalty consolidation services like Apple Pay, Android Pay, and Google Wallet.

## WIN Today

If you already have any kind of loyalty program, coach your team to ask customers about membership and demonstrate how being a member improves each sales engagement with a customer. Confirm that they can discuss the impact on price or future purchases to encourage larger immediate sales. Recognize staff members who are using the loyalty program to close more sales with a small but appropriate reward.

## Moving Your Marketing Message In Store

Marketing may seem like it only happens outside the store or website. But great retailers make sure their external messages are unified with their in-store experience. It's a disappointing slide for customers who are promised "the widest selection" to find a limited range of products Or the "best prices of the season" are only on a couple of items. Backorders lead to abandoned shopping carts. To make sure your store's external messages are harmonized with the in-store experience, follow these suggestions.

**Keep Your Employees in the Know**

Each week, every sales associate should know the current key marketing messages. It should be a topic of the weekly sales meeting (you do have one, right?) and a prominent message on the back-room message board. Help store employees by integrating the current marketing message with "say's and do's" each week. Sales and sponsorships should be mentioned in welcoming customers to the store, answering the phone and as a limited website message.

Create a message that associates can feel natural saying, like "Welcome to our store. If you're here for our February Clearance Sale, all of our sale products are in this aisle." Stay away from things like "Welcome to our store, where this week we are featuring a buy two get the third half off on every winter shoe over $25." That doesn't exactly roll off the tongue. The same is true for a phone message. Keep it short and helpful. But make it clear that marketing messages are a non-negotiable requirement for answering the phone.

**Match the Marketing Message to the Right Location**

Think of marketing messages as having one of three main goals: (1) attracting people into the store, (2) closing a sale in the store and (3) building loyalty for a return visit. Then match your locations to each message.

In a physical store, to attract people inside the store, you have three main locations.
1.  Outdoor messaging
2.  Storefront windows
3.  The front door itself

Outdoor messaging can be a sign with changeable letters, a sidewalk easel sign or even colored chalk. Depending on your brand's "voice" you can be very business-like or fun and approachable. Match the message to the way you talk to your customers to develop your "brand voice." The same "half off all boots" message can be written on a scrolling LCD panel, posted as a limerick on your store sign or drawn as a psychedelic graphic on a sidewalk chalkboard depending on your brand voice.

Storefront windows are like the title of a book for shoppers. The windows begin the promise of the experience inside. You can place a sign in the window that says you have creative paper solutions or hang 50 folded paper cranes in different sizes and colors to say the same thing. Savvy retailers use the products they sell in hundreds of creative ways to showcase exciting solutions inside. Hire a freelance local art student to help change the windows once a month if you are not creatively inclined.

If your message is about making a sale to people already in the store, use ceiling signs and the counter to deliver the message. But beware of how your store space is used. This is the message area that is most likely to become cluttered with overlapping signs. Look at the store with a critical eye and always focus on only one or two crisp messages. A sales call to action and perhaps a reinforcing loyalty message are common. Beware if there are overlapping messages like a "spring clean-up sale," "we carry your favorite brands," "become a preferred customer," "sign up for a service plan" and a charitable event message in multiple signs around the store. Rotate which message is primary. Focus on one message at a time. Be vigilant in removing old signs by making it a part of a standard first of the month opening checklist item.

Remember that your sales associates are also a part of harmonizing your brand message. If your target market is local businesses, a store uniform should probably consist of a button-down shirt with an embroidered logo instead of a T-shirt. Your store associates should look trustworthy and approachable to your target market. They are a part of your brand promise, which means that a written policy on appearance and hygiene may be in order. Reinforce messages with buttons or lanyards worn by your sales associates when appropriate.

For messages that are meant to build loyalty for a return visit, use your checkout, register receipts, bag stuffers, the bags themselves and the front door (again). At checkout, there should be a pleasant exchange with the cashier that includes an earnest invitation to visit again. Consider a counter mat that allows you to insert a changing message under its transparent cover to keep offers up-to-date. Here is where a customer is most likely to entertain an offer for a loyalty program, a service plan or consider home delivery. It is also where you can deliver a longer message about community involvement or sponsorships. Have brochures or other marketing materials available to the cashier so that they can quickly give an interested customer more program information. Use acrylic document holders to keep materials organized.

POS systems can deliver changing messages on customer receipts. Have cashiers remind customers of any offers on their receipts as they conclude the transaction. Bag stuffers should be calls to action for future events or reminders about home delivery or online shopping.

Critique your bag itself and make sure that it reinforces your brand. Today, bags are reusable items that will be taken on buses, to work and the beach if the bag is durable and cool enough. Make sure you provide a bag that customers are proud to use. Consider it a marketing expense – not an operating expense – that advertises your brand outside the store.

Finally, there should be a message that gives a customer a reason to return. This is your very last chance to communicate the brand to a customer – so please make it more creative than "Have a nice day."

## WIN Today

Critique the use of your windows and store space for key marketing messages. Designate one or two key messages each week and make them a focus at every sales meeting. Match message locations to the message content.

Institute a sign and message removal routine each month (or more frequently if your signs change more often). Each staff member is assigned specific locations to remove signs. Use a reverse reward system to recognize when signs are removed on time or left in place too long. For example, give out chopsticks to members who have signs "sticking" around too long. It's an easy and silly way to bring awareness to the issue without being overbearing.

## Build Your Network to Build Your Sales

When you picture yourself "at work" where are you? You probably said in the back room doing paper work or at the cash register with a customer or unloading orders and putting away products in the store. Maybe you said tweaking your website and taking picture of new products. In any case, you were working in your business attending to a task that had little to do with attracting new customers or marketing your business to potential clients. The most successful retail managers and owners spend dedicated time out of the store making connections and networking.

If you hate the idea of stodgy business mixers with Styrofoam cups of lukewarm coffee, exchanging grubby business cards, think again.

Approach every event as a networking opportunity. You do not have to be pushy or overly aggressive. When you approach networking as a chance to find out how you can help other people (that is why you went into the business, right?) then making connections begins to feel natural. Start where you feel comfortable. Perhaps your church, your pub or your children's school.

Create a natural way to describe what you do that is not what your store sells. So, when someone asks, "What do you do?" an office supply manager could say "I help companies and institutions project a professional image." An athletic footwear manager could say "I help athletes perform at their peak." Think about the customers and solutions your store sells. Not the products. That's bound to get an interested follow-up question or at least a puzzled nod. Then you can add more detail rather than saying "I manage a shoe store." See the difference?

Have a handy authentic follow-up. Ask what they do and what they are trying to accomplish and see if there is any common ground. Suddenly, you're networking!

When you own (or manage) your business, people will say, work *on* your business, not *in* your business. As long as you are working *in* your business, you cannot make the high-impact leaps in customers, revenue and visibility that are necessary to grow. Sure, you might keep your current customers happy and returning – but if your team can't do that for you, you have the wrong people.

Working on a network and building your business through networking does not come naturally for most people. You are not alone. Recognize networking as a skill that you have to achieve to run a successful business and attend to it each day.

## Create a Networking Strategy

Decide which customers you most want to acquire: Schools? Small business owners? Bowlers? Students? Identify whom you want to attract and then select networking events that have the greatest chance of including your target market. Consider who will be there and why. Decide what you will say about yourself. Describe what you uniquely offer to them. Let them know that you are an expert. Be available as someone they should turn to for that expertise.

Make sure you can feel as natural as possible in the moment. Select coffee/breakfast meetings if you are a morning person. Bring along a trusted ally if you feel odd being by yourself.

Perhaps begin as easily as selecting a half dozen stores that you admire. Ask for a meeting with the store manager (bring coffee!) and simply tell them what you like about their store and why. Ask them what they think makes them so successful. Listen to their answers. Chances are you can learn something you did not know about the secret to their success. Listen more than you talk. But tell them about what you think you do well in your own store and the kinds of customers you wish to attract. Be genuine. Look for places where you can help one another succeed. Perhaps in joint promotions or bounce-back offers?

Create a strategy for networking that will either bring you closer to your target market or that can put you in touch with people who influence your target market.

## Use Your Ears More Than Your Mouth

Great networkers listen to people talk and restate their comments so that they know they were heard. Want to be a dazzling conversationalist? Simply listen well, restate, then add an appropriate comment to show you are interested in hearing more. If a school administrator says something about budget cuts for example, offer a comment like "Making decisions about cutting budgets must mean you have to make some difficult trade-offs. How do you do that?"

You let the person know they were heard and asked a question that makes them more ready to open up to you. Once you listen well, you can see if it makes sense to either tell them about your ideas to save on consolidating school orders or ask if you could follow up with them about an idea you have. Explain that you have an idea, but you would want to make sure it could actually work – giving you the opportunity to follow up with a custom plan and approach at a future date.

### Follow-up and Follow-through Are Key

Networking develops your reputation for keeping your word and being a great resource. To gain that kind of a reputation, you have to be clear about when you have made a commitment and follow through on each commitment to the letter. This builds character strength that sets you apart from others and creates a kind of obligation for people to do the same for you. This leads to more business over time.

As you make introductions, suggest references and pass on tips to your growing network; never play down your efforts. When you are thanked, never dismiss the act by saying "it was nothing" or "don't give it a second thought." Instead, say "I know you would do the same for me." This reinforces the idea that your acts are favors that should be expected in return. Think of your network as a bank account. It is best to have more credits than debits in your account. But when you need to make a "goodwill withdrawal" you should feel comfortable that your past actions will be remembered and expect a positive response from your network.

### Use Your Network as a Business Tool

To use a network well, think of how you can make connections and links to help in your business. Look for people who may be able to make an introduction on your behalf or who should hear about your latest offering. Find ways to help your network work for you by offering friends and family business cards that are good for a discount when they pass along your card. Support a local event or charity and be sure you attend and work at the event to connect to as many people as possible and get your message out.

When you think about running your business, include networking events in your schedule and approach them with the same preparation and discipline that you would when placing an order and you will see your traffic grow.

Remember that networks are a two-way street and be a resource for others as well. Look for ways to build business connections for others and they will do the same for you. This isn't a fast track to success, but it is a long-term sustainable way to build traffic and loyalty over time.

### Use a Virtual Network

Facebook groups and local online communities are important places to network. Start by introducing yourself and offering advice. Do not immediately jump in with promotional or sales offers. Find ways to link your store to causes and events that will organically expand your shopper base.

Rather than selling the store, attempt to sell your store's expertise. Offer solid advice and take the time to research solutions. Make real connections by solving problems and keep every engagement online positive and uplifting. If you cannot stop yourself from arguing "when you are right" or worry that you cannot engage consistently, delegate the work to the right person on your staff.

## WIN Today

Review your local target market and events that you could attend that would connect you to that target market. Consider passing out samples at children's sporting events, fashion events, outdoor clubs, fraternity or sorority events, or street fairs. Join the chamber of commerce, Rotary, Business Network International (BNI) or other business-minded group. Offer to host after-hours events in your store or supply products for scout troops, charity breakfasts, walk-a-thons or other events that will link your store to a strong community institution. Actively engage in offering advice and answering questions online in group chats. Only mention your store in one out of every 10–12 responses to make sure that you are not seen as being too aggressive.

MARKETING

## Good Neighbors Make Good Customers

Whether managing a chain of hundreds of stores or a single shop on Main Street, store managers need to be seen as active members of the community. Facebook, Instagram and Twitter have made it easier to connect with potential customers outside the store, but gaining customer loyalty happens customer by customer.

For store managers, that means being purposeful about two channels: talking to customers outside the store and talking to shoppers inside the store.

Perhaps your best customers are other businesses. To connect with other businesses, it is best to frequent their businesses while consistently reminding them that your business exists to serve them. That means always having business cards with you and handing them out with a short offer. "Come in and get 10% off your first purchase."

Set aside time to send a short note and a business card to every business you interact with: dentists, barbers, the kids' football coach. If everyone you reach understands that they have a personal invitation from *you* to visit the shop, chances are you will be given a chance. At least once.

As the store manager, you are the "face" of your store. So many store managers are focused on the inside of the store – while your best customers are outside of the store 99.98% of the time. You should be seen attending as many community events as possible. Join the local business council and mentor a new entrepreneur.

In the journey from "I never knew your store was here" to "I tell everyone how great your store is" the first step is awareness. Make sure your potential customers are aware of your store and remember it when they next need what you sell. Consistent messaging and repetition are two main mechanisms for helping people remember your store. Your brand logo and easy-to-remember tagline should be repeated so often that you become tired of hearing it. Remember, you may say it a hundred times a day but your customers will only hear it once per visit.

The most you can expect your customers to remember is one strategic message about your business. It may be a convenient location, competitive pricing, outstanding service, delivery, environmental stewardship or in-stock selection. True: your business may provide all of those things. But your customers can only remember *one* to differentiate you from your competition. So pick your lane and stay with it by repeating your strategic message in every channel possible.

As a good neighbor, your goal should be to have your shop be the preferred supplier within a specific demographic and laser focus on that target market. If you are unsure of your target market, it does not matter how crisp your value proposition is. So select a market and be as visible to them as possible. If it is geographically based, that means posting your messages on bus benches, sending direct mail postcards and targeted offers and attending every community event possible. If it is industry-focused, your marketing strategy should include attending conferences, advertising in the trade journal and being active on online forums. The point is to do all you can to be seen as an active and accessible neighbor.

As you increase your visibility, chances are you will be tapped to provide promotional "free" items for benefits or other causes. Think carefully about each proposal. If the proposal fits precisely with your target market, agree to it. If the proposal targets a different target market, politely decline the offer.

Let's say a civic group approaches you to provide an offer for a coupon book they are selling to raise money for their cause. If the group is in your target market, the next thing to consider is the size of the audience that will see your offer and the likelihood that they are already a customer. If the group is large and primarily comprised of non-customers, provide a rich offer to entice customers to make their initial purchase with you. If the group probably contains many current customers, provide an offer to reward larger-than-normal purchases. For example, a rich new offer would be "buy one, get one free" while a rich larger-than-normal offer would be $100 off your $200 purchase. Both cut your margins by the same amount, but one has a much higher threshold (a $200 purchase versus a single unit purchase.)

Being a good neighbor means being adept at using the power of obligation with people. When another business person asks you to do anything above and beyond, you have an opportunity to graciously remind them that you are happy to comply... knowing they are a good customer who is loyal to you. Even if they are not. Saying that provides a kind of psychological obligation on their part to live up to your expectation. Work to create a relationship of trust and mutual reliance between business owners. Business people recognize that businesses are not run altruistically. There is an expectation of payment for services so as you provide excellent service, future loyalty is expected.

As a good neighbor, you can lift up the neighborhood. That means a clean and inviting store front. Perhaps a barrel of flowers at the entry is beyond your budget (or gardening skills). But every store can have entertaining and fresh window displays and a community bulletin board to help local causes.

As a good neighbor to other businesses, join the community merchant association to help drive business to your shopping area. Keep communication lines open about shoplifting, disposal services and parking issues. Unify behind common concerns that matter to a group of businesses to get attention and action from your city. When you are seen as the leader of a group of businesses, your voice will matter more and your business will get more publicity.

Finally, there is being a good neighbor inside the store. That means a cheerful greeting to every customer within seconds of entering your shop. Remind your employees that a greeting is "Good morning" or "Nice to see you" – not "Can I help you find something?" Then be sure that you provide an experience that reflects the neighborhood. Perhaps dress in the team colors on the day of a big game, post local notices in the store and display your relationship with a local school, hospital or charity. Finally, a heartfelt expression of thanks at the register and assistance getting their purchase out the door is what will set you apart from "the other guys." And give you a reputation for being a great neighbor.

## WIN Today

If you are not already a member of the local merchant community organization, join. If you are a member or there is no group, invite your business neighbors to meet you for coffee. Introduce yourself and talk about issues in common. All local businesses want to discuss safety, attracting new customers and hiring great people. Ask how you can help another business owner or manager reach their goals and you will convert them to a customer of your own store. Maybe suggest a mutual discount for all employees in the area or an event you can host in common.

# 7 Timeless Principles

RETAIL: The Second-Oldest Profession
© 2019 Flora Delaney

# Timeless Principle 6: Managing

## Build a Prosperous Team You Trust

Do you resist delegating sales or operations because you believe no one does it as well as you? If you do not believe your staff is capable of managing work to meet your standards, that is a reflection on your training. You will never be able to let go of tasks until you have trained your team and shared your knowledge. Set a goal for yourself to transition work to others on your staff by training them, demonstrating how to do the tasks and holding them accountable for achieving the results you expect.

There is one exception: staff management. If you do not spend enough time focused on coaching and improving the effectiveness of your team, your store will suffer. They are the key to the system of the store. Great managers find out how to deploy team members to be at their best. They set high standards and celebrate every time those standards are achieved. Build your staff's capabilities and let them have the independence to achieve their own victories to create a store or website that runs like a virtual system.

In the hustle of daily tasks, building the staff can fall to the bottom of the to-do list. But the truth is the *urgent* will always overshadow the *important*. And creating a strong, reliable, empowered staff is one of the most important roles of a business owner or manager.

Perhaps you no longer put the effort into training the way you once did because your experience with employee turnover is so great that it seems like new hires come in through a revolving door. There's a real burnout level many managers reach when they just go through the motions of training with their staff. And frankly, that can be the cause of that revolving door and high turnover. Employees know immediately if they are being challenged, observed and rewarded for their best efforts or if the way to survive in your organization is to just show up for their shift and keep their eyes averted around management.

Managing in retail is particularly challenging. Perhaps in other industries, management has more control over deadlines and timetables. But in retail, Black Friday and December 26th and every other shopping holiday will occur with severe regularity. You have to move out of one season and into the next or your customers will make you pay. Vendors deliver products at inconvenient times and there isn't much you can do when a delivery truck is at the back dock at the same time your store opens for business. And it seems like an e-commerce rule that websites never go down during normal working hours. But, if you are cut out for retail, you know that the pace of retail and the unknown about the day ahead are what make our industry exciting and invigorating. Truth is, you never have the same day twice in retail.

There are thousands of textbooks to teach you to become a better manager and hundreds of seminars every year. But managing in retail requires an unusual alchemy of drive, compassion and energy. Retail is always about people: customers and staff. Great managers know when to raise the bar to keep their staff striving to be better each day and when to ease up and show appreciation for jobs well done. In any day or week, a manager should probably do both.

Stores ultimately reflect their management. Management that deeply respects their customers will develop a respectful staff. Managers who call customers names in the back room should not be surprised by employees who disregard customers on the sales floor. Managers who browbeat employees to push add-on sales should not be surprised by customers who feel that the store is too pushy. Site managers who are incentivized to keep visitors on the site for as long as possible shouldn't be surprised when surveys show that customers are frustrated by navigating the site. Our stores become what we emphasize.

At the risk of sounding the same, I am afraid that *managing* is one of the Timeless Principles that absolutely needs to be on point. Because you can have the best strategy, the most desirable merchandise, an unequaled website or store location, but if you do not have the hearts and minds and dedication of a staff who will bring it to life, it will not endure.

## Attracting the Best Retail Talent

Retail staff turnover is amongst the highest of all industries. A 2016 Hay Group study of its members found that hourly retail employees had annual turn of 65% and that 35% of all employees who separate from retail left the industry entirely.[20] A recent analysis in the United Kingdom found that only 30% of retail employees who report being in their jobs for less than one year would be happy staying in their current position for more than one year.

Knowing that, every store manager finds a large portion of their time spent recruiting, interviewing and hiring staff members.

It is expensive, detailed, risky work. Even when done well.

Anything a retail manager can do to reduce the risk in hiring a new employee pays huge dividends. Employee longevity creates a stable team and a positive work environment. So how do you hire a team member who will grow with your company?

Let's start by assuming you already have a respectful, positive working environment for your team where trust thrives. Plenty of books and coaches are available to help you create a positive workplace. But even if you are leading a middling team, hiring a new employee is the perfect time to upgrade staff.

Every store manager wishes for employees who are reliable, engaged and positive while on the job. Yet more often than before, they complain about candidates who are not dedicated and move on to other jobs nearly as soon as training is complete

Managers worry about:
- Turnover in general
- Losing employees to competition
- Too few employees on staff
- Finding qualified candidates
- Getting an adequate number of candidates for open positions
- Getting employees who can work the hours needed
- Feeling confident in hiring the right person
- Training new hires
- Retaining new hires
- Keeping employees productive in their first few weeks

Your store staff's success begins before you post the open job notice. Is the job description accurate and up to date? If you need someone who will spend 50% of their time on the phone with new customers – but the position is labelled "store clerk" – do you think you will get candidates who will succeed? Your job description should be crisp and accurately describe the experience, qualifications and behaviors you want. Look at the job descriptions you use. What is most prominent? Selling skills? Customer service? Product knowledge? Your job descriptions are the foundation of all job postings. Get them wrong and you are bound to attract the wrong talent.

Consider including both a customer promise and an employee promise in your recruiting materials. If you promise your customers friendly, smart advice every single day, that may help make a candidate's decision to either apply or not. If you have a goal of surpassing environmental standards, providing a dog-friendly workplace or allowing employees to work from home once a month those are all promises that could tip the scales for potential applicants. If your company's passion is childhood education or charitable giving, include that in the hiring materials so like-minded candidates will be inspired to apply.

Think about the work environment. Your work environment is the brand you create within the community. How would you describe it? What is the word on the street? Is it casual? Fun? Nerdy? What makes it attractive to potential candidates? Remember the saying: you have to cultivate the field before you plant the seed. The environment you create can make a new employee flourish or wither in the first few weeks.

**Less Fishing. More Hunting.**

If you recruit employees with traditional approaches, that could be part of the problem.

Most retail operators wait until they have a job opening then post the job in the local papers, website, within the store, etc. They fish when they are hungry. To have vibrant recruiting consider less fishing and more hunting. Hunters are always noticing the signs in the woods. Even when it is not hunting season they notice when game is feeding, where water is located, where trails lead.

As a manager, being "on the hunt" means noticing whenever people show good customer service and selling skills. Restaurants, other stores, drivers and services that you engage with every day may help you find ideal people for your store or website.

Get clear on what you offer compared to others. Always have business cards on hand and train yourself to keep your eyes open. Stay on the hunt for people who provide great service and would fit into your company.

Don't be shy: everyone loves to hear that their good work is being recognized and that there are people who value them. Even if you get ten "no's"... one "yes" could change the dynamics in your business.

That also means you need to look the part while you are out in the town. Keep your appearance professional. Remember that you are representing your company while you are out.

Encourage others to help you find your next super-star employee. Give current employees rewards when their recommendation is hired and completes their first 2 months of work. If your employees are not giving you referrals, what does that say about the work environment you have created?

Tell people you trust what you are looking for in candidates. Make sure they can give a brief synopsis of what you have to offer and make sure they have a supply of your business cards.

## WIN Today

Make an effort to be in the market and community with your business cards and keep an eye out for great service.

Practice your delivery: "I couldn't help but notice what a great job you did handling your customers. I am always looking for people with skills like yours for my store. Even if you're not looking now, take my card. Because I would love to talk with you about opportunities in the future."

It's that easy. On your next day on the town, notice people at the dry cleaners, library, church, dentist, daycare, coffee shop or anywhere you see people who are engaged with their customers. Set a goal for yourself to give out five business cards in a week. Dress well. Be approachable. Find the great people in your community and bring them onto your staff.

## Selecting Staff That Will Stay

Finding great talent is something you can do. And if you have struggled in the past, you can improve. It is like baseball. You will not always hit home runs. But with practice and a good eye, you can strike out less often and make game-changing hits more often.

Break your acquisition process into five stages:

**Stage 1: Screening**
The screening phase is a time to be efficiently ruthless. In other words, reach out to candidates once. During that initial call, describe the position briefly and then dive directly into their current situation:
- Why are they seeking the position?
- How quickly could they begin?
- What specific talents do they have that will make them a remarkable team member?

Listen carefully for their answers and their tone. They should be professional and excited. Are they considerate of your time by being concise in their answers? If you find their responses reasonable and you think there is a purpose in moving forward with the candidate, schedule a longer phone interview at the end of the call. In this way, you can screen up to 10 candidates an hour.

*Note:* Do not re-contact a candidate who does not return your voicemails. That is the first indication that they are either not serious about finding a new position or their life is in such turmoil that they cannot follow through in a timely fashion. In any case, they are not the candidate for you. Move on.

**Stage 2: Interviewing**
To be most efficient with your time, interviewing should have two phases.

Set up a series of 20-minute, back-to-back calls when you can focus uninterrupted on each candidate. This is *the key interview* to detect whether candidates have the experience and knowledge to do the job.

Ask questions that give candidates the chance to show you their ability to shine. Ask for relevant examples of times they have been successful in situations that are comparable to working in your location. Listen intently for specifics so that you can ask follow-up questions to get a clear view of how they approach their work. Past performance indicates future behavior, so ask very specific questions about exactly what they did in past roles, their responsibilities and how they completed their work.

Complete all phone interviews in the session and then follow up with those candidates you wish to see in person. Be vigilant against spending too much time with the first or last candidate of the session.

Set up *face-to-face meetings*. Consider who else should interview candidates. Would it help candidates to talk to someone who is doing the job now? The questions you ask, the observations you make (and they make of you) reveal more than you may think.

Remember that they are interviewing you as well. Do you start your interview on time? Is there some eye rolling over "how crazy" the day has been or the last customer interaction? Did you already review the resume or are you reading it for the first time? Keep your engagement authentic and positive. Shake hands. Dress so they know that you think their interview is important.

Similarly, your ideal candidates should be on time, well-groomed and eager to engage with you to secure the job. A miss in any of those areas should be noted in your interview guide.

During the interview, first clarify any questions you may have about the resume or application. Keep that to less than 5 minutes. Acquaint each candidate with the role and expectations for the position. Be clear and honest about starting times, workload, flexibility and the pace of job growth. In many ways, your goal is to paint the role in a neutral to negative light so that all candidates can self-select to stay or remove themselves from the search. Gauge their experiences, ask for references and explain that you will be contacting past employers.

Then move into behavioral questions that reveal the candidate's approach to everyday work situations. Ask about times when they have had conflict with other employees or dealt with a difficult customer. Ask how they resolved the situation and why they selected that approach. Whatever your strategy, make sure that your questions are targeted to get information that relates back to the priorities of the role for which you are hiring. Do not create hypothetical situations. Ask them to provide true-to-life examples.

A face-to-face interview should be at least a 70/30 split in employer/candidate questions. Candidates should ask thoughtful questions about the expectations, training and work environment. A candidate who does not have questions about the position indicates that they may not have considered the job seriously.

While interviewing, what are you observing? Communication is 90% non-verbal. What is their body language telling you? Are they eager?

Relaxed? Thoughtful? Do they make eye contact? Do they seem genuine?

Remain neutral at the end of this interview. Do not offer a job, no matter how impressed you may be. You need time to call on references. If the candidate is truly outstanding, you can do that quickly and offer a job by the end of the day. But truthfully, this is a big decision that should not be rushed and you should take the time to properly assess the candidates.

After the interviews it is important to call past employers. This one step is the *most crucial in predicting success or failure in the job* – yet one that many prospective employers omit. Ask standard questions: When did they work there? What was their job title? What were the conditions of termination? Are they eligible for re-hire? Compare the responses to the candidate's application.

### Stage 3: Assessing

Assessing all candidates is where many employers will move mediocre candidates ahead just to fill the position with a warm body. Managers talk about the sense of a ticking clock in the hiring process. Ask experienced managers and they will uniformly agree that quick hiring decisions have led to most of their past "bad hires."

If you do not have a candidate or two that you are truly excited about hiring, begin the process again. Go to new locations to find new candidates. Consider local college career offices, advertise in church bulletins, give your current employees a "bounty" if they bring you a qualified candidate that you hire, network as much as you can to tell people about hiring. Yes, you and your team may be stretched thin as you seek a new supply of job candidates, but that is preferable to hiring someone who will wash out of the job within months or weeks after starting.

### Stage 4: Selecting

A good assessment should yield two or three candidates that excite you. Making the right selection requires a few things:

**Cultural fit** – Honestly discuss the norms of your company and the expectations. If your culture is one of strict adherence to starting times, breaks and uniforms, make sure the candidate understands that. Talk about how conflict is managed, the pace of the work and the likely frustrations in the workplace. Monitor how your final candidates answer questions and probe for attitude more than competence in the final interviews.

**Questions and suggestions** – Your final candidates should be mentally preparing themselves for taking the job. If they ask you questions, that is a good indication that the candidate is mentally preparing to take the job. Listen for how they can impact the company. Do they suggest ideas? Did they take the time to look into your business? Even if their suggestion is off base or has been done in the past, give them credit for thinking about things as an employee. While all candidates would like to understand hours, shift rotations and vacation policies, beware of candidates who focus solely on how the job will fit into their life without any questions about how to succeed in the role.

**Timing** – Discuss the start date and make sure your candidate can begin when they will get the best training experience.

Finally, you have to ask three critical questions of yourself:
1.   Do they have the talent?
2.   Are they a fit for your operation?
3.   Will they raise the bar for you and your team?

These questions are the key to improving your team through hiring instead of holding the status quo. Each new hire is an opportunity to access new talents and upgrade the current staff. Hire candidates that will flourish – not just be present – in the job. Hire candidates that will bring skills and energy to make the entire team better.

*A note on bench players:* If you believe that you have found more than one outstanding staff member consider whether your turnover rate is such that you should offer a position to both candidates. As you look to upgrade staff members, consider overstaffing to build a strong bench for the future. Frequent staff turnover is common in retail so that extra staff member will only be carried for a short period.

If you choose to only offer the job to your top candidate, do not notify the second choice until your first candidate has accepted. There are situations where candidates either get a better offer to stay in place or get cold feet after a job offer is made. The second choice may ultimately become a reliable staff member. As a professional courtesy, all job candidates should be notified that the position has been filled on the first day your new hire begins.

**Stage 5: Placing**
The first days on the job are critical. Placing the new hire into the correct role, with a well-executed training plan and a seasoned mentor are the best tactics for developing your employee into a long-term team member.

Be especially vigilant that new employees are not placed in situations where they will struggle to achieve early success. A positive experience that builds knowledge and skills each day will prepare your new employee to become a competent team member. Guard against short-staffing due to holidays or time off too early in your new hire's employment. Check in each day to briefly hear what they did and what they are learning. If they can see that you are taking a direct interest in their success, your relationship as a leader will be cemented quickly.

Make their first day a welcoming event. What do you do special to reassure a new employee that they made a good decision to join your team? Their first day is an exciting one for them. Do you treat it as any other day? How can you keep their enthusiasm high? At the end of their first shift they should walk away feeling excited to belong and eager to tell their family and friends about the great new job they started. Most new jobs begin with a day of paperwork and the most mundane tasks. Turn that upside down and make sure their first day is challenging and engaging. The paperwork can wait a shift or two.

Training should be focused on the number one priority for their role. Customer service, greeting and thanking customers and engaged conversations should be more important than cleaning, putting away orders or learning POS keystrokes. Anchor back everything they do to your vision and mission statements. For example, if you promise your customers friendly, smart advice every single day then showcase the steps in every customer interaction that make it friendly. Help them see that there is a difference between selling and providing smart advice. (Hint: the key is *listening* to customers before making recommendations.) It is important that they see what you expect in every area – not just read it in a manual. Explain and demonstrate each critical component so they absorb the expectations and recognize the standards you require.

It is important that the first weeks with the team are energizing and focused. Do not simply turn them over to the most seasoned employee and assume that job shadowing is the same as real training.

Finally, make sure that your employees get personal communication from you that you are confident in their ability to make a difference in your store. Let them know you will be particularly interested in their performance. Help them see that even in their first week they can have an impact on customers, the rest of the staff and your store. Do not let them believe that they need to "put in their time" before they will be valued. Positive communication from the first day will keep their new employee enthusiasm and funnel it into positive energy for the entire store.

## WIN Today

Review your job descriptions with an eye towards what it really takes to excel in the role. Edit them accordingly or ask for a review by human resources, with reasons why a stronger job description will help you attract the talent you need.

Review the first 4 weeks of training for new hires. Ensure that days 1–5 are focused on customer service and less on the administrative operations of the store.

Make sure there is a planned outcome each week for each new employee and that there are planned check-ins to engage new employees early in their careers with your company.

## Store Managers and Stage Managers

Ever plunk down cash for a movie ticket only to walk out a couple hours later disappointed and underwhelmed? The ads and trailer were just good enough to make you want to see it. But once it started you realized it was the usual story told in the usual way: bad guys, a normal guy caught in an unusual situation, a resolution that left it open for a sequel. Ho hum.

Where did it go wrong? The acting was OK. Maybe it was the screenplay? Was the budget too tight for decent special effects? Was it the director? What does the director do anyway?

Retail stores and websites can be the same.

From the outside there is something that draws you in. Maybe an ad for an interesting new product or a sale or a new location. You enter with expectations that you will find something you like so much you will give them your money to make it your own. But it isn't great. Prices are nothing special. The merchandise is in confused piles. It is unclear how much items cost. Worst of all, no one acknowledges that you have walked in to give the place a try.

Where did the store go wrong? If everything were corrected, would you still make a purchase? Hotter prices? Neat merchandising? Clear price tags? Someone who greets you and engages you in a conversation? Chances are the one thing that would have made the most difference was if there was a courteous and engaged associate who wanted to help you find something to buy. But in the end – like our movie – the fault lays at the feet of the store "director," the store manager.

If you are the owner or manager there is no greater force in the store for changing course than you. Employees take their cues from you. If you smile and greet each and every customer, you set the expectation that they are to smile and greet everyone as well. Scowl and stalk into the store grumbling about traffic and having a "bad day" and they will believe it is acceptable to behave the same way on their "bad days." The owner/manager sets the tone for the store.

Have you heard people talk about a store's personality? It comes across to customers as well. A store can be friendly/snooty, orderly/slapdash, vibrant/dull, trendy/basic, masculine/feminine, formal/comfortable. Each adjective can describe the store and usually aligns to the store management as well. It is rare for a store that is snooty, formal and orderly to be run by a manager that is friendly, comfortable and sloppy.

If you are the manager, step in front of the sales counter and walk every single aisle looking for your "personality" in the store. Are there half empty cases in the aisle because you tend to accept that tasks are left undone when something more urgent comes along? Are there handwritten signs because you prefer something fast rather than following a process to do it right? Are supplies neatly organized behind the counter because you believe in "a place for everything and everything in its place?" Do employees arrive late and leave early because you avoid conflict?

The store, how it operates and serves its customers are a direct reflection of the personality of the owner/manager in most small businesses. Even stores in large chains will show the same propensity to reflect management style on the sales floor.

Like actors, employees should be given good opening lines. Help them learn how to open up a conversation (not close a sale) with a customer by asking open-ended questions and following up with thoughtful suggestions. Questions like "describe how much room you have in your supply closet to house extra supplies" might help them sell more units than "Is a magenta cartridge all you need today?" Or "Tell me about the kinds of running you like to do" instead of "You want to see this in a size 10?" can help prevent future disappointment for customers.

Employees can bristle and be hesitant to "sell." Some do not like to follow a sales process but just "be available' for customers to ask questions. They should be reminded that it is more painful for a customer to return home with a new purchase that does not meet their needs than to answer well-intentioned questions from an associate at the store.

Good store associates need opening lines at three critical junctures:
1. As customers enter the store
2. As customers are encountered in the aisle
3. As customers complete their sale

Make it a practice to watch your team in action. When customers are greeted praise your employees for being friendly and welcoming. Remember that "Good morning" and "Good afternoon" are greetings. "Can I help you find something?" is not.

Customers should never be within 8 feet of an employee without being offered assistance. A customer should never make eye contact with an employee without the employee smiling and offering help.

Finally, every customer should be greeted and thanked at a minimum as they check out. From there, good associates can ad lib lines to be friendly, helpful and interested in the customer.

**Stage Managers Online**

Translating the "director" role to the online experience means making sure that product navigation is intuitive, images load quickly and online chatbots offer assistance. Online customers should know that they can have questions answered quickly. Toll-free representatives should be empowered to solve problems.

Many online directors have myopia. They are so close to the site that they no longer see it through the fresh eyes of customers. Customer research should be well-funded and varied. Insights from the research should spur action. Test fast and implement fast to stay ahead of competition.

Brick-and-mortar managers get myopia as well. Start outside: is the sidewalk clear? Windows clean and inviting? Are there enough notices on the door (hours and promotional offers) without too much clutter? Enter and notice the temperature of the store, the smell, the lighting. Watch customers to notice what they look at first. Make sure they see a well-maintained presentation of stock and new products.

Managers for online and brick-and-mortar stores set the stage for the show every day. The "show" is the dialog that occurs between employees and customers. And a sensational show leads to sensational sales.

## WIN Today

Walk your store and use the adjectives listed below to describe the personality of your store:

- Friendly/proud
- Orderly/slapdash
- Vibrant/dull
- Trendy/classic
- Masculine/feminine
- Formal/comfortable
- Serious/funny
- Complete/in process
- Uniform/disorderly
- Tidy/messy
- Predictable/unexpected

Ask employees to do the same. Compare notes and then make changes to align the store to the stage you really want for your customers.

Use what you find to lead a staff meeting where you use the movie analogy to talk about star performances, setting the stage, knowing your lines and creating a sensational show for sensational sales. Two tickets to a movie could go a long way to rewarding an employee who is getting it right. After all, employees who take care of their customers are the store's real stars.

## Time Management in a Busy Store

Ask store managers and owners about their day. Chances are they will list the unplanned tasks that "wasted their time." Customers, vendors, landlords, deliveries and employees conspire to thwart their plans. Sales reports reveal the damage poor time management has on the bottom line. Store managers struggle with setting goals and attempting to manage their time. They have had their plans scuttled so often that the very act of planning seems wasteful.

Sound familiar?

Think of driving a car on a highway. As you travel along at 60 miles per hour, where are your eyes?

Great drivers know their eyes should be where the car *will be* in 5–10 seconds. If you watched the pavement as it whizzed beneath your tires at 60 miles per hour, you would crash within minutes. The same is true of working in a store. If the management is focused on the immediate activities of the moment and does not look up and plan for where the business is going, performance will drift and decline in a virtual crash. Successful managers direct their store activities to meet the future without becoming victims to the day's operational distractions.

### Set Goals

The first step to take control of your time and productivity, is focusing on goals. As in the car analogy, the driver must have an idea of where they want to arrive. Stores need to have destinations as well.

Goals can be purely financial:

- Revenues +15% versus year ago
- 23% store profit contribution

Goals can focus on other measurements as a means to arrive at financial goals:

- Reduce employee turnover by 50%
- 60% of customers return every 6 months
- Ship to customers within 6 hours of receiving an online order

As in most organizations, there are many goals and many paths to achieve them. But the high-achieving store intensely focuses on a small number of outcomes rather than fragmenting resources across too many goals.

Remember that deciding what **not** to do is as important as deciding what to achieve.

Keenly focus your organization on just a few items to make progress. Think of watching a military unit on the ground from a satellite. If the infantry uses its resources to push out a quarter of a mile in every direction, it would appear to not move when seen from above. However, if it were to use the same effort to focus all of its forward progress in one direction and move 1 mile west every day, its progress would be notable. In a world where there is opportunity to improve in every area, the savvy manager selects just a few critical focus areas to generate real improvements and changes in the store or website.

**Set Priorities**

Most organizations wrestle with how to select the right priorities. The easiest way is to use the 2 x 2 matrix and delegate to capable store operators. The 2 x 2 matrix assigns a value to every goal based on its ease of implementation and its value. High-value/urgent goals are tackled immediately. High-value/less-urgent goals are also given high priority. Low-value items that are urgent require attention when resources are available. Low-value and not-urgent goals are usually eliminated entirely.

Managers who make priorities clear are able to rely on their key store operators (shift leaders, assistant managers, fulfillment managers) to handle urgent issues throughout the day. That leaves management with time to focus on what is important but not as urgent. Examples could include new customer acquisition, creating better training for new employees or developing more effective marketing campaigns. Because those kinds of important work streams are so seldom urgent, they are under-resourced.

| | URGENT | NOT URGENT |
|---|---|---|
| ALIGNED TO GOALS | Store management attention or delegate to capable operators | Store management attention |
| NOT ALIGNED TO GOALS | Delegate to capable operators | Eliminate or minimally staff |

Focusing resources propels the organization to meet its targets. But equally important is eliminating time-wasters in the bottom right quadrant. For example, if a site's goal is to increase sales by penetrating the small business segment, then spending time developing a marketing campaign for college students would be misaligned and not urgent. Curtailing employees who stray down a path that will drain productivity (even with the very best of intentions) is key to making a retail operation more successful.

In a store environment, customers will always be an urgent concern. That is why it is imperative to have a dependable staff who is fully capable and empowered to make real-time decisions in service of their customers. When a staff is fully authorized to make decisions in the best interest of their customers, managers will find three positive outcomes:
1. Customers expect and receive high-quality engagements with staff members who can take care of their needs.
2. Employees are more fulfilled and achieve more because they have

the power to make their customers happy.

3. Management is freed to focus on more strategic issues and better situated to achieve big picture goals.

## Track Success

In order to keep engagement high, management needs a tracking system to keep goals, priorities and results front and center with the team. High-level scorecards on a back-room bulletin board are common. Websites have real-time metrics scrolling across screens in public areas. For employees, they are easy to ignore and rarely motivational unless experienced staff members help translate organizational scorecards to employee goals.

Examples could be weekly or daily sales competitions, outbound call tracking, or add-on sale contests. Newer POS terminals allow managers to configure screens to give employees real-time tracking against goals. For store management, a visible to-do list with smooth handoffs between shift managers will keep momentum up across the board.

Units and dollars per transaction are key metrics for both online and brick-and-mortar retailers. Research into bounce rates and shopping cart abandonments can help an online retailer provide a better experience.

## Be Accountable

Finally, the most critical element in actually translating efforts into achievements is a management team that holds itself and the team accountable. Accountability is what separates the stores with the best achievement from the stores with the best intentions.

Most managers know how to do the first three steps (set goals, prioritize and use a tracking system.) But it takes a dedicated leader to hold the store accountable every day. One obstacle to accountability is a store management team that identifies too closely with a victimized staff point of view. They catalog the day's excuses for not achieving the agreed-upon goals. Vendors deliver late, customer rushes occur, employees leave ill, storms foul up traffic. But a mature store leader pushes through the daily setbacks to help store teams see that there is enough in their control (through excellent customer service and strong sales techniques) to overcome obstacles.

A strong team has contingency plans in place to make up for setbacks. Management teams who accept falling short as a natural consequence of good intentions do their staff a disservice in accepting sub-par performance in the face of obstacles.

It is just as true with stores as it is with individuals. The highly disciplined person who has prioritized their health and weight management will overcome the temptation to overindulge and get to the gym. Management teams who accept their store falling short let their team "become fat."

So, why set goals and priorities? Isn't it a waste when we know that there will be obstacles every day that requirement adjustments? President Dwight Eisenhower said that "In preparing for battle I have always found plans are useless but planning is indispensable."

Like an army in battle conditions, an organization that has done its planning well will know its goals and priorities. It will be able to make real-time decisions that are consistent with those goals. Every team member will be able to make choices they know are aligned to the organization's priorities.

Rather than taking away flexibility, planning gives you the ability to be flexible. Planning puts a store or website in the position to manage the controllable. To not plan makes it a victim of both the controllable and the uncontrollable. To sign off with a cliché: to fail to plan is to plan to fail.

## WIN Today

Collaborate with other store management members to list all the goals for your store in a 2 x 2 matrix. Include merchandising, staff development, marketing and customer goals. Be ruthless in assigning them to each quadrant. Align on the assessment and make decisions about the high and low priorities for the store.

Share your focus items with the staff. Make sure team members understand what are the highest priorities for the store on a daily basis (taking care of our customers!) and on a more strategic basis (attracting more female shoppers or selling more new items in the first month of their introduction to the sales floor).

## Delegate to Tackle Extra Projects

A true measure of your leadership is how well your operation runs without you. A company that requires the manager to direct every action and check the accuracy of every step is poorly managed. Only the manager can change the situation. Managers who are stressed, overloaded and behind schedule are often poor delegators.

As an owner/manager it is your obligation to hire the right people, document and train the essential processes to succeed and to reward the correct behavior. (See "The Power of the Checklist" in *Timeless Principle 7: Operations*.) With fundamentals in place, it is time to delegate.

Delegating routine activities is critical for a manager to be able to tackle extra projects. Trying to find time to build a new social media community, research a second location, streamline bookkeeping or penetrate a new market through direct sales calls? Improve your delegation.

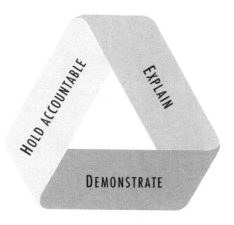

Delegation is easier with the training triangle. The training triangle requires the manager to explain an activity or process, demonstrate how it is properly done and then hold the employee accountable for doing it correctly. That means allowing an employee to do the activity on their own and being in a position to observe if the proper steps are followed to achieve the result. The manager should provide appropriate feedback and allow the employee to have opportunities to practice and perfect the routine.

Used correctly, the training triangle moves an employee from learning the basics to more refinement. A manager could train and demonstrate how to proof a cash drawer when opening a register. Then watch the employee do it themselves several times to ensure that they are proficient.

Then they can increase the skill by showing how to count down the cash at the end of the day or even create a cash drawer. The training triangle should start with simple skills and keep increasing the employee's knowledge and responsibility.

Many managers simply will not slow down enough and take the time to explain and document how to complete a task. When time is tight, an unskilled manager will continually complete the task on their own and then sulk because there is "no one else who can do it." Again, this reflects the management skills of the manager – not the staff.

When my boys were small, I could tie their shoes in under 10 seconds. Or I could show them how to do it and wait for them to tie their shoes. Which took somewhere between 4 and 40 minutes and was rarely done well enough to walk to the door without the laces coming undone. My mother calls teaching kids to tie their shoes "investing 10 minutes to save 10 seconds." But, as a parent, I needed to teach my children how to tie their shoes on their own. Yes, I could do it better and faster than them. But as long as I continued to do it, they would never learn and gain that sense of accomplishment and independence they needed.

The same is true with managing people. You must invest time to teach someone how to do something you can do better and faster. As long as you do not teach and delegate the tasks, the tasks will expand to fill your day. You will never accomplish the truly important items that will improve your business.

**What to Delegate**

Great managers know how to focus on what is important. They stay focused, not just busy. Managers struggling to delegate can use the simple 2 x 2 matrix to map out daily or weekly store tasks. Items that are in the upper right quadrant should get a manager's attention. Easy items to delegate are in the upper left quadrant. Even items in the lower right quadrant can be delegated, especially if there are several steps involved such as researching alternatives or testing several variations.

Frankly, items in the lower left quadrant should be dropped. If they are not important for a customer or a legal requirement, there is no reason to do them. Those are the "busy" items that prevent people from focusing on the most impactful activities.

**When to Delegate**

Delegating begins for an employee early on the job. Show them how to clock in, check the opening checklist for tasks to complete, demonstrate how to complete the tasks and then explain that you expect them to complete the same steps the next day. Review their work the next day. Then move to the next routine activity: accepting inventory deliveries, counting back-room stock, stocking shelves, pulling together web orders. Whatever the activity, teach and then stand back and let your "student" learn.

For seasonal activities like year-end inventory counts or window display changes, take the time to document your steps. Create a checklist and use it to train staff as well as to guide the work. Take the time to answer questions and to provide helpful feedback.

**How to Delegate**

1 Align on goals.

2 Set priorities.

3 Use a system.

4 Hold yourself accountable.

Let employees know the outcome you expect and why it is important. There is nothing more demoralizing than being given a task with no sense for why it matters. Many managers spoon-feed projects instead of giving employees the overall perspective of the work they are doing.

For example: "We are going to repaint the interior columns to match the new corporate sign package. So we need to clear off all the old signs and tape residue so they are prepped for the painters tonight" sounds a great deal more reasonable than "Clear off those columns and scrape all the tape residue off them." Give employees context and a sense for why their tasks (however small) are important. Without a frame of reference, delegated tasks can seem pointless.

Take time to inspect what you expect. Delegating is not abdicating. Your role is to hold people accountable for outcomes and provide feedback on how to deliver the outcomes more quickly, more consistently or more accurately. Acknowledge good efforts and give employees confidence that they are able to improve through practice. Conversely, be pointed and direct if work is not up to standards. Repeat the training triangle with consequences, if necessary.

What you cannot do is take the job back if you do not like how it is being completed. That is not delegating. Delegating means that you are giving the responsibility to someone else. It is now their job. They need to complete it satisfactorily to continue to be good at their job. If you take a delegated task back, you communicate to the staff that you do not trust them to be capable of growing in their role and you will stymy your own career and success.

For managers who need to expand how much they can accomplish, the only reliable strategy is to delegate. While delegating can feel like a loss of control, it is actually a better work balance that allows you to focus on what is critical and allows other capable people to contribute their talents more fully.

Delegating and transferring responsibility is essential to leave behind a legacy of leadership. With practice, you will become more comfortable delegating and your staff will recognize that you share responsibility and rewards. It can become a way to boost productivity while keeping yourself sane.

## WIN Today

Review your 2 x 2 matrix from the previous chapter and identify two items that you can delegate to others today. Be sure to use the training triangle to help them understand what to do and how to do it. Inspect for outcomes, but do *not* take the task back if it doesn't meet your standards. Continue to train and hold people accountable. Delegate today. Explain the importance of the task and give your staff the big picture.

Then use the time you have freed up for yourself to focus on the important items only you can do to drive your business forward.

## Yearly Goals Every Day

It's a simple question. Ask every employee you come in contact with for the next 2 days one thing: "What do you want to accomplish today by the end of your shift?"

Do they have an answer? Is it what you want to hear? Does it fit with the culture you want in your establishment?

If you hear responses like "What do you want me to do?" or "What do you mean?" those are red-light warnings. If you hear "I'm at the cash register" or "Putting away this morning's orders" those are yellow-light warnings. (more on that later). If you hear "Helping customers and selling $2000 or more to customers on the call list" or "The schedule said I'm completing the weekly cleaning duties and then creating POs for the monthly replenishment orders" congratulations – those are green lights. Your team is clear about what they need to do.

One of the signs of an immature manager is hesitant leadership in directing daily activities. Too often managers and owners believe their team "knows what to do" and the team drifts into lackluster performance over time. Sure, the store opens and closes and customers are helped, but there is no sense of progress over time – that this year is better than the last.

Leaders who run a winning team set goals and translate them to meaningful targets for team members *every day*. In a retail store or a website, where the team focuses its time is driven by managers. Time management is the difference between a productive, positive team and a deflated, unengaged place to work.

Translate annual budgeting targets to specific sales, inventory levels, new customers, new products or advertising goals. For example, if the sales target is to increase revenue by +15%, how will you get there? Is it +15% more transactions and the average transaction size stays the same? Is it +10% larger transactions and +5% new customers? Is it selling +15% more new products or +15% of the same products you currently carry? Getting specific about how the goal will be achieved is fundamental to translating the goal into achievable monthly, weekly and daily targets.

Take a look at some critical retail measurements:
- Average transactions per day
- Average value per transaction
- Average units per transaction
- Average hours of staff per week
- Average % new customers (or, conversely, repeat customers)

- Average orders by type: walk-in, phone, website
- % sales from new items
- % sales from clearance items
- % sales on promotion (sold with a discount)

Then set new targets for each relevant metric that would achieve the annual goal. Divide the goals so that each shift or team member can see exactly what they need to deliver. Track daily performance publicly. Specify goals for each team member. Set weekly sales or transaction goals and add them to the schedule.

If you work in a business that can sell to other businesses or reach out to institutional customers, consider measuring the conversion rate of cold calls to businesses over time. A sales manager determined that for every 12 cold calls, one turned into a warm call (a face-to-face meeting or request for more information). For every warm call, half placed an initial order. Initial orders were typically $300 for businesses. Once a business placed an initial order there was a 66% chance that it would make repeating purchases. Annual sales to small businesses averaged $1500/year. This company wanted at least $50,000 in sales from new customers.

Reversing the math, the manager can create weekly cold-call goals for its internal sales team to meet the annual $50,000 target:

- $50,000/$1500 = requires 33 new business customers in a year
- 33 customers from a 50% warm call success rate = 66 warm sales call per year
- 66 warm sales x 12 cold calls initiated = 792 cold calls per year
- 792/52 weeks per year = 15 cold calls per week

If the manager had simply said to the team, "I want you to make $50,000 in new business sales this year" they would have been paralyzed not knowing what to do. But a manager who says "I want you to make 15 cold calls per week and follow up on every opportunity for a warm call" will coach the team to success.

**Translating Annual Sales Goals to Weekly Team Activity Goals**

There is a tremendous difference between telling a team to achieve $50,000 in sales to new customers and telling a team to make 15 cold calls per week. That is the role of management: to translate the vagaries of strategic business goals into achievable tasks that team members can accomplish each time they start their shift.

Some positions within the store naturally fall into goal-driven roles –

sales, buyers, back-room managers. But even part-time clerks can have goal-driven duties that provide meaningful direction to their time on the floor. Tracking and measuring one simple metric: number of units per transaction – is a measurement everyone can affect. Meaningful conversations with customers nearly always have a positive impact on units per transaction. Combine that with attractive impulse merchandise and a store can drive significant profitability improvements.

Online, teams can drive for repeat customer visits by taking steps to make the site sticky. Email offers, requests for reviews, reminders of shopping cart items can bring back customers who did not complete their purchase. When new lines and high-affinity items are released, invite past purchasers back with discounts on shipping or other promotions.

A goal can even be created for people their *first* day on the job: greet each person who enters the store. That one simple step will have a positive impact on sales. Web team members should follow and track a customer's shopping path online to understand where they enter and exit the site.

Now, let's get back to the red, yellow and green lights.

**Green lights** occur when your team members have specific tasks they need to complete during their shift *and* they align to the store achieving its long-term goals. Look for actual numbers or other specifics in the tasks (call 15 customers, fill and ship all orders overnight, etc.). Even saying "Greet every customer who comes in the store" could align to a customer-service goal.

**Yellow lights** are usually just locations where the employee will be during the shift: cash register, back room, "on the floor." They don't have real goals, but a vague notion of duties associated with that location.

**Red lights** are when employees don't seem to have any notion of their role in the store for the shift. Showing up to work may be as far as they have developed the notion of "what to do" for the day.

Remember, in all cases, the responsibility for developing and clearly communicating the goal for the shift lies with management. If your team is unclear about what their goals are, the person responsible is the one in the mirror.

One final thought on goal setting for a retail team. There are two positive results:
1. People who can articulate their goals are more likely to achieve them.[21]
2. People who know what is expected of them at work are generally happier in their job.

It is counterintuitive that rather than chafing under the yoke of public goals, most employees flourish when they operate in an environment where goals are clear and consistent. And engaged employees are the source of productive stores.

## WIN Today

Annual Goals Translated into Weekly (or Daily) Goals

| Annual Goal | Weekly/Daily Goal |
|---|---|
| Improve customer retention by XX% | Email campaign to lapsed customers who have not purchased in past 45 days. |
| Reduce clearance inventory sell down from 120 days to 90 days | Restock clearance endcaps two times per week. Accelerate final markdowns on all items that are on the clearance endcap for 45 days or more to 75% off. Clearance pop-ups on every order before customer purchases online. |
| Improve impulse sales at the counter from 10% of all transactions to 20% of all transactions | Ask every customer if they would like the XYZ at the counter. Add a pop-up for high-affinity items prior to purchase on shopping cart screen. |
| Accelerate repeat store visits from every 8 weeks to every 6 weeks | Add bounce-back bag stuffers or packing slip offers to get a 10% discount next month on all transactions over $50 |
| Increase sales of private branded versus national brand products by +12% | Discuss the value proposition of our private brand with every customer who purchases two or more units of the national brand in a single transaction. |
| Reduce order fulfillment time from 3 days to 2 days | Pull web orders at 9 am, 12 noon and 3 pm for same-day delivery. |

## Why Managing Is *Not* the Answer

There is a reason winning sport teams have coaches, managers and team captains. They have different roles.

Coaches strategize, plan, make calls within the game and encourage their teams. Coaches hold the highly paid talent accountable and set high expectations. Team managers ensure that the logistics of clean uniforms, travel and equipment are always smooth. They oversee practices and scrimmages. Team captains lead the team by doing. They are role models and peers within the team. Think about your store and your role as a leader within the store. Which role do you play?

Typically, great team members rise to become supervisors or key-holders. Truthfully, they have proven themselves to be good role models and play the role of team captain. They know how to execute the tasks that need to be done to run a store well. They are trusted and necessary to any successful retail enterprise. But they usually are not prepared to manage a store successfully on their own.

Shops are usually run by a single store manager. Perhaps that describes you. With the role comes new responsibility for ordering inventory, managing vendors, setting prices, hiring and training new employees. Delegating tasks is critical to prevent bottlenecks from slowing down momentum. But for many (if not, most) managers this is as far as their management talent extends. They are capable of running day-to-day operations and balancing all of the crises that comprise running a store. Most stores operate with that kind of manager or management team for years.

One way to recognize if a store leader is behaving as a manager is to listen to conversations with other employees. If it is primarily assigning tasks, inspecting completed work and redirecting resources, then the person is acting as a manager. And everyone needs to be a manager at some point in the day. But great store *leaders* move beyond management to coaching to make the entire team better.

A coach watches the store and gives feedback to employees at least once a shift – if not more often. A coach in a store will recognize when an employee is struggling and make adjustments. A coach analyzes interactions with customers to see if employees need more product knowledge or a more (or less) aggressive sales technique. A coach provides feedback, encouragement and advice to the team to improve job performance. A coach sees his (or her) role as improving how the team delivers a great customer experience – not delivering the customer experience himself.

To transition from manager to coach, there are some fundamentals to practice.

**Be in a position to notice – and take the time to coach**. Make time in your schedule to watch the team as they complete their work and interact with customers. Understand that part of your role is to observe, analyze and thoughtfully advise your team. Do not jump in and do it for them – that's what a team captain does.

**Provide timely feedback**. Give feedback the same day an observation occurs. It should never come later unless there is real research you need to do. Feedback is most effective when it occurs immediately after the event.

**Be specific.** People cannot make the necessary adjustments with generalities. For example, an employee who hears "make better suggestions to customers" will struggle to improve while one who hears "when making a suggestion for a product, take it from the shelf and place it in the customer's hands" will know what to do differently next time.

**Be consistent.** First, make sure your standards are uniform and predictable. Then make sure every manager is in alignment so that employees understand the standards.

**Be fair.** There is a difference between "treat everyone the same" and "treat everyone fairly." It is the definition of an inspiring leader. Leaders draw the best out of individual players by challenging each one to reach their personal best. That cannot be done by treating everyone the same.

**Follow up.** Consistently evaluate the team and recognize when they create new habits or slip back into old ones. Set a tone of accountability.

Most people are hesitant about their ability to give direct immediate feedback. But it can be learned and honed with practice. The easiest way to remember the basics is to think of the Five E model. These will help you remember the flow of a coaching conversation: Event, Explore, Evaluate, Expectations and Encourage. It is a linear model. The conversation works best when you follow the flow.

| Stage | Conversation Sounds Like ... |
|---|---|
| **Event** – Clarify the event you will be coaching. Be specific so the employee knows what you are talking about. | "Susan, I'd like to take a moment and talk about that sale you just made to your last customer." |
| **Explore** – Ask for the employee's point of view on | "What did you learn about that customer? How did you think the |

| | |
|---|---|
| the situation. You may uncover some new information before giving your evaluation. This stage encourages self-reflection. Employees begin to evaluate their performance on their own. Ask what they learned and what they could do to improve. | conversation went?" |
| **Evaluate** – Give your point of view. Provide your feedback. Be specific. | "I noticed after you found the item for her, you walked away. I would have expected you to ask her if there was something else she was looking for. Suggest accessories like jewelry or mentioned our sale on shoes." |
| **Expectations** – You can co-create this with your employee. Set clear expectations with goals. Get their commitment. | "Let's agree that you will not walk away from a customer without offering to find them something else or offering a second item. If they refuse, always thank them before walking away." |
| **Encourage** – Show them and tell them you believe in them. Set a date or time for follow-up. | "I think you will enjoy your time on the floor more when you look for ways to delight customers. I will be watching you in the coming days and let's talk again by Friday. Plan to let me know how this new approach is working for you." |

Most employees succeed with coaching when the feedback is routine and attainable. It is best to focus on one item per conversation. When it becomes the standard way you talk with employees it becomes less uncomfortable – for you and them. Performance conversations are less tense. Because you give feedback about performance every day, employees know where they stand.

*Note:* Coaching isn't always positive. Sometimes people need to hear hard news to improve. Beware of telling someone "you're doing a great job" then coaching about ways to improve. Hold back telling someone that they are great until they are truly and consistently *great!*

To be an effective coach, a few things need to be in place. First, there has to be a shared understanding of what the job is and what is required. The employee must understand the prioritization of work (i.e., first, assist customers, then restock the shelves.) The employee must understand the required quality standards. Finally, they must understand how you will hold them accountable.

Beyond those "talking points" they must see you modeling and "walking the talk." So if you have a shared understanding that customers are the first priority, your employees must see you setting aside your tasks like vendor calls and email to assist a customer immediately. It will help build the degree of trust and mutual respect that is required to succeed as a coach and leader.

## WIN Today

Set aside a half hour at the beginning of each shift to observe the team and use the Event, Explore, Evaluate, Expectations and Encourage model to coach employees. Remember that your goal is not to step in and complete work or sales for them. Your goal is to consider each employee as an individual and provide personalized guidance for how they can become better at their job. Remember that people who succeed at their job enjoy their job more!

## When Good Employees Go Bad

M aybe he was a bad hire to begin with. Maybe you saw a lot of potential, but now he is late, calling in ill, disengaged with coworkers and customers. It is a tough conversation to have because he *is* already trained and who knows if the next one will be worse? And there are some days when he is focused and you still have hope. This is the internal dialog you may have with yourself for months before having the "turnaround conversation."

Tough conversations with employees come with the job. If you are avoiding a difficult confrontation, the first place to start is with yourself. What do you want? Decide if you want to salvage this employee or separate from the employee? Separation and the legal requirements leading to termination are different topics. But if you want your employee to change direction and deliver better performance, recognize that you will not get what you want as long as you keep accepting your employee's current performance. Silence is acceptance. Which means you must have the tough conversation.

The goal of a turnaround conversation is not to anger an employee, shake them up or fire them. The goal is to have them go in a new direction. A successful turnaround conversation will give an employee a new vantage point to see themselves not as victims of their boss or workplace, but as capable adults who can choose to be more successful by adopting new behaviors. A great turnaround conversation is a truthful recalibration of the value the employee brings to the workplace. It should be a liberating dialogue that allows both the manager and the employee to reset the course for the future. (Truthfully, there is always a risk that the employee may decide the request is too difficult and may choose to leave. A move that is empowering for both parties in its own right.)

First, ask yourself if you have properly trained the employee and if they are clear about expectations. Think of the training triangle, which says that for adults to learn, they have to (1) see the new behavior demonstrated, (2) be trained in how and why the new behavior is done and (3) be held accountable to do it so they internalize the new behavior.

If you know you have done the first two steps well, it is time to move to the third step and hold your employee accountable.

Confidence in tough situations comes from preparation. It is true for public speaking and for turnaround conversations.

**Prepare.** Write down what you explicitly expect and the direct observations you have made about the team member's behavior. Focus on behavior *not* intent. There is a wide valley between, "I expect everyone to clean the store at the end of the night. You did not do that on Tuesday and then we started Wednesday with dirty counters and floors" and "I know you think it is below you to clean the store." Anytime you assume you know intent, you are almost always wrong. You can observe *what* a person does. You cannot observe *why* a person does it.

**Be clear.** What would you have them do differently? "In the future, I expect you to follow the entire closing process, including cleaning the store before leaving for the night."

**Outline accountability and consequences.** Be detailed about the decision you will make if changes are not made. "If you close the store without the appropriate steps taken to clean it, you will no longer be a closing manager. As you know, closing managers are paid more than our day-shift managers."

While the conversation is one-sided, it also clearly sets the expectation, describes the expected behavior and outlines consequences for not adhering to the request. As the manager, it is your privilege to have one-way communication. It is also your responsibility to be fair about extenuating circumstances and, importantly, recognize good behavior as much as bad.

End your portion of the conversation with confidence in their ability to make the change. Encourage them to make the effort because it is within their power to change. Let them feel that you are a level-headed adult treating them the same way. They have the ability to make the change you are asking; you are being forthright in your expectation and nonpunitive.

If they should get emotional, explain that provoking emotions was not your intent. Give them time to pull together. But make it clear you want to complete the conversation before the end of their shift. Your goal is to end the conversation with their focus on what they can do (not what they did do) and how they will succeed in the new expectation.

Catch your team members doing the right things – and call out every example of it – to gain positive momentum. As Eliza Doolittle would say: "The difference between a lady and a flower girl is not how she behaves, but how she is treated." Find a reason to point out when people on your team are working well – even the ones that need coaching – and you will master the art of turning around the people who work for you.

For the team member who is unwilling to change, it is time to document your conversations and let them know that you cannot continue to have them fall short of the job requirements and keep the job.

## WIN Today

If you have been postponing a difficult conversation and need to redirect a team member, set time aside this week to have a private discussion with them. First be sure that they have been trained and clearly understand the standard to achieve. If so, use the direction in this section to be clear about what needs to change, what you expect and encourage them. Honest, mature conversations save employees.

## Three Skills Your Team Needs

New members to the team need training that sets the store up for success. What a new hire learns in the first few weeks on the job and its *sequence*, is critical to create a store culture that is founded on customer service, sales and operational excellence.

Most early training for new hires focuses on how the store operates: using the register, processing a return, properly bagging a purchase. New employees spend time learning how to operate machines such as compactors and postal scales instead of learning how to interact with customers.

If managers look at what is truly critical to developing a new hire into a competent team member, they would teach them these three things:

1. **Customer service and sales** – Providing excellent service to people in the store or online: learning how to interact with customers, ask good questions to make informed suggestions, greeting consistently and providing a friendly, helpful demeanor.
2. **Product knowledge** – Learning details about everything that is sold to make solid recommendations and provide helpful advice for customers making purchase decisions.
3. **Operational processes** – How to run the cash register, change online orders in process, accept deliveries, conduct an inventory, verify a purchase order, create a staff schedule, etc.

Too often, on-the-job training focuses entirely on the third area. Customer service and product knowledge is deprioritized until much later in an employee's journey. But the truth is maintaining a superior standard in customer service and product knowledge will make a store profitable more quickly than excellent operational processes.

For a store to meet aggressive growth goals every quarter, it must have an employee base that has a masterful command of a customer-focused service model and expertise in the products they sell. Most training ignores those topics because they are rarely written down. It is easy to write down the step-by-step procedure for opening a cash drawer or voiding a credit card transaction. It takes more thought and diligence to write down how to properly interact with a customer or keep a product database updated.

### Developing the Three Critical Skills

For store managers ready to take the plunge, there are uncomplicated steps for new hires and current staff to develop the three critical skills for success.

Create a customer service model. Simply put, write down the expectations for every customer, every day. Make expectations plain and reinforce it with modeling and coaching during every shift.

To begin, adapt this to your needs:

- Every customer will be greeted with a hello/good morning/welcome to the store *and* a smile within 1 minute of entering.
- Every customer will be asked if they need assistance by staff members on the floor whenever staff members are within 10 feet of a customer.
- Eye contact will be made with customers.
- Tasks are secondary to helping customers. Staff will interrupt stocking, pricing or other activities to offer assistance to customers.
- Before plunging into making recommendations, staff will ask customers relevant questions about their condition, budget or similar items to make thoughtful suggestions for purchase.
- Staff will offer to take purchases to the counter so customers can continue shopping.
- Staff will smile, be courteous and *thank* customers for their purchase during every single transaction. Customers will feel unique, attended to and appreciated in every transaction.

Employees need to watch and learn the customer service model before learning any other process within the store. A new employee must learn that helping customers in a friendly, attentive fashion is more important than making change or learning how to change a roll of register tape. The investment in learning the customer service model will pay off in the long term when all employees understand that their primary role is cheerfully helping customers purchase what they need and not standing at the register waiting to conduct a transaction.

**Create Customer-Based Product Training Modules**

Prioritize your primary business-driving categories first. Use more seasoned employees to build product modules. Pay your employees to write down four to five questions that help them narrow in on how to assess a customer's needs. Then describe three to four product attributes that meet those needs.

For example, questions about whether a customer is a private consumer or a small business, how many guests will attend a party, food allergies, typical commute distance and other relevant questions can impact the products a smart employee recommends.

Have more-experienced employees teach new employees how different products meet a variety of customer needs to build expertise across the entire staff.

Pay employees to read helpful websites and owner's manuals. Give employees permission to take a half hour every week to improve their knowledge of the products they sell. Then, to hold them accountable, ask them to either train the rest of the staff on what they learned or ask them questions about the content to ensure they understand how to translate their new knowledge to helpful advice for customers.

A smart way to make the translation is to use the "so what?" method of challenging each product feature. For example, if a product feature is "LED versus incandescent bulbs" the "so what?" for a customer is that the light will be brighter and the bulb will last longer, providing a lower cost to operate than incandescent products. That translation will help a customer make a purchase decision easier – and make the staff member a more trusted advisor.

**Document Internal Operational Processes**

Make them available online so that employees see them as they begin automated tasks or laminate job aid cards in appropriate locations to assist with manual step-by-step tasks. Rather than reward an employee because they have memorized the five steps to receiving an order, document the five steps and mount it at the delivery door. Operational procedures can be documented and you do not need have a direct training for each one. If your staff is focused on creating a customer-centric culture, the operational procedures can be relegated to need-to-know training that occurs as they are encountered.

Because so many store operators train new employees in the wrong order (procedures first, then product knowledge, then customer service), they actually create their own poor customer experiences. A store that begins with unwavering customer service first will be more successful and profitable than one that focuses on operations with its new employees.

## WIN Today

Ensure that the first training module for all new employees is focused on customer service.

Look for operational procedures in your store such as receiving deliveries, putting away orders, packing customer orders, changing online orders in process or counting cash drawers and then document the steps. Use Word or PowerPoint to create easy-to-follow instructions. Laminate and post the instructions in locations where the tasks are done. Have new employees use a dry-erase marker to check off the steps as they learn the process.

## Scheduling: Curing a Retail Headache

Making the schedule is the most dreaded chore for most store managers. Setting a store schedule that is fair, efficient and predictable is a difficult task. Most store managers find that associates want to work at the same hours that customers are least likely to shop (weekday mornings.) Retail hours that include weekends and evenings inevitably collide with family plans. Requests for time off, vacations and a little flexibility for illness or other unforeseen issues make it even more complicated.

First, scheduling has to fit within the budget. If a store has a $650,000 annual sales goal and payroll is 11% of the budget, only $1,375 is available each week for payroll. That's a tight limit and hours have to be allocated in the best way to match customer needs. Educate your employees that hours are allocated based on sales. Higher sales leads to more money for scheduling employees. Therefore, the way to increase take-home pay is to improve sales. Carefully monitor productivity of part-timers and reward discretionary hours to those employees who demonstrate high performance. Help employees connect their friendly greetings, sales techniques and appreciation at the cash register with the amount they see in their paychecks.

Next, look at the peak hours for assisting customers. Usually just as the store opens, over lunch and after standard work hours. Remember, customer needs come before vendor deliveries, back room tasks and other store operations. Use your POS system to track transactions per hour over several weeks or months and create a schedule that augments management during peak customer hours. Usually that means scheduling part-time assistance during evening and weekend shifts. Keep those shifts in mind when interviewing and hiring job candidates. Explain and reinforce that part-time positions require availability during your busiest times.

When associates withdraw or limit their availability, scheduling managers have tough choices to make. There comes a point when employees can make themselves so unavailable that keeping them on staff makes little sense. Changes happen. Employees who were steady weekend workers may suddenly only make themselves available for work on Monday and Thursday mornings. Address issues as soon as they come to your attention to reinforce the need to have employees work during high customer- volume hours. As a guideline, many retailers have a policy that says employees must commit to making themselves available for 30 hours for a 20-hour part-time work week or 54 hours for a 40-hour full-time work week.

**You Need *Flexibility*, They Need *Predictability***

It is a balancing act to keep a store operating efficiently and employees satisfied with their work schedules. Good practices are to:

Always post hours and schedules at the same time. Whether monthly or weekly, your employees should know when you post the work schedule so they can plan accordingly. Have schedules posted online or accessible via the web for even more convenient visibility. If you do not have a private intranet site, you can use other options to support your team, such as a private dropbox.com account, a closed Facebook group, teamup.com calendar or a private Google calendar.

Have a consistent policy for accepting vacation and other time-off requests. Make time-off requests public as soon as they are known so that staff members can see when multiple requests could be denied. Publish known vacations and approved time off early and consistently so that they are visible to the entire staff.

Establish consistent, fair and public consequences for tardy shift starts, unexcused absences and long breaks. While unreliable transportation, ill children and sickness happen for everyone, address issues quickly and balance being understanding with the needs of the store and the remainder of the staff.

When creating a schedule, it is easy to fall into a pattern that is repeated week after week. While it is critical to have a schedule that is not erratic, be sure to look at the schedule from the point of view of your individual employees. Are you relying on an employee to *"clopen"* (close the store one day and open the store the next) too often? Is one employee protected from working undesirable shifts, causing resentment within your staff? Are you making accommodations for seasoned employees that you do not extend to new employees? Do you have too many employees listed as "on call?" Review your choices objectively. Inspect your decisions for possible favoritism. Your "flexibility" may be seen as favoritism if you seem to show a bias for particular employees.

Prior to publishing a schedule, review upcoming sales, inventory tasks, changes to delivery schedules or other store events that could alter your staffing needs. Always make servicing customers the priority and make decisions in favor of overserving rather than underserving customers. It is a poor choice to augment staff to conduct an inventory by taking away hours to merchandise and sell products during regular store hours.

Not all business hours are equal. Make sure to schedule your strongest employees at your busiest times. A smart manager will ensure that the best sales people are on the floor when the most customers will encounter them.

Changing a schedule once it is published is sometimes unavoidable. But it should be an unusual occurrence. If your schedules change regularly after they are published, make it a point to discuss it at your next store meeting. (You have one at least once a month, right?) Get to the root cause of the changes. Are employees providing late notice of schedule conflicts? Do you have a poor system for recording time-off requests? Are schedules posted late? Are other tasks interfering with making the schedule? Make sure your team uncovers the real issues behind schedule changes and make an action plan to correct them.

For those rare occurrences when the schedule must be changed after it is published, have a process for informing everyone on your team of the change. Consider texting and other real-time notifications so that store associates are not caught unaware of schedule changes.

For many employees, "retail hours" cause burn out. Be aware of the toll long hours can have on employees and their families. Look for ways to acknowledge them with surprise pizzas over the dinner hour shift, a breakfast pastry box for early shifts and hand-written thank you notes (a *free* way to acknowledge staff!) when employees demonstrate praiseworthy flexibility or reliability.

Finally, have a consistent recordable method for clocking employees in and out. Employees need a consistent process for reporting their work hours and absolute confidence in accurate paychecks that reflect hours worked and paid time off.

If there is one critical item to outsource to experts, it is getting payroll done correctly for every employee every time. Even a single hiccup can cast doubt in the most important element for engaged workers: their wallets.

## WIN Today

Review the last 2 months of schedules to see if there are some employees that are incorrectly utilized by "clopening" too often or only working the most (or least) desirable shifts. Review availability with your staff and resolve to create a more balanced schedule that allows your staff to plan their lives around their schedule. Set a specific time and day that your schedule will be posted. Share that with the staff. Every time you miss that schedule, bring in coffee and pastries. Do that enough times and you will stop being late when posting the store schedule.

## You Can Prevent Theft

Shoplifting isn't just a crime against your store. It is a crime against all customers. It's a "cost of doing business" that gets built into the price of products in all stores.

Just as good online retailers build anti-fraud steps into their transaction process, there are steps store managers and employees can take to reduce theft and make their store an unattractive target for would-be thieves.

### Internal Theft

The majority of theft occurs internally. Stores that have loose reporting leave themselves open to employees who take advantage of the situation for their benefit or to benefit their family and friends.

Areas to focus on are: receiving goods, processing discounts, returning products for cash or credit, gift card sales and taking out trash.

You cannot see what you cannot measure. Put processes in place and regularly review reports to identify all "shorts" in comparing packing slips to receipts coming into the store. Make sure all receiving processes require identifying who is receiving the goods.

Look for patterns. Are shorts happening when a certain supervisor or lead is in command? Is it specific to a particular vendor or carrier?

The same is true with discounts, returns and gift card sales. Look for report variances and identify the cashiers on duty. Look for patterns where cashiers have higher-than-normal discount or return percentages. Watch vigilantly for incidents. Then sit down with the individuals and reinforce your policies.

Taking out the trash is one of the easiest ways to hide merchandise. Trash disposal should be done in pairs. (And it is safer for employees in an alley.)

Take immediate action. Once employees know that you have a zero-tolerance policy for internal theft, two things usually happen. Either theft rates reduce or employees decide to leave.

### External Theft

External theft occurs from all manner of people who come through your door. There are amateur and professional shoplifters. Both sets typically work in pairs or groups and will attempt to distract your employees while helping themselves to products on the shelf.

Here are steps to prevent shoplifting:

1.  Whenever possible, avoid situations where only one person is in the store to watch the cash register and the door. Keep a minimum of two people in the selling area of the store.

2.  Assign someone to the front door as both a greeter and to look for signs of shoplifting. Stores that greet every person put shoplifters on notice that they are seen. Shoplifters may wear large bulky clothing when it is too warm for such apparel, perhaps walk stiffly to conceal items and appear to watch employees more than shop.

3.  While they are in the store, simply asking to assist and keeping a vigilant eye on suspicious people will often send them out the door to an easier target down the street.

4.  Put high-value, easy-to-steal items behind the counter or in a locked case. While making it more difficult to steal, realize it also makes it more difficult to sell. Since customers cannot help themselves to items or browse the goods, always station assistance nearby to get products for any shoppers interested in making a purchase. Keep tempting items directly in front of counters where they are in view of both cashiers and shoppers.

5.  A tidy store with good sight lines will help employees keep an eye on goods. Eliminate blind corners. Place a mirror or cameras to allow management to have full view of all areas. Consider cameras at the front door at a minimum to allow police or others to identify perpetrators should a crime occur. Keep signs about shoplifting and persecution visible at all entrances.

6.  Strictly monitor policies such as checking bags and packages brought into the store, requiring receipts for returns or refunds, destroying discarded receipts immediately and stapling or sealing bags after purchases to prevent other items from going into the bag after a small sale.

7.  Keep a watchful and friendly eye out for your neighbors. Shoplifters will move along a street or shopping area. Immediately let your neighbors know when you have had an incident and keep communication lines open to make your shopping district safer.

8.  Institute a code name for suspected shoplifters in the store as well as an actual stealing incident. A message like "Derek to the front desk" can mean that there is a group that appears to be working the store for an incident and all employees are to have eyes up. While a message like: "Jessica is needed in the back room" can be the signal for an active theft in the store. All employees' eyes on the door while a manager approaches the suspect.

When an incident occurs, have plans in place and continually reinforce training to your team. Address someone taking something, by asking "May I ring that up for you?" Remain calm and professional. Assume that a misunderstanding has taken place. Treat the suspect in a polite, yet firm and professional manner to avoid a slander, false arrest or discrimination lawsuit.

Have plans in place to determine when and who calls the police, if necessary. Have a standard plan in place that is applied fairly for determining when to persecute versus simply getting the goods back.

Vigilance, a clear plan and consistent communication with staff and customers will make your store less attractive to thieves and keep your merchandise out of the wrong hands.

## WIN Today

Explain to staff that besides being friendly, a greeting to every single customer gives notice to would-be thieves that they are identified. Most shoplifting occurs in stores where there is little interaction from staff. An engaged customer-service model where customers are always greeted and attention is paid will not only increase sales but also decrease theft.

Take time this week to have a conversation with your neighboring stores in the mall or street where you operate. Talk about rates of shoplifting and agree to open communication lines between stores to alert one another when there are amateur or professional "hits." If you are not a part of a merchant association or chamber of commerce, invite a police representative to join a few of you for an informal coffee to discuss preventing shoplifting and what to do when it occurs.

## Five Ways to Sabotage Your Business

Is your store stagnating? Is the ebb and flow of revenue a repeating pattern? Are you achieving the growth you once dreamed of? If you are ready to make a change, the first place to start may be *you*.

### 1. No One Does It Like I Do

I call this *getting the leader out of the way*. Store leaders who believe that only they can handle customers, vendors, merchandising, pricing – even clean the bathrooms – to their strict standards should recognize that they are creating a bottleneck. The message that the staff receives is: I don't have to do my best because I will fall short and the job will be re-done by the boss anyway.

Leaders who delegate properly, train, communicate and encourage their teams. The goal is to empower the staff and give them autonomy. Staff accountability is undeniable. But first, store leaders must be able to accurately convey exactly what they expect and give the staff a safe place to practice.

Employees improve their skills under managers who have the discipline to not take away delegated tasks after each mistake. A manager who can help staff members link their tasks to the company's strategy will be able to keep motivation high for even the most mundane tasks. Remember: give staff the final goal, the one or two things you expect and the one or two things you cannot accept. Then let them complete the goal. If you find yourself ordering people around, you will get a bare-minimum performance. And always be in your own way.

### 2. Hiring the Wrong People (Ones Just Like You)

Take a look at the staff you have hired. Do they look and sound a lot like you? Did you hire people because you wanted them to be like you? Are you disappointed that they are not motivated by the same things you are? Great managers hire people who are different from themselves to shore up their weak areas.

Do you love customer service, but hate details? Hire someone detail-oriented and understand that their penchant for minutiae will make you crazy at times. Prefer back-room operations to sales? Hire a strong "people person." Let them have the freedom to interact with customers without requiring them to do inventory or tasks that will make them unhappy. If you are an ideas person, get someone who is very focused on project planning and makes checklists. If you are the checklist person, hire a creative person and let them try out at least one unusual idea a month.

The critical requirement in hiring right is to both hire for your weaknesses *and then* maintain composure as their differences annoy you month in and month out. It is when you blend the strengths from many different talents that your store will break out of the current limits you've created.

### 3. Focusing on Operations

Yes, your store staff must learn how to use the register, void a transaction and put inventory away. But if those are the first tasks in your training program for new hires, you are setting yourself up for lost sales. The first training component should **always** be focused on your customers. The first thing any new employee should learn is how to greet customers, how to help customers, how to be approachable and recognize when a customer requires assistance. Every other training module should link back to customers. There is a surprisingly high expectation set with new employees when their first training day is focused on customer service and *not* how to use the cash register. Examine what you emphasize the first day on the job with new employees and make adjustments so everyone knows that the most important job in your store is taking care of customers.

### 4. Falling Victim to Being a Victim

Looking at sales every night and week can lull a manager into believing they are like a bobber on the ocean. Some waves lift the bobber and some troughs drop the bobber. Many store managers see customer traffic and sales the same way. Do you say "I can't sell to them if they are not coming in the door?" Or "I can't sell if I don't have what they want?" Like all sayings, there is only a kernel of truth in those retail clichés.

Truth is, managers need to ask:
- Are we getting better?
- What can we do to get better?
- Was every customer acknowledged and helped?
- Was there an authentic conversation about their situation that brought them to the store?

If so, each customer could have been inspired to purchase an extra item or two. If each customer was genuinely appreciated for their visit, your business will seem to grow on its own. Because your customers will do your marketing as they walk out the door with a great experience.

There is always something a retail manager can do to make a

difference. Post an immediate promotion on Twitter for a slow afternoon, step out of the store and call on other retail neighbors and see how you can help one another, clean the store's curb appeal and make sure you have a fresh new window display to entice customers. Managers who lean on the counter and complain about a lack of traffic are buying into the victim mentality.

## 5. Knowing Enough

Even basic retail technology usually has more capability than anyone in the organization uses. Think about something as simple as a Microsoft Excel spreadsheet. Chances are, you use Excel. You may even think you are a proficient user. But do you actually use everything in the menu? Know how to create a single-stroke macro to quadruple the speed of repeated tasks? Build a scenario? Use conditional formatting to highlight exceptions? Chances are you do not.

Now think about your POS system, your HR system, your bookkeeping system. If you are like most store teams, someone on your staff knows *just enough* to do the same weekly or monthly tasks. Or create the same routine reports. Meanwhile, there are new insights and ways to improve your store's business locked in those systems because no one has taken the time to learn all of the capabilities in the systems you already own.

Consider using your bookkeeping system to look at profitability by customer, by sales person, by time of year. Use the scheduling system combined with the POS system to track sales by shift leader. There are dozens of new ways to extract the information that is locked in your invoicing, receiving, scheduling, merchandising, POS and other systems that could give you a breakthrough insight. Profitability is locked away because no one has made it a priority to learn more than "enough."

Retail is tough. Customers have so many choices. But a retail leader has to recognize that there are many choices made each day that will lead to profitable growth or stagnation. That is not in the hands of the customer. It is in your control.

## WIN Today

Look at your habits and note if you have any self-sabotaging characteristics. Use the topic to guide you to more empowering behaviors as a store leader.

Spend an hour reading the user's manual or "Help menu" or watching YouTube videos to learn how to do something new with a system that you feel you only know "enough" about. Teach yourself how to do something new or ask another store manager you envy to show you how they build reports or track measurements that are helping them run a better store. Force yourself out of your comfort zone with a system to become more proficient and use it to make your store more profitable.

## Who's to Blame When Employees Disengage?

Experienced managers can walk into a store or back room and immediately sense how the business is going. Energy levels are high, employees are on their feet and conversations are open, trusting and focused. They understand the connection to a profitable store.

Businesses in crisis are just as easy to spot. The back room is quiet, customers are watched before being approached (if at all) and hushed conversations are punctuated by cynical laughter, usually at management's expense. The difference is engaged employees.

But I distrust that term: *engaged employees.* Because it makes it sound like it is 100% on the employee to engage with the business. Truth is, the first day on the job, every employee is an "engaged employee." But in the weeks and months that follow, their managers will determine how long they will be able to retain that original enthusiasm for their job and company. Managers determine whether their team is energetic, focused and supportive or if they are defensive clock-watchers.

And by now, there are certainly members of your team that are disengaged. Despite perhaps years of investment on your part in training and routine performance conversations, you may still have a significant portion of the staff that is either overtly or covertly disengaged. According to a UK study[22], a worker on the average 8-hour shift is productive only 3 hours of the time. (Over 2 hours surfing the web, 31 minutes eating and drinking, 45 minutes on personal calls and texts, an hour talking about nonwork things with coworkers. You get the idea.) It's expensive to replace those employees. So how do you get them to re-engage at a high level with their job and your customers?

Notice them. Personally. Every day.

Part of the reason workers lose interest in performing at their best is they believe their work goes unnoticed. As the initial guilt of stepping away from their work becomes replaced with a sense of business as usual, they can get the signal that management will look the other way (literally and figuratively) when they no longer give 100% to their job.

Your job is to be their coach. Coaches watch their team play every single minute of the game and they watch them in practice. Then they provide **lots** of feedback – especially when a player has made small improvements to their skills.

Your job is to be so close to the employees that you can see and recognize when they are making efforts to improve. Even if they are just trying something new, make sure to give them encouragement and support. Let them know you think they are capable and that their efforts make your company a better place to work.

Yes, it also means being close enough to point out when they are falling short – but if you remember the 5::1 ratio (five items of encouragement for every correction) you will see that even severely underperforming employees will rise to the challenge. For some poor performers, the diligent coaching may help them choose a different job.

## Listen to Them

Actively listening to employees means understanding what they mean – not just what they say. Employees communicate a company's culture with comics or signs. Dilbert cartoons in the IT department or signs that say "yesterday was the deadline for all complaints" at the customer-service desk indicate that a base of your employees are actually asking for help. The humor points out that they know they are not being heard. They are not providing the kind of service they are capable of.

Ask to shadow someone on staff, just to learn what it is like to spend a day in their shoes. You will have to work to break down barriers. Be real and nonpunitive. Ask open-ended questions. Listen for obstacles. Investigate their causes. Work on making changes. I'm not suggesting that every request be fulfilled. But listen to them complain about response times from other team members, lack of visibility to timelines from suppliers and other issues that are within your control to adjust.

**Warning:** This *will backfire* if you commit to do something about an issue and nothing changes. You must go into this with the intent to listen, learn and take action. Not on every item. Not immediately. But if you commit to addressing an issue you *must* report back to your team quickly on what will change.

## Believe In Them Again

It takes work to be optimistic in the face of a disgruntled workforce. But if you do not demonstrate belief in their ability to make the company succeed, there is nowhere else for that optimism to come from. Only management can provide sustained belief in the future. No one will have more optimism than you.

Any well-intentioned employee's voice who cheerleads the team will quickly go silent in the face of a disengaged culture. But a manager who finds even one optimistic employee can work together to change the attitude and the productivity of the entire staff.

### A Word About Dark Forces

As you re-commit to your team, get closer to it every day and provide consistent feedback; there will be some who will sit on the sidelines and watch. About 15% will quickly buy in. About 15% will always fight the power. And about 70% will decide which side is winning and then commit. There is hope for them. These are the employees who are waiting to see which attitudes will win: the culture of cynicism and malaise or the power of positivity and energy. They can be led by good managers back to high productivity.

A small percentage of people will make it a personal mission to fight management. You will always be the enemy and any other stance will always be "selling out."

First, no matter what you think you know, you may not actually know who those people are. Sometimes the toughest cases are the ones who most want to believe again. Frequently, the opinion leaders within the team that initially seemed the most intransigent ultimately become the most passionate when they fully engaged.

Sometimes it is the most talented (and perhaps the most bored in their current capacity) who take on the role of rebel leader within the team. Working closely with them to re-awaken their passion can yield tremendous productivity across the team. Those "spectators" will change shortly thereafter. For this reason, it is important that you embark on this effort with an open mind toward every employee.

If an employee has made the choice to stay disengaged and will not change, it is important to have a turnaround conversation about the specific behavior needed to succeed in their role. Talk about behaviors – not attitudes or intentions – and have a deadline. As the employee realizes that there is a change afoot they may choose to leave. Or escalating conversations may lead to their departure. In either situation, a very clear message will reinforce the change with your remaining staff. The malaise of the past is in the past and the team is operating at a new level.

Notice that employee engagement begins with management. If the team in your operation is disengaged, there is only one way to eliminate it and reach new profitability: manage your way out.

## WIN Today

Put yourself in a position to notice how team members work and communicate. Look for something encouraging that you can say to each team member. Watch their reactions. Do they believe you?

Ask to learn how they do their job and what they think could make the task they are assigned easier or more efficient. Do *not* defend the current process. Listen and consider. If tomorrow you still think the current approach is best, explain why. But do it in a way that helps them see what the underlying goal is.

For example, they may question why they have to answer the phone a certain way. Maybe the repetition is boring. Maybe they cannot muster the right excitement in their voice. Ask them how they think the phone should be answered. Explain the key things you want conveyed in answering the phone and ask them how they would do that. Let them start to find solutions to the things that bother them.

If they know you will listen and consider their suggestions, they will be more likely to bring ideas to you. Act on those ideas and give them credit to keep engagement high.

## Why Team Members Quit Their Jobs
### (and how to keep the ones you want to stay)

If you have high turnover and your management team is constantly hiring and training, it's time to examine the employee experience in your shop. Remember "People quit their bosses, not their job."

The *Wall Street Journal*[23] found that 50% of people leave because of their manager. Yes, the other 50% leave because of a change in transportation, another job opportunity or family issues. But half the time, people would like to stay but management has made the job intolerable. If you have high turnover and some employees leave without another job offer, look at how management is contributing to the turnover. Are employees scheduled with enough hours to make ends meet? Are there consistent expectations from shift to shift? Is there a positive atmosphere where productivity is rewarded?

Part of the turnover issue can stem from a store that is overly dependent on part-time staff. Part-time positions by their nature are created from a more transitory work force that experiences high turnover. A full-time position is more commitment from both the employer and the employee. While full-time positions usually require more benefits and pay, in the long run, they can be the more profitable choice. Employers can save money on hiring and training. Employees who feel well-cared for will be more productive. Full-time roles can attract more experienced and professional candidates.

If you operate more than one location and require the flexibility of a part-time staff but have employees who need full-time hours, consider sharing some positions across stores. An employee who can work 20 hours in two stores and still receive full-time benefits may be the win-win solution.

According to the Society for Human Resource Management,[24] the cost to lose a worker is about 6–9 months of their annual pay. Details to help employers understand the true cost of separation (things like separation pay and other costs for the organization to uncouple from the employee) and the costs of replacement (attracting candidates, interviews, training) are on their website. There are also hard-to-quantify costs in morale and lost productivity amongst the employees who remain. Retaining talent and keeping employees engaged is at the top of the list for every manager and store owner.

### Real Reasons People Leave Their Jobs
**They don't like their boss.** It really is that simple. Somewhere along

the way from eager first-day employment until the day they serve their notice, the employee and manager have created an "us versus them" environment. They are no longer on the same team.

**They don't see room for advancement.** This is especially true in a small organization with an owner/manager who "isn't going anywhere." Even dedicated, long-term employees will eventually ask themselves if their career has hit a dead-end. Unless the job is meeting other needs (flexibility, stability, high pay) to such a degree that it outstrips a need for challenge and advancement, this will eventually become the rock in the shoe that causes an employee to change.

**They are offered a better job.** And that usually means more pay. Sometimes employees are not "looking" for another job. Sometimes another job looks for them. Through family or friends or even competition, a good employee can be lured to a new company. And those employees are rarely the ones you want to see go.

For many workers, a job is a place of stability and a fair trade of their time for money and other benefits. But over time, an inevitable restlessness causes employees to question their decision to stay. At that point, what really affects people is their sense of how they are doing versus other people in their peer group. How they are doing compared with their dreams and expectations at this point in their life.

That restlessness is predictable. Life events are trigger points that cause reflection and searching. Events like landmark birthdays (30, 40, 50) class reunions (job searches increase +16% after class reunions!) and work anniversaries (especially at 5 and 10 years) are powerful self-evaluation moments. Weddings, babies and parents becoming ill or passing can also cause unwavering employees to begin questioning their dedication to a job or company.

### When Employees Are "Looking"

Be proactive with information about near-term growth and opportunities that are within striking distance. Talk about something they can do to achieve a goal and be rewarded rather than general information about overall company growth.

"You know, Bill, you are nearly to your quarterly new-client goal of 30 new clients. Sign on five more and you will be eligible for a new-client bonus in your paycheck in March." Or: "The store is ready to take on another full-time manager. If we hit our revenue goal for the first quarter, we will need to promote someone into that position." No promise of guaranteed reward, but such conversations may help an employee see short-term opportunities they overlooked before.

This is far more effective than waiting until there is a competing job offer in hand and then preparing a counteroffer. When a manager is fighting that far back on their heels, they are very unlikely to succeed in the long-term.

### The Risks of a Counteroffer

Imagine that, despite your best efforts, an employee that you rely on has another job offer. What are the risks of the counteroffer?

First, for a person to make the decision to leave, there are more issues at stake than money. Many reasons contribute to the decision to leave. Maybe it is stability, benefits, room for advancement, working with friends. If an employer only addresses one issue ("We will give you more money to stay"), usually the employee will not stay more than 2 years before leaving for good. Money only buys a portion of an employee's loyalty. The only time a counteroffer works to get a good employee to stay for the long term is when all of their concerns are recognized and addressed.

For example, if you know that the length of a terrible morning commute is at the heart of the problem, offering a flexible start time and more leniency on starting time might make a good employee stay on – assuming the job and the money are comparable. Or if short-term family pressure due to illness or children are the cause, offering work-from-home options or other ideas could be effective.

But if the issue is that the employee sees opportunities with another company that you cannot match, offering more money will not be the answer. Mature managers wish their employees the best and remind them that if things do not turn out as they expect, the manager would be eager to welcome them back.

### Retaining Employees

Take a moment and think about your "best employees." Are you tempted to assume your best employees are not at risk? The best employees have a lower tolerance for sticking around once they become disengaged. They do not have a high tolerance for "waiting it out" to see if things get better. They are more likely to be confident that their skills and work ethic can result in a better job if they concentrate on it.

In fact, Gallup studies[25] show that even employees who are technically "engaged" – meaning they are dedicated and positive about their company and their jobs – are at risk:

- One in three admits to not putting in their full effort.
- At least one in four will leave within the year.

- Two in four have low confidence in their coworkers and the company.

It takes true (authentic) relationships to understand the goals employees have for themselves and to realistically create a future vision for them that achieves their goals while remaining at the company. *Engagement* is nearly the same as *connection* – but not quite. Engagement means I show up every day and give my best to the job. But connected employees believe they are part of something bigger. They have a connection to their company that hardens them to competitive offers.

High performance does not always mean high potential. A great employee who may excel on the sales floor with customers can flounder when given new management responsibilities. The engineer who loves the technical details of a service counter may not want to the same responsibilities for creating an employee schedule or maintaining the books. Some high performers do have high potential and will succeed when provided new challenges. But beware of the Peter Principle: taking stellar performers and heaping so many new tasks and responsibilities on their back that they struggle in their new role. In those cases, management can cause an otherwise dedicated employee to question their worth and value as they grapple with new responsibilities.

High performance also does not mean high aspiration. It requires a personal relationship with an employee to understand their dreams and goals. Beware of misidentifying an employee because they show up with a positive attitude – it does not always mean they are looking for advancement. Fast promotions can be as much a driver in leaving a company as lack of forward career progress. Capable but proud, ego-driven employees who reach the breaking point and begin to struggle for the first time will often leave a company because they do not have experience in asking for help.

If you have a stellar employee, don't delegate their management to other people. Talented people need to know they are valued and have access to decision makers. Let them know that they are a critical asset to the company and that they have a bright future. High performing employees who report to merely adequate managers are more likely to accelerate their job searches. Regular interactions with higher management and concise advice about honing specific skills as a prerequisite to career advancement can keep star performers engaged.

Make sure that promotions and accolades go to those who deserve it. Beware of any whiff of nepotism or favoritism. They can derail months of encouragement amongst the entire store staff. Even employees who are not considered "top talent" will work harder when they see that good things happen to people who deserve it.

Don't keep your employees in the dark. Treat your best performers like the assets you need them to be. Make sure they understand the strategy and goals behind promotions, marketing campaigns and decisions. Let them know that you value their understanding and agreement. Give them a chance to provide input, if possible, before making general announcements to everyone on staff.

## WIN Today

Sleuthing for the employees that are about to jump ship is risky business. Instead, make sure that you have conversations with your best, moderate and even poor performers that link their actions to rewards.

Let them know that there is a path from the role they are currently in to a new one. Connect more money or responsibility to learning new skills and becoming independently proficient in new areas. Talk about how the work they are doing (even if it is taking cardboard to the compactor) supports company goals.

Every job is meaningful in retail. Your job is to communicate that to retain employees.

# 7 Timeless Principles

RETAIL: The Second-Oldest Profession
© 2019 Flora Delaney

# Timeless Principle 7: Operations

## Drive Out Costs and Be Efficient

A store that simply hums with energy. Isn't that the goal? Customers being helped and happily buying even more than they planned. People efficiently transitioning from one task to the next. Goods that are swiftly moving from the back door to the sales floor and out the door. Or accurate orders that are picked and delivered to customers on schedule. It's the nirvana of retail. To create a living system or structure within a retail organization, people have to know what they are doing, why they are doing it and how to do it efficiently.

There is perhaps no higher compliment in retail than to be called a good operator. A good operator can walk into the chaos of a mismanaged store and whip it into shape. Good operators have their people in position to meet customer needs. They evaluate reports and measurements early enough to take the right actions before sales tumble. Good operators understand their customers so well that they can anticipate customer demand – even for unique new products. Good operators recognize waste when they see it and make calculated risks to invest in new ideas when they are right.

Sort of sounds like sorcery, doesn't it?

This chapter may not intrinsically make you a good operator. But it will teach you how to do the things all good retail operators do. And by mimicking the steps, before you know it, you will be able to dance. So, get ready to examine not just what you and your team do, but how you do it. Much of being a good operator is making the tacit knowledge of your organization explicit. In other words, most of what is known throughout your organization is known inside people's heads. It is the wisdom of the elders. Handed down from employee generation to employee generation, it is malleable and changes over time. Good operators write down tribal knowledge that exists in the organization. As geeky and dry as process flowcharts sound, they are the backbone for high-execution companies. When people know the standards and how to achieve the standards, they can replicate success despite changes in people or products.

To succeed, you have to be ready to question *everything*. Good operators ask basic questions. Sometimes elementary questions.

- How do we clean the bathrooms?
- Why does the head cashier count down the drawers alone?
- How often do we retrieve shopping carts from the parking lot?

- How long has this can been on the shelf?
- Why do we compact some cartons, but not others?

It isn't easy to approach your operations with the eyes of a new hire – especially for someone who created the business or worked their way up for years. But asking the most basic questions and listening to the answers without judgment will set the stage for making breakthrough changes. Now is when you have to be honest with yourself. Are there reports you never look at? Columns of reports you do not use? You either need to learn what to do with them to become a better operator or streamline them to make better use of internal resources. If you have online services, do you use all of their offerings? We all postpone advanced learning for "when I have time." But in the hectic world of retail, those urgent tasks consume that extra time. Carve out time to learn more about the resources you are underutilizing. Hire someone to teach you how to use Excel better or force yourself to use a vendor web portal to place orders more quickly or sit with the social media team to learn the kind of content they expect from you to stay engaged with your followers.

The point is, operations is where the rubber hits the road and when we must look internally at what we do instead of allotting blame to lazy vendors, difficult landlords, stubborn employees and pesky customers.

Action is the measure of true success. As the **WIN Today** portions of this book have pointed out, there are actions that must be taken to apply the 7 Timeless Principles to your business. In every situation where you move from theory to action ... from thoughts to activities ... you can improve your retail operations. This chapter on operations is the pinnacle of the **WIN Today** approach. Every action in operations can make your store easier to manage, easier to service customers and easier to move merchandise through profitably.

## The Power of the Checklist

Great customer service and sales begin with efficient store operations. Preoccupied team members who prioritize store tasks over customer service drive down sales. Conversely, people who exclusively focus on customer interactions stand idle while their cluttered, dirty store degenerates around them. Both extremes are problems for the store management.

The most common way to prepare the team for an efficient sales day is to habitually use checklists. Checklists support managers.

- **Expect.** Make sure employees know what is expected of them.
- **Inspect.** Follow up to find out if/how it is being done.
- **Respect.** Give good performers respect and they *will* respect your expectations.

The checklist every store needs is the daily opening and closing checklist. There are also weekly, monthly and quarterly checklists. Usually quarterly tasks are rotated into the monthly tasks. To be effective, checklist usage has to be a non-negotiable. Checklists must be used every day by every manager or employee and use of the checklist must be verified. It's like counting calories in a diet: it only works if it is done for every single meal.

To begin, define your expectations for store standards. How should it look every single day before opening? Write out the expectations by location within the store and then build the checklist around it. For example, you may say that you expect the checkout counter to be clean, with fully stocked bags, pens, register paper rolls, a tidy selection of impulse-sale items, the till stocked with sufficient cash, an empty trash bin, and a smiling employee wearing a name badge. Write out similar expectations for the restroom, the stockroom, the entry way and your merchandise areas. To prepare the checkout opening checklist, use your standards and you are on your way.

An **opening checklist** should include: turn off the alarm, prepare the cash register, verify internet and systems connections, adjust the thermostat, clean the counters, floormats and door, restock any empty shelf locations, merchandise products to the front of the shelves, clean and restock restrooms, turn on music, turn on the Open sign. Smile.

A **closing list** would include: turn off the Open sign, lock the front door, run sales or POS reports, run computer backups, count cash and make either a bank or a vault deposit, secure petty cash, clean counters and floors, restock bags, return any stranded goods to their shelf location, survey the sales floor for damaged goods, adjust the thermostat, remove garbage, turn on the alarm, lock the back door. Smile.

Each day's opening and closing checklist should be posted in the back room with a place for initials  and when each step is completed. The general manager is responsible for reviewing the opening and closing checklist. Include additional items to meet your store's specific needs. Using the opening and closing checklist should be a part of all new employee training. The goal of the checklists is to create consistency and accountability. Each day your store needs to open "customer-ready." Postponing opening tasks until after the doors open leads to poor customer service.

Weekly tasks should include: review the employee schedule, run weekly sales, inventory and payroll reports, deep-clean restrooms, clean and remove old items from employee refrigerator, clean and remerchandise rotating sections of the store to include baseboards, shelf cleaning, product dusting, etc., remove old sale signs, put up new sale signs, adjust product price change labels, review non-sale item stock (register paper rolls, bags, cleaning supplies, pens, toilet paper) and reorder as required, review and rotate stock to sell oldest product first (in critical businesses, this may be done daily), restock literature throughout the store, replace light bulbs as needed, conduct weekly team sales meeting.

A monthly task list would include: create the upcoming month's staff schedule, run monthly sales, inventory and payroll reports, return any accumulated products to vendors, cycle count scheduled physical inventory categories or products, monthly store performance meeting with staff recognition, change windows and interior/exterior signs. Cycle in other key items like smoke detector tests and fire drills, following up with notes or calls to key customers, social media posts, and community activities.

The advantage to creating lists is that you can use them as tools to manage your staff. They become the basis of training. You can "certify" employees on each step on the checklist as they move from part-time employees to full-time managers. The steps in the checklist graduate in responsibility and become the basis to rationalize a variety of pay levels as employees gain mastery of each component. Similarly, checklists provide documentation for accountability. It is easier to have performance discussions with employees when you can review accurate and timely checklist tasks completed. Or, in the case of poor performance, when you can review missing checklist items. As with all management tools, the key is consistency and uniform application  with all employees. Managers who use checklists find it easier to communicate priorities and provide baselines for improvement.

Checklists can also help when creating store staff meetings. You can choose to concentrate on key items or rotate through the items as you ensure that everyone is aware of management priorities and expectations. Include sales goals and you quickly have your agenda for a staff meeting completed.

Every well-run store uses checklists to ensure consistency and smooth operations. A store with a routine of checklists will have happier employees who understand what is expected of them and are well prepared for the day's operations. Poorly run stores fatigue employees with constant fire drills that could have been prevented with proper preparation. Adhering to checklists keeps operational fire drills to a minimum. Using a checklist every day and every week keeps maintenance costs down, improves customer service levels and makes for a more enjoyable working and shopping environment. Just don't forget the last step: *smile.*

## WIN Today

Create an opening and closing checklist for every staffed position in the store. If you have a large enough staff, delegate this task with a 1-week deadline. Discuss the weekly and monthly checklists with staff members from a diverse perspective to make sure you include loss prevention, receiving, payroll and inventory tasks.

Consider having your checklists printed on carbonless forms so that you can keep records of the checklists. With enough IT resources, create a digital version of the checklists with automated reminders and exception reports when tasks are not completed on time.

# OPERATIONS

## Efficient Operations = Retail Profit

Efficiently handling store operations can make the difference between a store with a positive profit contribution and a going-out-of-business sign in the front window. Operators who sustain profits over the long haul and withstand economic downturns always operate in a streamlined fashion. They know that work steps must be logical, repeatable and waste-free. Whether the process is receiving a truckload of produce or emptying the waste bins, every process in a retail environment can be optimized for efficiency.

Signs of an inefficient operation are easy to spot: Different people do the same task different ways. Only the most senior staff members know how things are done. Information lives primarily on Post-it notes or notepads. Work is unevenly distributed because only certain staff members know how to do things. Some operations have to be suspended when key staff members are on holiday. Tasks are often left half done at the end of a shift. If that sounds like your operation, it's time to build and document standardized operations.

To generate more profits, savvy managers put themselves in a position to observe and notice how work is completed in the store. The largest opportunities are processes that are repeated often throughout the day or week, done by multiple employees or large investment items.

Examples are:
- Receiving and putting away inventory
- Picking and packing web or delivery orders
- Conducting transactions at the register
- Returns and exchanges
- Physical inventory counts
- Opening and closing the store
- Making deliveries to customers

The key to developing the most efficient processes possible is to understand how the process is completed currently. In other words, someone has to take the time to write out the steps of the process. Or, if you are more tech-savvy, the easy way is to use a smartphone to video the steps in the process. Start with the person who is most efficient or who most commonly completes the task. Use the video to document:
1. *What steps* are in the process
2. *What materials* are needed to complete the process
3. *When* is the process *completed*

**Sample Checklist: Putting Away an Order**

The steps in the process are:
1. Check in the goods received against the purchase orders and packing list.
2. Enter the stock into the store inventory.
3. Merchandise fresh merchandise behind current stock on the shelves.
4. Place excess inventory in the back room.

The materials needed are:
1. The original PO
2. A hand truck
3. A box cutter
4. Access to a computer

The process is completed when the entire order has been "worked into the store."

However, every person may do the process differently. Is there room to improve accuracy and speed by counting the stock in a certain way? Do the best employees also use their time re-stocking the shelves to dust the shelves and current inventory? Do they reprint missing price stickers? Do they put away stock in a well-labelled location so everyone can find it or just the nearest empty spot in the back room? What if the order is incorrect and product is missing? Watch people, ask questions and document the process to devise the most efficient process possible.

Let's say that you have documented the most efficient process to do anything: cleaning the store, changing prices, closing the books each month. The best operators know that *managing the processes* is what sets well-run stores apart. There are three keys to managing processes:
1. Setting up the team for success – training and tools
2. Consistency – predictable, unwavering rhythms
3. Measuring outcomes – inspect what you expect

To set your team up for success, the first step is training the process to new hires as well as current staff. There should be job aids where the process takes place. It can be as simple as a checklist or as sophisticated as an online program to track job status.

Think of two different processes: cleaning the bathroom and preparing a web order.

To clean the bathroom, there should be a set of tools in one place (bucket, mop, disinfectant, towels), a scheduled rhythm for completing the task and a notice when the job is completed. The steps may be clean mirror, clean sink, clean toilet, mop floor every day at close of business and date and initial cleaning checklist on the back of the bathroom door. The job should take 15–20 minutes. The job should be inspected in 1 minute. Explain this to the person being trained. Assign them the duty and inspect it until it is completed correctly. Expect it every day (consistency) and be in a place to notice if it is being done completely each day. Have an easy system for replenishing supplies and that process can be considered well-managed if it meets the standards for cleanliness when it is expected each day.

To prepare a web order, the process is the same: Set up the team for success by giving them a dedicated space to pull and print orders, a systematic way to select inventory to meet the order, a standard way to package and label the order and a rhythm of picking up completed orders every day. Time the steps to complete different kinds of orders and manage labor hours to meet those needs. For example, if a consumer order (less than ten items) takes 6 minutes to process and there are 10 orders, expect to complete those in an hour. If a commercial order (over 25 items) takes 15 minutes to process and there are 10 orders, expect your employees to complete that in 2.5 hours. Evaluate labor hours against order completion rates to manage the outcomes effectively. Actively measure order accuracy.

While process management may seem like it requires heartless focus, the truth is a manager can be well-liked and drive an efficient team. Teams that know what is expected of them, who can rely on a consistent process to complete tasks and who have the tools and equipment to do their job right are happier because the tedious tasks of the day can be handled swiftly. Leaving more time to be creative in sales or merchandising. Staff members quickly get disgruntled when "normal" day-to-day operations are handled differently by different people or if only the most tenured people really know where things are or how to do something. Operations are smoother and more reliable when you document your processes while holding the team accountable to meeting standards every day. We call it a frictionless environment. And in retail, "friction" is waste. To increase profit, reduce the friction in your processes.

## WIN Today

Select one critical process each week that is not documented in your store. Video someone completing the process and document it. Use PowerPoint or Visio if you have those tools. Otherwise, it can be Post-it notes on a wall. Once you have completed the initial process "map" ask for feedback from the team on steps that can be improved to make the process more efficient and consistent.

Each week focus on that process and then communicate to the affected staff the new process and expectation to complete that task. Begin to manage and measure the process to make sure that it is being followed and yields the results you expect.

Place your process documentation in a public place where staff members can find it: a shared network drive or online data center or at the appropriate location for the work.

## Pushing and Pulling – Which Is Right for You?

Retailers either use a push or pull inventory system.

**In a *Push* Operating Model**

A corporate resource selects products, develops a sales forecast, delivers products to stores to supply that forecast and replenish products from a headquarters system. This is common in fashion retailing where new lines are sent to stores in one or two waves throughout a season. Typically, stores cannot determine which products they receive or how many cases will be allocated to their store. Store team members receive the product and then merchandise it as directed by headquarters or a regional office.

In a push model, it is critical that the headquarters is very competent in predicting sales trends and forecasting sales by store. Otherwise, customers are disappointed by out of stocks. Or there are gluts of stranded products that have to be marked down at the end of the season.

One of the benefits of this model is that store teams do not have to select their own assortment. It keeps hard-selling vendors out of the stores. Vendors are typically limited to influencing the corporate location and stimulating sales with consumers. Vendor sales representatives would waste their time in stores trying to influence store managers as they have no control over purchasing.

Centralized control has other benefits. Purchases are made at volume discount levels. Stores are uniformly managed and merchandised. Vendors are held to delivery standards. There is more financial control for the organization within a corporate budget.

The drawbacks of centralized control are the risks involved anytime decisions are so far removed from the end customer. The buyers may not understand the competitive situation in the market or the regional taste of the customers. Furthermore, the forecasting model has to be tremendously accurate to eliminate out of stocks and overstocks at the store level. Store conditions can deteriorate quickly. Loaded pallets stack up on the sales floor some months and empty shelves are a blight other months. There has to be a fast-response feedback loop from the stores to the central location for this model to be efficient.

Another drawback is the lack of engagement at store level in the push model. It is easy for store team members to portray themselves as victims when products do not stimulate sales or poor replenishment systems cause out of stocks. Without the responsibility to successfully select and price products, the store team can disengage in the process of selling them.

**In a *Pull* Operating Model**

Stores select which products and how much they will carry. This is typical in most co-op models (like True Value or independent grocers) or franchises, like Hallmark stores. The store management selects among the breadth of products offered by the wholesaler(s) and decides what they will carry, where it will be merchandised and how much inventory to carry.

Replenishment is at the discretion of the store through store-created purchase orders. To automate the store orders, the sales data may be transmitted to the replenishing warehouse where automated orders are created to maintain a minimum inventory level. Vendors who call on these retailers typically devote substantial sales resources to influence stores or store groups. Stores have authority to purchase new product lines, change prices, support promotions and increase order levels.

The benefit of a pull operating model is that the decision about product selection, quantities and timing are closer to the customer and should anticipate true sales rates better. Thus, a store owner in Dallas can receive garden supplies in February while a store owner in Minneapolis can delay them until May if spring is particularly cold. Store management can meet niche product requests and manage the inventory better in the store for the true store conditions.

Generally, store teams are more invested in the success of the products they select themselves. Since they see vendors on a regular cadence, they may get more education and training about new products and how to present them to customers.

The drawbacks are that there is little financial control in place to prevent poor decisions from scuttling store performance. Also, stores can vary wildly in their presentation to customers. Inventory bulges and shortages can crop up unpredictably across the system. Vendors may wield control over inexperienced managers suggesting merchandise that may not be in the best financial interest of the store. There is more unpredictability in the financial performance of the entire system.

Purchases can be made without reaching full volume discounts. Vendors can multiply as each store finds their own source for common goods. So, power-buying opportunities are lost when vendors are not consolidated.

In the extreme version of a pull model, online storefronts use vendors as their fulfillment houses. The online storefront showcases products that are shipped and delivered by its vendors. For online retailers who are in that lucky position, the risks of excess inventory fall on the vendor.

However, vendors usually require a minimum monthly or quarterly volume to agree to those terms. Consider how to strike a balance by bringing best-selling SKUs into your inventory while fulfilling secondary SKUs directly from the vendor.

### Many Retailers Use a Blended Model

Grocers typically use a blend of both models. The center of the store uses the push model. Product is controlled from a central location. As sales draw down store inventory, more cases are delivered to the store. Replenishment is managed to meet the estimated demand based on market trends and known future price changes. Meanwhile, the perimeter departments use a pull model. The produce manager, bakery/deli manager and meat/seafood manager make their own purchases from local sources to ensure the freshest selection.

In your store(s), there may be a combination of conditions that will determine your optimal operating model. The push model requires systems that can accurately forecast sales and allocate inventory across stores. That requires investments in both people and IT. Once a small chain expands past a handful of stores, the buying power and financial control of a push model is usually justified. The pull model remains a darling of companies like Whole Foods and others who insist on making decisions as close to the end customer as possible. To succeed, pull models require savvy store managers who shoulder the financial accountability for their store's investments and performance.

## WIN Today

Identify the inventory and replenishment model used in each department of the store. Review the risks of each model and take steps to mitigate them.

In push models, store teams become distanced from the products. Make sure you have training in place that explains new products and projects excitement behind their new benefits to customers. Work on keeping your feedback to corporate resources as updated as possible to make sure that they are fully aware of your customers' unique needs and your store conditions.

In pull models, carefully monitor aggressive vendors who can oversell products. Have a repeatable process for testing and measuring new product success rates to help you improve your batting average on selecting winners. Leverage your online storefront to help select winners quickly before moving inventory into your brick-and-mortar stores.

## Is Inventory a Verb or a Noun?

Is inventory something you *do* or something you *own*? First, remember that the goal of inventory is to satisfy customers. In a perfect world, every customer who enters a store or online storefront finds enough stock of everything they want for sale.

*Managing inventory* reduces the chance of running out of stock and losing sales or holding too much stock of low-selling goods that require deep discounts to reduce to reasonable levels. *Taking inventory* is a practice well-run retailers do regularly to account for store stock, ensure that books accurately reflect the sellable goods and to identify and prevent internal or external theft. It is a critical step in inventory management called **inventory control.**

Your stock or inventory of goods reporting should reflect the quantity of products you have in the store and warehouse for every SKU. As products travel into and out of your store or warehouse, there are several points where there should be an accuracy check.

The first point is receiving goods. As vendors or distribution centers ship products into the store or fulfillment warehouse, there should be a process of thoroughly counting the goods received and verifying the received quantities against the purchase order quantities. Any abnormalities should be directly noted and addressed with the shipper immediately. Most shippers have locked procedures to keep high-value items secure. Mis-ships happen whenever received quantities do not match the PO-requested quantity. Any additions to stock should be reflected immediately in the store's inventory reports.

Another way that product can be added to store inventory is when customers return sellable goods. When a customer returns a product previously purchased and it is in reasonably good shape for sale to another customer, it must be added to the store's inventory ledger. Damaged goods should be entered into a damage/destroy account or a "return to vendor" (RTV) account. When a customer exchanges a product, a secure practice is to add the returned item to inventory before deducting the new item from inventory. That way there is a clear record of the transaction should there be a question of fraud in the future.

Products are typically deducted from the inventory as they are sold. Most retailers have a daily reconciliation of the inventory in the store with the day's sales deducted. Products that hit a critical inventory level trigger a re-order to keep shelves full. E-commerce retailers usually process inventory reconciliation in real time and do not postpone it for a nightly batch report.

# OPERATIONS

The daily processing of receipts and sales creates a live inventory stock ledger that accurately reflects the stock on hand in the store. To conduct an inventory count, some retailers hire a third-party service. But for those who will do it themselves they will need to freeze the inventory stock ledger and count the physical goods to verify the ledger's accuracy.

To prepare for an inventory count (usually conducted when the store is closed or the warehouse is not operating) it is a good practice to prepare by doing the following steps:

1. Conduct a merchandising sweep of the sales or warehouse floor moving all products to their "home" location. If products are in multiple locations (on a shelf and at the cash wrap or on an endcap) note the secondary location at the home location.
2. Conduct a back-room sweep moving all products from the back room to the sales floor, if possible. Otherwise, organize the back room into logical segments with all similar SKUs grouped together and accessible. Count all back-room stock and move the back-room counts to the home locations.
3. Organize the inventory counting by assigning employees to specific product lines or sections of the store or warehouse. Provide them with the live ledger and have them note the physical counts on the live ledger.
4. Double-check inventory count accuracy by randomly selecting SKUs from the ledger and conducting a second count. Use any discrepancies to teach employees better methods for maintaining inventory accuracy.
5. Conduct second counts on any SKUs that deviate from the live ledger.
6. Once you are certain that all inventory counts are fully accurate, reconcile the live ledger and stock-on-hand reports by deducting or adding stock to the variant SKUs. Delve into discrepancies and look for root causes such as: improper intake processes when receiving goods, damaged goods improperly deducted from inventory, theft, improper accounting for returned goods. Use inventory counts to look for ways to improve training and accountability among your staff.

Inventory is a great time to develop the staff. First, putting a junior manager in charge of this critical process can begin to encourage growth and responsibility to expand their skills in leadership, communication, process management and accuracy. Be clear that this is a development exercise and an important step in their maturation into a full-fledged manager. Use the process to observe how they handle decision-making and communication with other employees. Take time to provide feedback and coaching.

Inventory can be a time for team building as well. Set goals with the team for accuracy levels (98% accuracy is a world-class target). Take a pizza break, a karaoke break or a lottery break to keep the task of counting products livelier. Once inventory is completed, share back results with the team and reinforce the goals with a small recognition or a team reward.

Depending on the inventory fluctuation, the value of the inventory and the sales churn within the store, you can determine the frequency of conducting physical inventories. Some retailers only conduct inventory once a year but "cycle count" key products (conduct a mini physical inventory) once a month or once a quarter. Obviously, a car dealership will require 100% accuracy and will establish a practice to reconcile inventory every day. A grocery store may only conduct its inventory once a year, but cycle count high-value razor blades, medication and gourmet foods monthly, for example.

One of the main benefits of analyzing inventory is to rebalance inventory levels. Use your reporting to calculate average inventory levels and look for imbalances in inventory to sales ratios. Products naturally move from introduction to mature life to decline. Be alert to sales indications that a SKU is moving from one phase to the next and make inventory and re-order level adjustments. Creating a tighter but more balanced inventory-to-sales ratio will make your inventory investment more productive.

Useful inventory measures include *average cost of inventory* or *cost of goods sold* – COGS - (which should be managed as a specific percent of sales based on your margins and pace of growth), *inventory aging* (to alert you to pockets of underperforming products), *inventory turn* (the number of times the inventory churns through your store based on its annual sales rate and its average monthly inventory level) and *gross margin return on inventory* (GMROI) to understand the productivity of turning dollars invested in inventory into profit. Every key inventory management measure must first be grounded in reliable inventory control practices.

]

## WIN Today

Align your inventory physical counts with the best practices outlined in this topic. Elevate your role to overseeing the process instead of counting products. Use your next inventory count as a development exercise for a junior manager. Take note of employees who are particularly accurate and encourage them to use their attention to detail for other critical processes each day. Measure your inventory investment against sales rates using GMROI, inventory turns and aging to make sure that your purchases are meeting customer demand.

## Turning Inventory into Cash

Wouldn't you like to predict how well you turn inventory into cash? You can by using the most common operational measurement in retail: GMROI or *gross margin return on inventory* (or GMROII – *gross margin return on inventory **investment***).

You can turn inventory into cash a couple of different ways:

- **Turn and churn** – A product with a very low profit margin that sells quickly can yield a high GMROI. If you keep your inventory turning quickly and replenish the product before it is ever out of stock, this is an ideal situation.
- **High margins** – Slow-turning stock needs to earn its keep on your shelves (or in the warehouse). It can do that by providing rich profit each time it sells. Think of a Rolex watch. There are a lot of inventory dollars tied up in that watch, but you only need to sell one to make a very handsome profit.

It is important to understand your GMROI – the average for your range of products and the specific GMROI for each product you carry. Once you do, you can create a strategy for increasing your GMROI – which means making your store more profitable.

First, let's do the math:

$$GMROI = \frac{Annual\ Gross\ Margin\ \$}{Average\ Inventory\ Carrying\ Cost}$$

So, if you carry $20,000 in inventory on average (measuring the monthly ending inventory and averaging that for the last 12 months) and your annual gross margin profit is $50,000, your GMROI is 2.5. For every $1.00 you keep into inventory, you usually get $2.50 in profit each year. GMROI can be calculated by the month or the week. But in a highly seasonal business, those measures can be misleading – especially with clearance and closeout products that sell off quickly without being replenished.

As a retailer, carrying inventory is a cost of business. It is an investment in the business and as such, it is a balance sheet asset. As an investment there should be constant reinvestment of the balance sheet asset into more inventory to keep up with customer demand. But it will change over time as your business grows or shrinks. Savvy retailers keep it a fixed percentage of forecasted sales. The sales forecast drives the inventory investment (known as *open-to-buy*). Indeed, it should be a managed resource and planned for, just like scheduling store associate payroll hours.

### How to Improve Your GMROI

**Reduce your stock levels to more closely align to your sales levels.** Investing in 36 units of a product when you only sell 12 units per month is a drag on GMROI. Look at sales rates and reduce your purchase quantities while increasing your purchase frequency to improve GMROI. This should free up inventory dollars to be reallocated to different stock or other investments. Or you can move the inventory investment from the balance sheet to the bottom line of your profit-and-loss (P&L) statement. This will likely cause you to:

**Buy more frequently.** To keep inventory turns brisk, plan to rebuy (and restock) more often. Beware of front-loading seasonal and holiday products, which will cause a drag on inventory turns. Retailers who purchase holiday items and store them from September until November are banking on high sell-through. Most negotiate extended terms to keep the inventory off their books for as long as possible.

**Buy in lower quantities.** Of course, those volume discounts from your vendors look appealing, but if it loads you with months of inventory gathering dust, is it a real bargain? Only buy in larger quantities than necessary if the vendor is willing to make a special payment offer (like letting you pay for the goods with an additional 60 days of financing). Speaking of payables terms:

**Increase your payables terms.** If you can increase your payables from 30 to 45 days and you can increase your stock turns to 12 times/year you will, in effect, sell your stock before you have to pay for it, making your GMROI on that product infinite. *That* is the golden goose of retail. (And lest you think that is impossible, it is *not*. Easter candy is a great example. Many retailers carry vast quantities of Easter candy because their vendors will take back any candy that is unsold after the holiday and the payment for the candy inventory is not due until after Easter. With a deal like that, why wouldn't a store fill up its shelves with Easter candy?)

**Move to consignment sales.** If your vendors have a consignment option that makes sense for your store, consider changing to that program. Magazines, milk, bread, batteries, greeting cards, candy and many other businesses are consigned, meaning that the vendor owns the inventory in your store and you only "pay on scan." When you sell those goods to customers, you pay the vendor for the number of products sold. Think of it like the vendor fulfillment model in online retailing. For most retailers who have a GMROI measurement, consigned goods are excluded in reports. But the more product that is moved to consignment, the less the retailer has to invest to achieve sales.

**Cut your losses.** Know when that sludge inventory is dragging you down. If your customers have seen the same product four or five times and are not buying it, chances are they are not going to any time soon. Inventory dollars that are tied up in products no one wants prevents you from being able to reinvest those dollars into new products they *do* want. Accept the fact that you bought something undesirable. Every retailer strikes out from time to time and even the best can "fall in love" with a product their customers don't want to buy. Markdown the product, move it to the clearance rack and be grateful to get anything you can (even losing money) just to be able to buy something new that will entice your customers.

**Increase your margin.** I realize in today's economy, raising prices is unacceptable and expenses have been cut. But in the real world of retail, any way you can improve the margin while still being price-competitive is a sustainable strategy. If you must raise prices, consider offering a lower price to club members or during special shopping events. (Amazon Prime is this model taken to the extreme.) It allows you to keep an attractive price in the marketplace while limiting the number of transactions at a reduced price. Use coupons, which have a "breakage rate" of people who buy the product without the coupon when you must raise prices. Ask yourself if you can display product in a more simplistic and impactful fashion such as cut cases, floor stacks and other easy-to-merchandise ways to cut down on the labor to merchandise products. Any way you can make your margins richer while maintaining sales will improve your GMROI.

**Know your bogey for more inventory**. As in golf where bogey is one shot over par, GMROI represents your "par" for investing in more inventory. Your forecasted sales and margin have to be over your current GMROI for a new item (or more inventory on a current item) in order to be accretive. Otherwise, you will be diluting your GMROI and slowing down your profit-making machine. Using the example above where GMROI is 2.5, a case of 12 new items with a wholesale cost of $54.00 and a retail price of $69.48 (each piece costs $4.50 and sells for $5.79) needs to sell at least 9 cases in a year to deliver 2.5 ROI. Make sure you look at the required turns and margins when buying new products and be realistic about the sales forecast in light of GMROI.

Remember that while some retailers have GMROI under 1, that is in unhealthy level of inventory productivity that cannot be sustained. To have a healthy store that can weather difficult business cycles, GMROI on every item should be over 1.0.

## WIN Today

Review your GMROI and inventory turns at the total store level and then within each level of your product hierarchy. Look for departments that are dragging down inventory productivity and review the methods listed in this topic to improve inventory investments to make your inventory turn to cash more quickly. Of the many tactics listed, you may only have control over a few of them. If nothing else, review your merchandising and see if you can improve GMROI by placing products in a more visible location.

For online retailers, look at how to share inventory risks with your vendors. Then analyze the navigation to get to unproductive departments. Is it intuitive to your shoppers? Should there be multiple access points to the products? Should your hierarchy or menu system change? Can you test new filtering techniques to make it easier for your customers to find and purchase products on your website?

## Why Cash Flow Is More Important Than Profit

Even the best retailers can find themselves in a cash crunch. Cash flow is the single biggest issue retailers face. Profitable companies can find themselves without access to liquid cash when inventory purchases outstrip sales. As a retailer, getting your hands on cash and keeping cash flow moving through your business can mean the difference between managing through tough economic times and closing up shop. Critical retail measurements like inventory turn and profit contribution are early indicators of a healthy cash flow cycle.

The best possible cash flow situation is when there are purchase deals from vendors that are longer than sales cycles. For example, let's say a vendor offered you a payables program where a $700 purchase needed to be paid in 90 days. Your price markup takes the retail price of that wholesale purchase to $1,000. If your stock sold in 60 days, you would have a positive situation where you sold your goods before you had to pay for them. You would gain 30 days of "float" in your cash flow where you could earn interest on the full sales price of the product ($1,000) before paying out the wholesale price to your vendor ($700).

Now imagine the same scenario where the 90-day purchase took 120 days to sell. Even though the profit rates or margins are the same 42% markup rate, the first situation is far better from a cash flow point of view.

Smart retailers review their financing terms from vendors, control their inventory (stock) and rely on management reporting to maintain visibility to their cash flow.

As important as managing the outflow of cash is managing the cash coming into the organization.

To keep receivables as liquid as possible, encourage cash, credit and debit card transactions whenever possible. But be vigilant in reviewing merchant transaction fees from credit card processors. Transaction fees can eat up profits quickly. If necessary, consider a minimum purchase requirement to use credit or debit cards. (Generally, $5 or $10 as a minimum recovers the transaction fees within a tolerable rate.)

If you have business accounts, keep them on a short payables schedule and monitor accounts receivables to keep customer payments on schedule. Offer longer terms (60 days+) only when you are given a broad concession such as an annual contract or other significant commitment. Invoice all business customers promptly at the close of every business cycle. Make deposits the same day as checks are received. Charge interest and penalties for late payments and offer discounts for early payment in your standard business account terms. Do not offer payment terms to customers without both a background check and a probationary period for timely payments. Aggressively collect payables every business cycle.

Manage your own accounts payable just as aggressively. While it may be good for your credit history, it is a bad cash flow practice to pay every bill when it arrives. Set your timing to pay bills as they come due. If available, use online banking bill payment schedules to manage payables to the exact due date. Ask for discounts from vendors for early payment and ask for longer payable terms when taking on new products or lines from current vendors. After a history of consistent payment, ask for longer payment terms. If you are willing to pay in an electronic direct deposit, *always* ask for a cash discount.

Use a budget of expected expenses (use monthly averages for payroll, rent, utilities, supplies, etc.) combined with planned sales and purchases to create a monthly cash flow budget. Manage your store to that budget by adjusting purchases, pricing and payroll based on weekly sales rates. Give yourself visibility to early warnings about cash flow difficulties and take steps to abate them. If you must, consider talking to your banker about unique situations where cash flow shortages are expected (especially prior to holiday or other seasonal inventory build ups.) Ask for a line of credit – the interest on short-term loans will be cheaper than bank overdrafts and late payment penalties.

Balancing purchases with cost of goods sold each month is critical. The most simplistic early warning indicator for cash flow health is making sure that inventory purchased does not exceed cost of goods sold for any given month. Naturally, there will be specific times of the year when inventories build up in anticipation of seasonal sales. But keeping an eye on inventory purchase levels is a smart gauge to measure cash flow.

For most retailers, poor buying decisions lead to poor cash flow. Obsolete inventory ties up cash. It requires close monitoring to maintain the appropriate level of stock. Spend time to review aging inventory and adjust prices to sell slow-moving products and free up the cash to purchase more attractive merchandise. When possible, automate reporting so that store and shelf inventory older than 60 or 90 days is flagged in your reports then take abatement steps.

For all merchants, taking unplanned markdowns is difficult. Build a small expense budget each month called "unplanned markdowns." Then, when stagnant inventory seizes your cash flow, use a planned markdown strategy on the most troubled products to induce customer sales. The markdown can be offset by the "unplanned markdown" expense line and not have as devastating of an effect on profitability because the markdowns were already built into the budget. Consider setting aside a specific percent of sales each month that is reasonable to cover unplanned markdowns. Begin with 0.5% and adjust as you gain more insight into this troubling issue. Over time you may need to set a fluctuating percentage as inventory from back to school, end of year and holidays may need to be aggressively marked down. Tracking and managing an unplanned markdown budget should also start to reveal patterns about your buying habits and your customer's purchasing habits. Typical patterns to look for include a local affinity for particular colors or flavors that varies from the national average.

Savvy merchants create a markdown plan for stagnant inventory. Product that is non-seasonal and simply is not selling may go on a 25% to 50% to 75% markdown plan where the price changes automatically every 30 days until all of the product is eliminated in 90 days. Seasonal products typically need a more aggressive markdown plan that may be a 50% to 75% markdown completed within 45 days.

Selecting a specific back endcap or other permanent store location for clearance goods is a good merchandising practice. First, it removes poor sellers from the most valuable sales locations in the store. Second, it creates a destination for your bargain-minded shoppers who will regularly shop the discount areas. Bargain hunters can actually accelerate the cash flow and give your store a reputation for having great prices.

As a retailer it is tempting to covet the margins suggested by vendors with their manufacturer's recommended price (MRP). But remember, that their job is to sell you product and yours is to turn every dollar invested into inventory into fresh cash from your customers as quickly as possible. Keep close tabs on balancing inventory and sales to keep cash flow high.

## WIN Today

Make sure that your month-end reports include COGS and inventory purchased as lines within the report. When COGS is larger than inventory purchased, it is an early warning that out-of-stocks could occur. (Thus, sales transactions will be smaller, customers will be unhappy and business will decline.) When inventory purchased is higher than COGS, inventory turns can slow without promotional or seasonal sales to spur increased purchases in the weeks ahead.

Drill into the balance of these two measurements at the department and category level to make adjustments and keep ahead of sales trends.

When people in retail talk about using reports to look into the windshield (predict the future) instead of the rear window (to see performance history), this is what they mean.

## Managing the Back Room

Every retail store has a back room or warehouse. For the purpose of this topic, we will refer to it as the back room – but know that it is the warehouse for online retailers. For brick-and-mortar and online stores, it is truly the heart of the operations. Despite the importance of the sales floor in setting the guest's perception, it is the back room that often sets the tone for the entire store.

All back rooms have the following common critical components:

**The delivery area** – The delivery area is typically a secure area and a transitional zone where product enters the store through a freight dock, is counted and swiftly moved to either the sales floor or warehouse racks. As a staging area, this needs to be large enough to be easily accessed by forklifts and pallet jacks.

**The back-room warehouse** – Typically racking that houses unopened case goods.

Most brick-and-mortar retailers follow the motto "If it's in the door, it's on the floor" to keep back room inventory lean and increase inventory turn. The back-room warehouse should only be used for fast-turning, high-cube product that require daily replenishment to keep sales locations full or high-value theft items that need additional security. High-value items are typically locked and monitored. A secondary back-room warehouse would house all supplies that are not for sale. Shopping bags, forms, cleaning supplies, excess shelving components, sign holders and other functional supplies are in the supply warehouse.

For online retailers, setting up the warehouse and racking is critical in creating the most efficient picking scheme possible. Warehouse management systems ensure that the most common items are stored on the same aisle to make order picking as swift as possible.

**Returns** – Product awaiting pickup or shipment to vendors or recyclers. Again, this product should be secured to prevent theft. Products should never sit in a returns area for more than 1 week.

**Outbound shipping** – For online retailers, a staging area for packages to be shipped to customers. Outbound shipping can be staged in trucks at docks (for very large operations), bins on wheels or stacked neatly for the UPS delivery person. This should be a tightly secured area with locked access and 24-hour monitoring.

**Staff area** – Whether offices, desks on the floor, lunchrooms, lockers or restrooms, a certain amount of back-room space is needed for the comfort and function of the team. More than any other part of the store, a savvy manager can assess the culture of a store by scrutinizing the back-room staff area. Signs of an efficient store with a positive culture include a clean, well-stocked break room, clean restrooms, posted internal metrics (sales, units per transaction, traffic count), personal attention to birthdays or community outings with a positive, fun personality. Dismal backrooms include filthy restrooms, disorganized break rooms, sarcastic comics or notices, passive-aggressive notes (that usually end with "this means YOU...") and general untidiness.

A focus on a tidy and functional back room will make a store easier to operate and a happier place to work.

To create an organized back room, create the zones listed above. Depending on the store, there may also be a repair zone, a fabrication zone, a steam station for apparel or other defined areas where a specific back-room task is completed. Use colored tape to partition the back room into the zones. Make sure that all required tools and components for the zone are within each marked area. A common sign of disorganization and inefficiency is multiple required elements outside of the zone.

Move zone by zone through the back room creating a tidy "home" for each major element. For example, designate a specific location for hand trucks and pallet jacks. Mark the space on the floor so that it is clear where they belong. Much like a carpenter's pegboard tool outline, use outlines to designate the home location of critical tools.

For the warehouse, use colored signs to create categories. Put the fastest-moving items near the door to the store. Use moveable or temporary signs so that categories can ebb and flow throughout the year. An organization scheme (by vendor, by brand, by type, by size, etc.) can make finding things easier for staff members in a rush to help customers. The goal is to be able to scan the shelves and quickly identify every product on the shelf. If there are single items, place them into a bin that is clearly marked with each category name.

If there are seasonal products or decorations, consider moving them to an outside storage location or a high shelf that puts the products out of the way during the rest of the year. Handling products multiple times increases the likelihood of damaging the goods and reducing their value.

To maintain the back room, follow these guidelines:
- Maintaining the back room is everyone's job. However, there should be one single person who maintains each zone. The warehouse manager has responsibility for the back room and its maintenance.
- In a small store one person will maintain every zone. But it is a very

rare group of people who will maintain the back room without a single point of authority. Keeping the back room maintained is critical to maintaining a positive culture and that means each employee should be empowered to hold other staff members accountable to meeting the standards. Give one person time to attentively maintain the back room every 2 weeks and the entire store will operate more efficiently.

- In a large store, a warehouse manager is a full-time job that reports to the store manager. The store relies on a warehouse manager to maintain an easy-to-understand system that funnels inventory into the store as efficiently as possible. A warehouse manager has critical safety responsibilities and must run their operation in compliance with all mandated safety standards.

- In an online retailer, the warehouse is the core of all operations. Warehouse management is key to have room to create permanent staging areas for every operation of gathering, aggregating and shipping orders. In online retailers, the receiving manager, picking manager and shipping manager are likely to be separate team members.

- Standards for put-away and trash. There must be standards to require stock to be put away and turned oldest to newest to maintain freshness. Standards include all delivered goods much be put away before close of each shift before punching out. Trash must be removed and placed completely in its receptacle at the end of each shift. Cardboard must be broken down and compacted each day. Simply stating the standards and not accepting deviations will begin to set the right expectations with the staff that proper back room maintenance is non-negotiable.

- Security and lock-up. Be very clear about which product must be secured and why. Have security procedures in place for each shift lead and train staff on how to properly lock up and open secure areas. Lax security always ends up with theft and should lead to terminations. Store management needs a "trust but verify" approach that lets staff know that following security protocol is a requirement for employment. Video surveillance is recommended for high-theft locations like docks, shipping and returns.

- Invest in back-room amenities. Provide lockers for purses and personal effects for each employee. Purchase see-through plastic bins, uniform shelving, label makers, colored tape, bathroom cleaning supplies, bulletin boards, microwaveable tableware, chairs, waste bins and other requirements to make the back room easy to maintain and a reflection of the respect you hold for the team and the store.

Without setting a tone of respect and professionalism with your team, it is hypocritical to expect respect and professionalism from them towards customers. A back room that is organized and a respite from front-of-house chaos will give your team the environment they need to recharge and return to the floor in a positive frame of mind.

## WIN Today

Examine your back room or warehouse to verify that your work stations are distinct and prominently marked. Ask team members about the tools and equipment they need in each zone and create a system for housing each element in a convenient permanent location for each zone.

If you are unclear about how to set up a more functional back room, connect with your local business community and ask to tour a local printer or production plant to see their warehouse configuration. If you are in a mall, ask to share best practices with back rooms with other mall retailers to build a communal approach to shared back hallways and receiving docks. Use the opportunity to network for your business.

# OPERATIONS

## Cost Cutting and Expense Splurges

Midway through the year every retailer starts to get nervous about making the annual sales goals. The 6-month point is the time to review the store budget and make adjustments while you can still affect the third and fourth quarter.

If you are in the enviable position of being ahead of your planned budget, it will be tempting to make some long-delayed splurges in the business. Running behind budget? Most react with a meat cleaver approach to expenses.

But businesses set up for long-term success have a plan for cost cutting and expense spending that aligns with their strategic plans.

Here's how to make that work:

First, it is important to have a prioritized set of strategic goals. Examples could include:

- Penetrate the local business market (focusing on medical, dental and health businesses, then schools).
- Gain market share in households with elementary and pre-K children.
- Have the lowest prices in the market on commercial-grade replacement parts then use those to build traffic for ongoing supply delivery to local businesses.

In any case, there should be a plan that the company is mobilizing behind that is meant to attain the required sales and profit to meet your budget goals.

When evaluating expenses, weigh each one against the strategic goals. For example, if the plan is to offer outstanding customer service that is equivalent or slightly higher priced than the market, it would be advisable to cut advertising expenses before cutting store employee hours. The advertising may not provide a strong price message and cutting hours could lead to a reduction in careful customer service. Each expense needs to be justified by upholding the company's strategic goals when there are shortfalls and cuts need to be made.

The first places to search for expense cuts are secondary marketing and operating expenses that do not directly support either the bull's-eye in the center of the target market or the operational plan. Usually, these involve pet projects and are difficult to address. However, "nice to have" donations to local sports teams or community events are not critical if sports teams and their members are not the target market. There is usually some argument about getting the store's name in the community. But each event or donation must be looked at as a marketing investment – not a charitable contribution – when a retailer has to make budget cuts. Look at marketing and advertising budgets and critically review the payback for your investments.

Next evaluate the inventory and operational costs within the store. Use measurements that tie investments to sales. Look at the gross margin return on inventory (GMROI) and gross margin return on advertising (GMROA) when making decisions. Both of these concepts consider the profits generated per year in dollars invested in inventory or advertising. Changes in sales rates, pricing and costs can change the measurement. For a more thorough discussion of using these metrics, see GMROI in "Turning Inventory into Cash". Many point-of-sale systems have a standard report on GMROI for customers who are using their system correctly.

Are there areas where you could invest in "cheap inventory" to give your store a full look but cut back on higher-priced, slow-moving products?

Ways to fill the store with low inventory include:
- Use inexpensive products like reams of paper, bleach, or soda to create an attractive display to take up floor space and make a visual statement.
- Use mannequins or create vignettes to highlight key products from throughout the store while using just one item from inventory to make your "display."
- Eliminate shelves or peg hooks from fixtures and hang graphic panels or signs on the backer board of the fixtures to take up shelf space. Make high-quality graphics with customer messages to make it appear that you're not just cutting back on stock. Many retailers do this during slow-selling seasons and then replace the graphic panels with shelves and inventory when the high-selling season kicks into gear. Messages can include reminders about home delivery, set-up, guarantees or brand name reinforcement to remind customers that you carry their favorite brands. Many times, vendors will reimburse the production expense if their brand is featured prominently as it considered an in-store advertising sign.

Operating costs (garbage removal, electricity, taxes) cannot be negotiated, but there are many choices about operating standards that can be adjusted to impact those costs. Different lighting fixtures, interior thermostat settings, frequency of cleaning services are discretionary changes that can be adjusted if cost cutting is dire.

Let's look at the other side where sales are above budget providing an opportunity to invest more than expected. Again, there has to be the same judicious eye to evaluate every spending opportunity as a chance to reinforce the strategic plan for the company. Too often, store owners or managers are attracted to a new marketing idea: Let's sponsor the town bike parade or invest in Google AdWords or buy a billboard or take an ad in a local magazine. But each additional investment must be evaluated against delivering the core brand message that the company believes differentiates them from the competition. If your competitor sponsors the town carnival, that may not make sense for your shop. If you are targeting small businesses, it may make more sense to sponsor a coffee break at a local meeting of business owners than to participate in a parade.

What is critical is to create a budget each year and the strategy that will deliver the budget. The budget must be based on that strategy.

Investing in a website or investing in an employee training seminar are both great ideas. But only one makes sense if your strategy is to beat the competition by making each team member engagement a delightful experience that builds loyalty. It is normal for most businesses to have more spending ideas than cash during each budgeting cycle. Place the items that didn't make the cut on a prioritized list. Share the list with your employees and let them know that if the budget is exceeded, those items can be reinstated. It's a good way to develop employee engagement and make them feel their efforts tie into the overall destiny of the company.

## WIN Today

Set aside a half day every quarter to review your financial results compared to your budget. If you do not have a budget, use last year as a baseline. Then create a simple increase or decrease based on a plan like: sales of hardware up +10% because I am advertising in local construction trade journals this year that I didn't do last year or expenses –5% because I have a new contract in place for IT and server security, etc.

Use your actual versus budget to make adjustments that are aligned to your strategy as outlined throughout this topic. Make sure your adjustments are delicate at first and not reactionary. Make each adjustment a thoughtful decision that sets the store on a path to a achieving the budget by the end of the year and not a radical shift that changes each month. Careful monitoring each quarter and thoughtful adjustments are more effective than to recalibrate every month and upset programs in motion.

OPERATIONS

## 4 Reports for Brick & Mortar Store Managers

In retail there are endless ways to look at information: by customer, by product, by day, by location. But for a store manager with limited time and a need to make good decisions – not just analyze data – there are four that are critical to lead a successful store.

**1. Sales Report**

The sales report *must* be detailed enough to drill down into issues but also have a summary screen or page that aggregates sales into meaningful units. For most managers, it is possible to lead the team using monthly sales reports. But during peak periods or for high-turning categories, weekly or even daily reporting may be better.

A simple report has:
1. Time periods
   - The week and the month and quarter to date or year to date
   - The same time periods last year for comparison
2. Measurements
   - The expected sales (budget) for this year's time periods
   - $ sales for time periods this year and last year
   - Sales % change versus last year and budget
   - % markdown sales
   - Gross margin $
   - Gross margin % change versus last year and budget

If the measurements are reported by category or department, you can pinpoint where sales have exceeded or fallen short of the plan. A top-level view focuses on areas that are exceeding the budget plan to help identify new merchandising, pricing and inventory decisions to lean into the sales growth trend. Or identify underperforming categories that need a closer review to prevent an inventory glut.

The *% markdown sales* indicates promotions that over or underperformed as well as excess inventory sold on clearance. Markdowns predict gross margin challenges even when sales meet the plan.

Of course, this top-level view is not effective unless there is detail behind it. There are a couple of summary levels under the category or department that are particularly useful. To move to a SKU or item level is not as actionable as to have a subcategory level or a vendor-level summary before the item level.

Vendor-level summaries are helpful in negotiating pricing and promotional discounts. Showing a vendor that he is not meeting the standard margin rates or sales rates of his competitors is usually all it takes to get adjustments. I have often screened the competitive names to "Company A," "Company B," "Company C" and shown the actual report to prove my point with vendors.

Driving down to the item level allows you to make decisions about promotional effectiveness, pricing changes, inventory levels, merchandising and other critical retailing tactics that can only be done at the item level. The best store managers can rifle through sales reports in a few minutes and find the exceptional high- and low-performing areas that need immediate attention to bring performance back to plan.

**2. Expense Report**

A monthly expense report that highlights key variable expenses and variance from plan and a year ago is critical.

Main expense items should include:

- **Payroll** – The largest single item for most retailers. Set a target %-to-sales ratio for payroll and manage employee hours accordingly. Review last year's sales trends by week to create employee schedules. Be mindful of fluctuations to prevent overstaffing during slow weeks and understaffing during high- volume weeks. Note outside influences such as weather, city events, tourism rates, school openings and holidays to make your scheduling more precise each year.
- **Supplies** – Supplies and travel are typically easy to manage and schedule to coincide with high- and low-profit months. Consider placing a supply order when months are more profitable so that the store is not caught short during lean sales months when it is harder to find cash flow.
- **Advertising/marketing/promotion** – Like payroll, advertising and marketing expenses should be managed to a target %-to-sales ratio. But like payroll, there is a minimum investment necessary to "keep the lights on." Decelerating marketing investments whenever there is a sales shortfall can send a store into a steep decline. Instead, monitor the marketing expenses in conjunction with your sales report to conduct marketing experiments. Test months with and without brand name promotional items, test different vehicles and timing. Learn how to make your marketing spending as efficient as possible.
- **Utilities** – Perhaps the least easy to modify, utility expenses can be managed through more efficient lighting and heating as well as by implementing conservation practices with your employees. Still,

monitoring utilities prevents expensive errors from draining bank accounts when there were billing mistakes or employees keep loading doors open throughout August!

Proactive managers use the expense report to modulate future spending plans while still maintaining good morale among the teams. Be cautious about whipsawing your team members from freewheeling spending to miserly penny-pinching month to month.

### 3. Payroll Productivity

A critical personnel management guide is payroll productivity reporting. Begin with a baseline measurement of the total sales dollars produced per employee hour. Calculate the sales dollars per payroll hour by week of year, by day of week and by hour of day. Consider all payroll hours the same. Calculate cashier, sales and management hours aggregated and then (if you wish) separately. Look for patterns.

Look for specific people and managers who increase or decrease sales productivity during their shifts. Act and adjust. Look for over- and understaffed periods and make changes to improve your overall production. While your payroll expense reporting can help you manage the total payroll budget, payroll *productivity* gives insight into which employees and positions are most critical for success.

### 4. Contribution Report

With a contribution report, every retail asset (inventory, space, payroll) carries its own balance sheet. For inventory, there is the asset of gross margin and the debit of COGS and carrying costs. For space, there is the asset of gross margin and the debit of rent and prorated utilities. For payroll, there is the asset of gross margin and the debit of fully loaded payroll, training and administrative costs. If you carry the concept of an asset balance sheet to a category level, you can compare the contribution of each of these assets to the overall contribution of the category.

To illustrate, imagine you sell cell phones or diamond rings. If you look at the contribution of each asset you would find that sales increase with an increase in inventory and payroll but not with an increase in space. Cell phones and rings do not require much space and adding more of it does not contribute nearly as much as adding more knowledgeable salespeople or more spectacular inventory selections. Conversely, if you sell denim jeans adding space and inventory is likely to yield a higher contribution than adding sales staff since customers help themselves and most want a wide variety of options.

Evaluating a contribution report can indicate how to drive better sales by investing in the right sales assets for each category.

As a manager, no one likes time spent on paperwork. (With computers, should it be called "screen work"?) But a practiced manager can quickly scan a few key reports and diagnose issues that need to be addressed. Reports can alert managers to symptoms before business issues move to a critical stage.

## WIN Today

Review the standard reports available to you. If you are not in the habit of reviewing reports regularly, review the reporting screens available through your point-of-sale system. Share reports and train your inner leadership team in how to read and interpret each measurement. It will sharpen your understanding as well as provide training to other key leaders on your team. Make it clear what you do or do not want shared with the entire team. Align with your leaders on the key metrics to review regularly and tolerance levels for every metric that will trigger new action.

## 4 Reports for Online Store Managers

Reporting and data are the life blood of all online store managers. Unlike brick-and-mortar managers, reports for e-retailers are usually in real time and reviewed every day. Interestingly, the same is true for television shopping channels like QVC and HSN which operate very much like an online retailer.

**1. Website Health Report**

General metrics about the speed to load the website, the number of pages visited, time on site, acquisition sources, security and mobile access are standard for all websites. A commerce site should also measure their user's experience, their path while on the site and the key search terms they use while on the site.

**2. Visitor Conversion Report**

Conversion rate (how many visitors purchase) is a key metric. For most sites, 4% is the goal. Customer metrics in standard online reports include average units and dollars per transaction, % of abandoned items in carts and average value of abandoned items. Critical in abandoned cart tracking is understanding when it occurred in the purchase. (Items left in a cart? Items left when user login/guest checkout was required? Items left when the payment was requested?) Make sure your checkout process is as easy as possible and send a friendly reminder to those that bounce out before checkout to create a conversion.

Individual campaign measurements can be tracked to understand how customers shopped the campaign. Think of your site like a set of stage gates and measure customers passing through each one:

- Viewed home page or landing page
- Browsed collection
- Viewed product
- Favorited a product
- Added product to cart
- Completed order

Capturing email is key for ongoing messaging and to understand how frequently former visitors shop. Monitor the open rate as well as the unsubscribe rates to learn how to improve your lead list.

### 3. Click-to-Ship Report

Online customers are loyal to companies with a strong reputation for fast shipping and delivery. E-retailers who monitor and shorten the time between a completed order and a complete, accurate shipment will improve their return customer purchases over time. Sometimes referred to as a click-to-ship report, it usually monitors both order fulfillment rates and tracks shipping speed.

Order fulfillment includes picking accuracy, packing costs and time to ship. Working with shipping partners, it can also include metrics on their delivery time so that the end-to-end time from a customer placing the order until it is delivered to their door is measured.

### 4. Returns Report

Online retailers manage a higher return rate than brick-and-mortar retailers. Because customers do not actually see the products, try on the clothes and often order the wrong item, online retailers have to be vigilant to keep returns as low as possible. Returns are expensive transactions if a customer cannot self-manage them online. If returns require a call center, order look-ups, data entry, return authorizations and third-party logistics, the entire profit for the transaction can be consumed. Retailers who automate all of those steps for customers online not only hold down their costs, but also build a reputation for high customer service.

A returns report should align to both the product hierarchy and vendors. A daily review of returns codes will pinpoint immediate action to be taken when a product description is inaccurate or a vendor is not conforming to expectations. Take swift action when a color listed as "violet" online is returned regularly as "wrong color" because it is actually "lilac" or if a vendor has a consistent pattern of over-sizing or under-sizing garments.

Return labels should identify if returned goods are fit to return to the warehouse for sale (wrong color or size) or if they need to be returned to the vendor for credit (incomplete good or not functioning). Keep handling costs down by requiring your vendor to unbox and process returns from consumers. If possible, work with your shipping vendor to provide customers with a mailing label that directs those goods directly to the vendor's disposition warehouse.

## WIN Today

Post individual and group accuracy levels each shift to emphasize the importance of accurate and complete order fulfillment. Set aggressive goals and offer rewards for hitting each goal. Currently, US retailers (other than Amazon) average 4.3 days from click to ship. Leading retailers are shaving 48 hours per year off their click-to-ship times by implementing automation and efficient processes.

Listen to your order-picking team and implement their suggestions to make orders more accurate. Setting up new products with images for every item that are visible to order pickers and accurate weight measurements will improve order accuracy. Warehouse locations that are clearly marked and even automated (using lights or beacons) to accurately pinpoint the exact location of every item improves speed to pick rates.

Finally, refine your products every day to make them more descriptive and accurate – not just to improve sales – but to reduce product returns that can destroy 100% of the profitability of a sale.

# What to Do During The 4th Quarter of Each Year

At the last quarter of each year is the time to make adjustments that can impact how your business will end the year. Corrections made now have a significant impact on year-end earnings results.

### 1. Make Your Customers Smile

It is the busiest time of the year and customer tempers run high. This is when a patient and thoughtful smile and extra customer attention goes a long way. Make your store attractive. Make transactions easy.

Consider bringing a large coffee pot into the store and adding cider and cinnamon sticks to it every morning. Offer customers small paper cups of mulled cider. Most customers are happy with a 4-ounce cup or none at all. But the store will immediately smell like the holidays and help your customers relax.

Be fast and friendly. Tell customers you understand how much they have to get done this time of year and show them you are happy to speed them along their way with hopes they will return when they have more time. Offer a special pre-holiday delivery service for a week or two just because you know this is the worst time of year to be caught without essential supplies. Make it your holiday gift to your customers and announce it on every social media site you can access.

### 2. Tweak Your Merchandising Every Week

Impulse sales are at their highest this is the time of year. Keep your store fresh by moving different impulse items every week from the shelves to the checkout counter and high-visibility tables at the front entrance.

Have a contest with your sales team each week to see who can suggestive-sell the most key add-on items. Contest winners can win anything from small gift cards to a coveted day off work on December 24. Remember: not all rewards have to cost you money!

Update your store by highlighting different items for shoppers that could be purchased as gifts, used for decor or entertaining. Now is the time to make sure clearance products are looking their best because store traffic will decline shortly into January and they will be even harder to liquidate.

### 3. Review Inventories and Shrink

Before you have to manage the end-of-the-year sales and inventory bulge, take time for high-value stock counts and balance your physical stock with your inventory reports. Reinforce policies for locking high-value items and security practices for selling and bagging them. Have a clear picture of your inventory situation prior to the end of the year and be prepared to cancel or postpone orders if sales are slow by November 30 so that you are not left with high volumes of non-sellable goods at the end of the year.

Review your goods not for resale inventories as well. This includes everything from cash register tape to shopping bags, bathroom cleaning supplies, extra sales racks and light bulbs. Ensure that you have enough supplies on hand to see you through the end of the year.

Additionally, clear out old merchandising stock that you will not need from the back room. Summer clearance sale signs, back-to-school signs and other unnecessary clutter should be thrown in the dumpster to make way for holiday and new model year product.

### 4. Adjust Delivery Dates

There can be a tremendous difference in your balance sheet between accepting delivery on December 30 or January 2. Depending on your year, consider moving up January payments into December to create expenses to reduce current year profits. Or, postpone supplies and inventory into January to keep future liabilities lean for December 31 statements.

### 5. Review End-of-Year Deals

Expect vendors who are close to reaching milestones to offer unprecedented deals if you place your order by December 31. If you have the financial flexibility, let vendors know you have funds available for the right deal. Press for extra allowances if you accept delivery by December 31.

### 6. Review Performance and Development Goals

Review the performance and developmental conversations in the past year with your team and make sure you are on track to meet the goals. Look at written records as well as your memory. Make sure goals that were recorded in May or June are not forgotten at year-end. Give your team members the support and challenges that you agreed to earlier in the year.

Delegate operational tasks to capable team members. Now is the time to step away from daily tasks that prevent you from interacting with customers. Delegate operational duties to develop your team. Now is the time to make sure you are seen giving customers your best.

### 7. Stay Connected

To set yourself apart from all those other shiny holiday cards, send a personal message to key people *before* the holidays begin. Tell key staff members, vendors, suppliers, neighbors and customers that with the holidays bearing down on, you appreciate having them in your corner all year long. Explain that while everyone else is wishing them a happy holiday season, you want to thank them for helping you get through the year and making it to another holiday season. Add a personal item you are especially proud of from the year or a reason they are included in your appreciation. Then wish them a prosperous holiday season and assure them that you consider their ongoing support or patronage to be the best holiday sentiment they could send back your way.

### 8. Plan for Post-Holiday Recovery Now

Have a plan for how you will transition after the holidays and schedule it by day. What happens on December 26? December 30? January 2? January 15? Have a plan in place for ensuring that your holiday messages are retired in a timely fashion and that your store looks as good after the holidays as it did on December 15.

Plan for messages that take you from New Year into February. Ask team members to recall last year's biggest post-holiday issues and put a solution in place now that will make the transition easier. Make sure every cashier is trained on how to accept a gift card and how to execute a return and exchange. Document this year's issues and suggestions and keep them filed for reference next year.

Even for a well-run store, the last couple of months of the year can be nerve wracking. Take time to adjust. Your customers, your employees and your bottom line will acknowledge it.

## WIN Today

In October, review each of the eight elements in this topic area. Create a November through January calendar and place each item on a date on the calendar. Delegate them to key team members or take responsibility for each item yourself. Use the calendar to keep focused on what really matters during the holiday season and rise above the daily chaos that will inevitably ensue.

Remember that Eisenhower quote about war: "In preparing for battle I have always found that plans are useless, but planning is indispensable."

OPERATIONS

## What Gets Measured...Gets Done

Retail is an industry with innumerable measurements to indicate business health. But far too often, store owners get fixated on one or two. Too often total revenue, profit contribution or sales versus last year are the only metrics that are regularly reviewed. But smart retail managers know that they need to keep their eyes on over a dozen other measurements to really see where the business is headed. Like a plane's cockpit, there are different dials that managers should watch to see the future and take appropriate action.

### Sales Metrics

In trying to drive top-line sales and revenue, there are really three major components:

1. **Shopper traffic or website visitors:** How well do you do attract potential customers to your website or storefront?
2. **Customer conversion rates:** How well does your website or customer service team turn those shoppers into paying customers?
3. **Average purchase value:** A combination of the number of products purchased in one transaction and the value to the items purchased. An indication of providing a full-service shopping destination. Not just a fill-in shopping trip or a single-item driven purchase.

For online stores, visitor counts as well as acquisition sources are easy to track. They are part of the usual standard website health reports that you can easily access from Google. For physical stores, automatic door counters can be installed to count the number of people entering and leaving the store. A more economical hands-on method can be as simple as staging a greeter at the door with a hand tally counter or "clicker." Measuring shopper conversion is then a simple division of the total number of transactions during a defined time by the number of people who entered the store. It is best to consider counting shopping "groups" as one person since children and spouses rarely make separate transactions.

There are two ways to increase top-line sales with traffic metrics: increase the number of people through the door or to the website (by extending hours, increasing promotions and marketing, increasing bounce-back offers) or increase the conversion rate (by increasing store associate customer service conversations on the sales floor, reducing out of stock and back order rates, and sending notices when online shopping carts are abandoned.)

Two components drive an increase in the average purchase value.
1. Increasing the units per transaction
2. increasing the average item value per purchase

Selling your customers more items can be as complex as adding service contracts to power tools or major appliances or as simple as adding impulse items at the cash register. Increasing the value of each item sold is the slow process of raising open price point items or creating a higher tier of products so that customers move along a *good > better > best > premium > ultra-premium* continuum to higher price points. The most effective way to improve the average purchase value is to provide helpful, knowledgeable assistance from team members in store or online chatbots or 24/7 call center associates who are prompted with additional items to make sales suggestions.

### Profit Metrics

Profit is best managed by reducing costs of operations and improving product mix rate within transactions.

Operational metrics such as cost of goods sold, payroll, rent and utilities as a percent of sales and *selling, general and administrative expenses* (SG&A) are all smart ways to look at operational costs. Some retailers "fully load" costs into each individual item by dividing costs across all products in the store. This is called *activity-based costing (ABC)*. They prorate rent, utilities, returns, labor, and all other cost components to each item in the store to understand exactly how much each item costs before setting the full markup.

The formal practice of SKU rationalization identifies the contribution of each product to the overall sales and profit mix and is a common consequence of completing an activity-based cost analysis. From this exercise, a retailer could learn that simple $1.00 items (that cost $0.45 to purchase) are actually money losers since costs to order, receive, stock and sell that item may be more than $0.55. Driving profit can be done in two ways: sell more profitable items and sell less money-losing items. In other words, from a profit and loss standpoint, it benefits the company the same if you sell two items that earn $2.00 each or if you stop selling one item that loses $4.00 each time you sell it.

While every industry expects management to contain and limit costs, in retail there is the additional component of managing the product sales *mix.* Competitive pressure requires most retailers to promote popular products at rates barely above cost from time to time. To offset the profit squeeze, add high-margin items to the transaction. An example is when a retailer sells a printer at cost but sells it within a "bundle" that includes photo paper, extra ink cartridges, cables and a protection plan within the bundle. Overall, the printer may have a margin of less than $5.00, but taken all together the total package may yield upwards of $75.00 in profit. Thoughtfully managing the mix of items in a transaction can offset low-margin items.

### Customer Metrics

Customer-retention rates, repurchase cycle frequency and customer engagement levels measure customer health in retail. Customer Net Promoter® score measures the likelihood that a customer would recommend your store to a friend in the future. While it is a trademarked service, it is an open-source concept and therefore can be used by any retailer for no fee. In fact, SurveyMonkey and other online survey tools offer a standard Net Promoter® template to help you get started in soliciting direct feedback from your customers.

For most retailers a loyalty program or frequent customer card and CRM database is the best way to monitor customer metrics. But even simple paper files of commercial clients with regular quarterly service calls can be used to detect changes in shopping patterns. Creating a customer email database and measuring its growth can turn into a more robust tool when services like Constant Contact or Mailchimp are used to measure the open rates of emails. Offer unique promotions and track coupon redemptions. It may sound like you need a tech team, but all you need is to start to test rates (10% off, 15% off, 20% off) and you can build your own customer offer elasticity rates.

A broader customer metric is market share or share of wallet, which measures your retail store's ability to capture the consumers that you service versus your competition. Rarely available at a micro-level, it is a key metric for national and regional retailers who want to measure the percentage of the total market that they are satisfying. Nielsen and IRI are common US sources that measure what people buy across all channels and sources and then provide reports to both retailers and vendors. A common way to use their reporting is to understand the market share to identify opportunities in a retailer's business model.

For example, let's say that Grocer A has an overall market share of 15% in Chicago. Diving deeper, Grocer A discovers that it only has a 7% market share of cereal while it has a 22% share of milk. (Perhaps because it has a convenience strategy that makes it easy for customers to get a fast gallon of milk during a fill-in trip.) Grocer A could determine how much more sales it could achieve if it were to drive its cereal sales to its fair market share (15%). In our example, Grocer A could expect to slightly more than double sales if it could achieve its fair share of cereal sales. Since Grocer A has an over-developed milk business (22% market share versus the average of 15% across the entire store) it could devise a promotion to try to convert its milk customers to also purchase cereal. Since the increase in cereal sales can be modeled, Grocer A can even set a realistic marketing budget to achieve its cereal sales goals with a high degree of certainty that the investment will pay off.

## Social Metrics

It is impossible to ignore the power of online, mobile and social interactions and feel confident in your future viability. Monitor your online reputation with Yelp and Google as well as your followers on Facebook, Twitter and Instagram to give you insight into your digital following. At least once per month look at all the relevant social sites and track your followers. Assign one person to monitor any real-time customer interactions by linking their email with the account. Set expectations that all customer comments will be acted upon within 24 hours. Include social metrics in quarterly business reporting and look for ways to improve your social metrics by asking for advice from the most socially savvy team members.

## Employee Metrics

While retailers get caught up in their products and customers, most would agree that the true source of wealth and growth are their team members. Quantitative and qualitative measurements of your staff are key to building a sustainably profitable retail organization.

Quantitative metrics should come from your HR function or can be tracked internally and include things like turnover rates, average length of time in position, salary rates and average increases by job title or department and payroll hours per week. But be judicious in reviewing the measurements. Turnover can be a lazy metric because it is easy to measure but it has so many causes. For example, a turnover report that shows that turnover is highest amongst your part-time cashiers and overnight warehouse workers does not mean that you have a problem in those areas. After all, turnover will be high due to the nature of the work and position. It does not tell you if the overnight warehouse manager is a bad manager or a good manager. So when looking at employee reports, make sure you are examining them and diving in to find out what you really want to know.

Quantitative metrics can help you understand if you are meeting your financial plan. You can measure if your payroll hours align to the monthly budget. New hire rates can help you predict the demands from HR and IT. They can also help you understand how your company is doing in the market place. Are you paying to scale in the market? Are you losing employees to specific competition and acting as their "feeder system?" Measuring your employees means understanding the questions you want answered and challenging your HR team to help you uncover answers.

Qualitative metrics tell you about the *why* behind quantitative measurements. Most retailers think of engagement surveys that are typically done once per year from an objective third party. To be effective, employee surveys must be both anonymous and actionable. Most retailers can conduct the surveys, but it is rare for them to have the resources to analyze and interpret the results in a way that improves conditions for employees. Some questions about safety or equipment can be answered and acted upon. But it takes insight and rigor to uncover the honest conditions behind answers when an employee is happy with their pay but hates their boss. If a survey uncovered that women score the company low on benefits, but like the flexibility, does that tell you if they are likely to leave? Surveys yield results. But that is altogether different than giving you insight that can help you strengthen loyalty and fulfillment on the team.

If you are considering a survey, seek outside assistance. It is easy to turn to SurveyMonkey or other online providers to conduct the survey. But the rubber hits the road when you get the information back. Apply the same kind of rigor to getting information from your employees as you would from your customers. If you gain a reputation for asking questions but not doing anything, the mere act of conducting employee surveys can be demotivating.

If you cannot afford an outside service, consider using small focus groups to ask the questions you want answered and *listening* to them. Listening to employees is no less important than listening to customers. Let's image you create eight groups of four people. Ask the same three or four questions of every group. Have a scribe take down responses. (Do not record the sessions unless you seek legal counsel based on personal consent issues.) Look for patterns of answers across all or most of the groups. It is important to ask the same questions of every group and to keep the discussion focused. When conversation goes out of scope, the findings will be inconclusive.

Finally, some of your most honest feedback will be in employee exit interviews. First, determine what you most want to know. Are people leaving your company for better pay? More growth opportunities? To escape a bad boss? Work with HR to create a set of four or five questions and diligently ask every employee who leaves the same set of questions. You must know what you want to know and then ask those questions directly to departing employees.

### Goal Progress

While all of the metrics listed so far have been ongoing health measurements, every company should have focused initiatives that are moving their business ahead. Aligned to strategic vision, major company projects could include store openings, new IT systems, vendor or market expansion, employee training, or other important overarching goals that need to be met to build a strong future. Owners and managers must monitor all strategic initiatives to ensure that there is continual progress. In the bustle and urgency of daily customer and vendor interactions, it is easy to let time slip without making progress. Using a Gantt chart to track milestones and development status is a simple reporting tool that will give you a current projection for attaining important goals.

## WIN Today

Review your metrics and ensure that you are getting a well-rounded overview of your business each month or quarter as you review your business financials and health. A "balanced scorecard" includes employee, customer, sales and profit metrics. Regular updates on company initiatives and external metrics like market share and social influence should integrate on a regular cadence.

Think of reporting as a form of listening. As the leader of the team, you must listen to the various voices that are telling you about how well some portions of the company are meeting needs while other components are struggling. Be vigilant that your reporting is well-rounded and that you are not omitting blind spots that could give you an early warning from customers, employees or vendors.

There is really just one final thing to say to help you Win Today in retail:

**LISTEN – to your customers.**
**LISTEN – to your team members.**
**LISTEN – to your vendors.**
**LISTEN – to your marketplace.**

# OPERATIONS

# Footnotes

1. Greg Buzek and Lee Holman, "Debunking the Retail Apocalypse" (IHL Research) August 29, 2017.

2. PEW Research Center, "The Lost Decade of the Middle Class," August 22, 2012.

3. Larry Selden and Geoffrey Colvin, *Angel Customers & Demon Customers: Discover Which Is Which and Turbo-Charge Your Stock Portfolio,"* 2003.

4. Piper Jaffrey, "Collaborative Consumer Insights Project," Spring 2017.

5. Greg Buzek and Lee Holman, *Debunking the Retail Apocalypse* (IHL Research) August 29, 2017.

6. Deluxe Corporation internal research, 2016.

7. Chris Anderson, *The Long Tail: Why the Future of Business is Selling Less of More* (Hyperion), 2008.

8. An even-numbered scale metric (e.g., 4) rather than an odd-numbered scale metric (e.g., 3 or 5) is always preferable because it forces ratings that are either positive or negative – never neutral.

9. Clay Christensen, "Milkshake Marketing," *Harvard Business Review,* Feb 14, 2011.

10. The Pareto principle is also called the "80/20 rule." In retail it refers to 80% of the sales typically coming from 20% of the products.

11. Chris Anderson, *The Long Tail: Why the Future of Business is Selling Less of More* (Hyperion), 2008.

12. Thomas Gruen and Daniel Corsten, *A Comprehensive Guide to Retail Out-of-Stocks in the Fast-Moving Consumer Goods Industry,"* 2008

13. Herb Sorenson. *Notes from Inside the Mind of the Shopper.*

14. The "cost of money" refers to the interest rate that money could accrue in a financial instrument like a bank account or other safe investment instead of being used for the riskier inventory investment. Thus, if interest rates are at 2.5% per year, the opportunity cost of 2.5% must be accounted for in evaluating how much money to invest in the forward buy.

15. This assumes that your goal in carrying the new technology item is sales and inventory turns. However, you may make a strategic decision to sell a very slow-selling new technology item because you want to make a statement to your customers about your leading-edge position in the market. It can lead to engaging customer interactions and a possible change in your brand's perception. Just don't expect a lot of sales for a long while.

16. The *only* time I would recommend storing seasonal product from one year to the next would be if the product had a very high value, an evergreen appeal *and* was not in the store during the peak seasonal period this year. For example, a crystal Christmas ornament that was not put on the sale floor until December 21 might be a good candidate for storage. But not gift tags (low value) nor a dated ornament (will not be appealing next year) nor the same crystal ornament if it was on the sales floor from November 15 – December 31.

17. Amy Gallo, "The Value of Keeping the Right Customers," *Harvard Business Review*, October 29, 2014.

18. Accenture, "Customer Service, Nor Price, Remains Top Cause of Customer Churn, Accenture Study Finds,"November 18, 2008.

19. Colloquy, "2015 Loyalty Census: Big Numbers, Big Hurdles"

20 Kornferry.com, "Retail Employee Turnover up as Black Friday and Holiday Shopping Season Nears, according to Korn Ferry Hay Group Survey of Top U.S. Retailers, November 16, 2016

21. Forbes.com, "6 Ways to Achieve Any Goal", March 14, 2013

22. Vouchercloud.com, "How many productive hours in a workday?"

23. Lauren Weber, "What Do Workers Want from the Boss?" *Wall Street Journal*, April 2, 2015.

24. Society for Human Resource Management, "Placing Dollar Costs on Turnover," 2015.

25. Ben Wigert, "Talent Walks: Why your best employees are leaving," (Gallup.com).

## About the Author

Flora Delaney is a former retail merchandising executive with over 25 year of experience working for brands as large as Best Buy and Ahold and as small as single-store boutiques. She is a global retail consultant who helps retailers re-discover what makes them successful. She works with store leaders to reinvent their customer experience and create loyal customers and profitability. Her clients include Target, Whole Foods, PetSmart, The Good Guys (AUS), Family Dollar, Dell, Petco, Sears, and many small chains and nice shops. She is a sought-after speaker at trade events and retail meetings.

At the insistence of past clients, Flora has documented what the best retailers know and how everyday retail employees, department heads and store managers can make their store more profitable as well as a more fun place to work and shop.

## Did this book help you?
### Could I ask for help in return?

*You did it!* Congratulations, retail maven! Reading to the end of the book means you've got the makings of someone who's ready to truly win at retail. I hope you will return to this book again and again to make improvements for your store and your career. Thank you again for giving me your valuable time to try and help your retail operation.

If you enjoyed this book and would like to help, then you could think about leaving a review on Amazon, Goodreads or anywhere else that readers visit. I would appreciate your honest review and other readers would like to see what you thought as well. Thanks in advance to anyone who does ... It means a lot.

If you would like to find out more about future books or invite me to speak at your next event, then please visit my website for full details. www.floradelaney.com

Also feel free to contact me on Twitter @floradelaney or through the website. I look forward to hearing about your retail journey.

~Flora

Made in the USA
Coppell, TX
11 January 2020